Mothers and Their Children

A Feminist Sociology of Childrearing

Jane Ribbens

SAGE Publications

London • Thousand Oaks • New Delhi

First published 1994

SAGE Publications Ltd
6 Bonhill Street
London EC2A 4PU

SAGE Publications Inc
2455 Teller Road
Thousand Oaks, California 91320

SAGE Publications India Pvt Ltd
32, M-Block Market
Greater Kailash – I
New Delhi 110 048

British Library Cataloguing in Publication Data

A catalogue record for this book is available from the British Library

ISBN 0 8039 8834 6
ISBN 0 8039 8835 4 (pbk)

Library of Congress catalog card number 94-068659

Typeset by Mayhew Typesetting, Rhayader, Powys
Printed in Great Britain by Redwood Books, Trowbridge, Wiltshire

Contents

Acknowledgements

This book is the outcome of more than ten years of work; along the way I have received advice and support from many people. I would like to mention Pamela Abbott, Pam Calder, Leonore Davidoff, David Morgan and Barbara Richardson. The Women's Workshop on Qualitative Family/Household Research has been a wonderful source of inspiration and encouragement. Karen Phillips has been a tremendous help towards the production of this book. I owe a great debt to Miriam David, who led me gently towards feminist ideas; without her support the project would never have been completed. With Rosalind Edwards I have shared a loving friendship and hours of invaluable discussion, while Louise Jane has cherished and supported me in my personal and daily life throughout all these years. Thank you to one and all.

The research was also supported financially by the Economic and Social Research Council. Figure 3.1 is reproduced by kind permission of British Telecommunications plc.

And of course, I owe a great debt to the women who gave me their time and their thoughts on their children's lives. Particular thanks go to the 'case-study' women, who have allowed me to come and go in their lives over several years.

Lastly, however, I wish to dedicate this work to two very lovely people, Jonathan and Catherine Ribbens, and to Suzannah McCarthy, my new daughter who will arrive in the world before this book makes its appearance.

Introduction

Childrearing is a central part of the lives and concerns of the majority of women, particularly mothers. The experiences of those women who do not become mothers are also significantly affected by the centrality of childrearing for the identities of women, and there are widespread social expectations that closely relate the identity of woman with that of mother. Yet, in this key area of women's lives, we have largely allowed 'expert' ideas and theories to dominate public discussions and literature of childrearing. There has been considerable concern by feminists and others to highlight and counteract the takeover of childbirth itself by 'experts' (particularly by male-dominated medical professions), and yet we continually fail to listen to and respect what women themselves have to say about how they bring up their children. Indeed, this almost amounts to a failure to acknowledge that mothers do indeed have views that can be expressed and listened to at all.

Childrearing is a highly emotive and politically sensitive topic, one that is very hard to discuss without immediately making controversial assumptions. There are also more deep-rooted assumptions that we tend to take for granted, that are difficult to reflect upon at all. This book arises from a project whose original title was to have been, 'Bringing up our children'. It was a study that sought to be non-judgemental about differences in childrearing, and to question the assumptions embedded in the concepts we use to describe such differences. However, over time I came to realise that every word in that original title carries cultural assumptions: (1) that children are a separate category from other humans, (2) that they are in some sense a possession, or at least attached to particular individuals, and (3) that they need to be 'brought up' rather than just 'growing up'. Jane Lazarre – a white American woman, married to a black American – observes insightfully about her own attitudes to children and those of her husband: 'When all the intellectualising was said and done, James, the child of a poor family who had not given their children all the minute attention we continuously gave ours, still basically believed that we do not *bring* children up, they *grow* up' (1987: 163, emphasis in the original).

At the time I began the research, in the mid-1980s, feminist debates on motherhood were largely expressed in terms of the limitations women experience as a result of having primary childcare responsibilities (see chapter 2). There was some optimism that many men really were reassessing their own responsibilities for childcare, and that the way forward for women lay in equality within the worlds of paid employment. In the years since then, however, there has been increasing recognition, both in Europe and the United States, that there has been little fundamental change in men's childcare involvements, and that women have only entered paid work at the expense of accepting a 'second shift' (Bjornberg 1992, Boh et al. 1989, Hochschild 1990).

Furthermore, it has become increasingly apparent that women themselves value and prioritise their childrearing activities. While there have been striking changes in some aspects of childrearing (most notably the increase in births outside marriage), it is clear that most mothers still put their childcare responsibilities high on their personal agenda (Boh 1989, Gieve 1990, O'Donnell 1985, Judith Stacey 1986). A survey was conducted of the women readers of the progressive middle class British newspaper, the *Guardian*. This is a group of women we might expect to be at the forefront of change in gender roles, but even among these women, the conclusion was reached that, 'Probably the most staggering result of the survey was the high priority women continue to give to their families' (*Guardian* Women, 7 March 1991: 21). At the same time, the position of fathers in relation to their children's care has become increasingly anomalous, caught between ideologies of shared parenting and increasing trends towards absent fatherhood (Bjornberg 1992, Ribbens 1993a).

Public debates have raged (and continue) about the supposed demise or otherwise of 'the family'.[1] Yet children continue to be born, to live with and to be primarily cared for by their mothers. In Britain it is predicted that one in four children will experience divorce in their families before the age of 16, if divorce levels remain at their 1988–89 levels (Haskey 1990), while it is currently estimated that one in eight families with children is a step-family (Robinson and Smith 1993). On the other hand, in 1991, 85 per cent of dependent children were living in a household headed by a married couple (*Social Trends* 1992). In 1989 71 per cent of births outside marriage were registered by both parents, and of these, 72 per cent gave the same address (Cooper 1989). The majority of children live with their natural father at least until adolescence (*General Household Survey* 1982) and, on the whole, people continue to regard such domestic units as 'families'. We need to be very careful about how we discuss such statistical evidence, and tease it out from the political positions embedded in the terms of the debates. In particular, as researchers, we may sometimes need to use the concept of 'the family', and at other times to deconstruct it (Bernardes 1985a, 1985b, Rapp 1979). Yet such deconstruction need not deny the existence of the family as a significant concept in people's lives, and indeed, I shall describe in chapter 3 how women themselves may actively work towards its construction as a meaningful social unit.

In this book, then, I shall argue the need for a specifically feminist discussion of childrearing, since this is such an important area for women's lives. I describe this work as feminist sociology, and both these terms are crucial. I have always found sociology to be a fascinating and fruitful discipline, and we need some of its insights to help build a different sort of analysis of childrearing. But sociology needs a full feminist input if it is to realise its potential contribution. In chapter 2 I set out the grounds on which I describe this work as feminist, and in chapter 9 I reassess some sociological issues for the difference that might be made by a feminist analysis of childrearing.

My own experiences of mothering occurred in a particular context, and I chose to conduct research on women living in quite similar circumstances to my own (see chapter 2). I am a white woman from a reasonably prosperous background. At the time of new motherhood, and for a further 16 years, I was married to a middle class white man, with a middle income range, living in owner-occupied housing in South East England. I willingly terminated my own employment at the birth of my first child, although I returned to part-time employment a year after his birth, continuing on through the birth of my second child, a girl. Motherhood was for me an overwhelming experience, and one which I have largely enjoyed (and continue to treasure). Indeed, at the time of writing (August 1994) I await the imminent arrival of a new daughter, and am thus embarking on motherhood again at the age of 43 and under quite different circumstances with a new partner. This volume represents the culmination of the resulting project that has spanned ten years of my life. It is not possible to incorporate all aspects of the original project within the limitations of one publication. What the book does represent is the core of the research – namely, listening to how mothers themselves talk about their childrearing, and exploring the preoccupations and perspectives that are apparent in their childrearing accounts.

The emphasis is therefore upon the voices of the mothers themselves in relation to the upbringing of their children – what I call an 'insider perspective'. I shall argue that we also need an 'outsider perspective' to develop a full picture and analysis for a feminist sociological understanding of childrearing. While the second and last chapters point to some of the issues raised by such an 'outsider' analysis, material from the original report (Ribbens 1990a) concerning the overall context and circumstances of the lives of the women I interviewed has been largely omitted. I have paid sustained attention elsewhere to the complex, localised and quite self-contained social worlds in which many of the women I interviewed lived their daily lives with their children (Bell and Ribbens 1994). I also pay more attention elsewhere to the analysis of women's position and experiences of being a mother (Ribbens 1990a, 1993a); while the difficulties of finding an appropriate language for describing women's domestically based lives are discussed in Edwards and Ribbens (1991). Mothers' perspectives on their children's lives in relation to schools and education are discussed in Ribbens (1993a and 1993b).

These aspects of women's lives with their children have received very little research attention, though they all constitute important features within which women develop their childrearing concerns and perspectives. What I am able to set out in some detail in this present publication is the main focus of the research, which is what mothers have to say about how they bring up their children. I pay less sustained attention here than in the original report to any explanations we might develop about variations in women's childrearing perspectives, although, again, I do point to some of these issues in the opening and closing chapters. The heart of the book, then, is based upon the women's own voices as they talked about their children. In this undertaking, I move between broader themes concerning the cultural understandings and social contexts for contemporary Western childrearing, and more detailed and individualised accounts of the women's lives and concerns with their children.

Chapters 1, 2 and 9 are the places to look if you are interested in how I place the present study in relation to existing psychological, sociological and feminist debates, both theoretically and methodologically. In chapters 1 and 2, I thus set out my argument that there is at present an enormous gap in sociological and feminist discussions. Women's everyday concrete experiences in their lives with their children have been largely overlooked and have certainly not been considered on their own terms. This gap, for reasons which I also elaborate in chapter 1, is not one that can be filled by the psychological literature on child development. The one way in which the social circumstances of childrearing have been extensively examined in the existing literature is through debates concerning social class patterns of childrearing. I examine these debates in some detail to reveal their fundamental weaknesses, and demonstrate how they are based upon assumptions which continue to marginalise women's lives within core sociological debates. I thus set out my case for a specifically feminist sociological study of childrearing. Chapter 2 also includes a discussion of methodological issues related to these theoretical concerns, and provides some background to my own study. Chapter 9 reviews the material presented in the main part of the book, but also returns to some of the issues raised in the first two chapters, as well as extending the discussion and analysis further.

Readers who are not interested in these wider debates may decide they would prefer to launch straight into the discussions about childrearing that constitute the heart of the book: chapters 3 to 8 inclusive. Chapter 3 discusses cultural themes of individuality, family and childhood, while chapter 4 explores mothers' concerns with their children as social beings via their acceptability and involvement within informal and localised social contexts. Chapters 5 and 6 present detailed case-study 'portraits' of the childrearing accounts of four mothers, setting out each account as a more or less coherent whole and also exploring both their similarities and their differences overall. Chapters 7 and 8 broaden out the discussion beyond these women, while still paying direct attention to childrearing issues, in terms of the images of children that mothers draw upon and evoke (chapter 7), and how these different images are elaborated in relation to concrete issues of time, control and independence as significant childrearing themes (chapter 8).

Overall, I hope to show that the feminist sociological study of childrearing can reveal and respect the diversity of women's own childrearing views, a diversity which is rooted, not in contrasts between 'good' and 'bad' mothering, but in much wider issues of social and political philosophy. I hope therefore also to show that any sociological theorising which marginalises the lives of mothers and children is not only sexist but also seriously flawed.

Note

1. For examples of how academic opinion can diverge on this matter, see Chester (1986), and Bernardes (1985a, 1985b, 1986b, 1987).

Part I
Childrearing in Context

I
Childrearing, Psychology and Sociology

In order to establish the case for the feminist study of childrearing, I begin by examining prevailing discourses within psychology and sociology, starting with a discussion of psychological approaches to 'child development', and moving on to examine how sociologists have discussed 'socialisation'. Throughout these debates, I refer particularly to issues surrounding social class patterns of childrearing, which, I suggest, highlight the deficiencies in existing psychological and sociological approaches, revealing how these disciplines have marginalised women's perspectives and experiences.

Psychology and childrearing: 'child development', 'socialisation' and 'social class'

Psychological discussions of childrearing have been steadily elaborated in recent decades, and childrearing has been increasingly defined as a psychological process (Newson and Newson 1974). Nikolas Rose (1989) has traced the history of such psychological 'discourse', and argued its pervasive impact on everyday family lives. Developmental psychology can itself act as a form of social regulation (Ingleby 1986), and Walkerdine and Lucey (1989) suggest that expert theories of appropriate childrearing can be a source of oppression to women.

The nature of childrearing, and what counts as 'good' childrearing in public debates, may be increasingly conceptualised and evaluated by experts, very largely from one particular gender, class and racial group (Phoenix 1987). Certain theoretical psychological ideas may be taken up because 'they give scientific legitimation to significant cultural or political values' (Dingwall and Eekelaar 1986: 67). These ideas are then used to define appropriate maternal behaviours, and indeed, to extend the range and content of maternal roles. There has been increasing emphasis on mothers' roles as educators (David 1988) and health workers (Stacey and Davies 1983). There has also been a growth in Britain of new organisations and movements concerned with how parents (mothers?) should bring up their children (for example, Exploring Parenthood, the Dobson tapes and the Dreikurs movement),[1] some of these organisations being based in the United States. Morgan (1985) suggests that family matters generally have been increasingly medicalised, taking them out of the realm of 'lay' expertise. Furthermore, it is mothers in the more vulnerable social groups that are most likely to be negatively evaluated by such discourses, and subjected to the imposition of expert-defined models of 'correct' mothering (David 1988, Edwards 1992, Jane Lewis 1986) (perhaps because they are more resistant to expert ideas?). Indeed, in Britain at the time of writing, an expert report recommended that child benefit payments should be dependent upon attendance at parenting classes (Abrams 1994). As one journalist commented, the Year of the Family could feel like the Year of Parent-Bashing – 'We're arguing about who controls the next generation' (Freely 1994: 24).

Yet psychologists actually know very little about how children are brought up in their everyday social settings, and even less about how mothers themselves regard their childrearing (Phoenix and Woollett 1991). The significance of the social contexts of childrearing has been increasingly recognised by some developmental psychologists (e.g. Bronfenbrenner 1979, Martin Richards 1974, 1986, Woodhead et al. 1991), yet it seems that psychology lacks the theoretical and methodological tools to know *how* to incorporate an analysis of social context as *intrinsic* to the developmental process, rather than just the 'icing on the cake' (M. Richards 1986: 1).

Bronfenbrenner in particular has argued that: 'Much of developmental psychology, as it now exists, is *the science of the strange behaviour of children in strange situations with strange adults for the briefest periods of time*' (1979: 19, original emphasis). Bronfenbrenner's own analysis concerns a complex hierarchy of 'nested' social settings as the context for individual child development. There are considerable difficulties with this approach, however, linked to his rather functionalist form of social theorising. There is a danger of describing social contexts as though they exist independently of the people who construct them, and of regarding 'subcultures' as providing clear-cut boundaries for social contexts, rather than considering the possibility that boundaries are themselves social constructions, whether of members themselves or of academic observers.

It seems that the biggest difficulty for a social psychological account of childrearing is that it starts from the notion of the 'individual' child, and cannot overcome the fact that from the outset it splits the individual off from the social, rather than seeing the individual as intrinsically social (Ingleby 1986). In a major review of the literature on the social formation of personality, Burkitt concludes: '. . . the basis of human difference and individual identity is to be found within society, in the social relations that exist between individuals . . . when we look at society and the individual we are viewing exactly the same thing – social being – from two different angles . . .' (1991: 189).

The notion of 'the individual', which is so central to psychology (Adlam et al. 1977, Harré 1986), is itself a particular feature of post-industrial Western culture (see chapter 3). Furthermore, the notion of 'the child' is also increasingly recognised to be culturally specific, such that 'childhood' itself is open to analysis as a social construction (Alanen 1990, James and Prout 1990, Qvortrup et al. 1994, Wartofsky 1981). This is not necessarily to argue that developmental psychological theories are 'wrong', but we need to consider that they are developed within particular cultural groups and processes and so necessarily have limitations. Some psychologists are themselves concerned to acknowledge these limitations (Triandis 1987, White 1981).

If psychological theories of child development are culturally limited, how do they come to appear as if they have universal scientific validity? This largely occurs through the concepts used, which obscure the assumptions upon which the theories are based. I have already noted the questions that are now being raised about the concepts of 'individual' and 'child'. There are further questions to be considered. The notion of 'development' itself implies moving onwards to a more desirable situation – 'to come or to bring to a later or more advanced or expanded stage' (*Collins Concise Dictionary*). Concepts such as 'growth', 'development' and 'maturation' can give writing a spurious appearance of objective assessment (Cole 1981), unless we question *what counts as development*, or growth – what are the goals towards which children are said to be growing, and by which childrearing practices may be evaluated? The feminist psychologist, Carol Gilligan (1982), has made a highly influential critique of the gendered terms of reference of traditional theories of children's moral development, which define the goals of such development in terms based upon masculinist concerns. Similarly, Woodhead (1990) provides a telling analysis of the different ways in which the concept of 'need' may be used, so that value judgements may be hidden within arguments about apparently inherent imperatives in children's natures. Such theories may lead to judgemental attitudes about different approaches to childcare, due to the failure to recognise the value-laden aspects of some of the most basic underlying terms. The emphasis upon apparently 'objective' and 'scientific' research methods within psychology serves to further mask such underlying assumptions and impede cross-cultural research (Taft 1983).

Such hidden value judgements are particularly apparent in psychological descriptions of social class differences in childrearing and in parental values. Such patterns have received considerable attention within psychological research, for example Duvall (1946) and Bronfenbrenner (1958) in the United States, and Newson and Newson (1965) in Britain.[2] There are considerable difficulties with this work, leading to a self-perpetuating cycle of value judgements that are hidden within an apparently universal scientific discourse. These difficulties concern an oversimplification of complex data and an over-reliance on structured methodologies, leading to evaluative judgements of differences in childrearing that appear objective while being based in cultural values. These judgements are then fed into professional expertise and used to drive further research based on similar assumptions.

The first difficulty, then, is the tendency to overlook the complexities of the data. Social classes are frequently dichotomised into two clear-cut categories – middle and working class. This leads to a neglect of variabilities within these categories, including curvilinear relationships between childrearing and social class, and data that show no social class patterns at all. Yet a close examination of much of the data on patterns of childrearing reveals that such complexity is common (see e.g. Newson and Newson 1976, 1978, Newson and Lilley 1989). The position of women married to routine white collar workers appears to be particularly ambiguous, while social class differences are often only clear-cut between the extremes of the classification systems (e.g. Blaxter and Paterson 1982). Examination of data on how social class patterns in childrearing have changed over time (e.g. Newson and Lilley 1989) also reveal complex changes that appear quite random and difficult to explain. In a review of social class and socialisation, Kerchoff concludes: '. . . although social class seems to be an important variable throughout the socialisation process, it can explain only a rather limited amount of the variation in the process and the outcome' (1972: 125).

The second difficulty in these debates is the heavy reliance on structured methods. Whether relying on interviews or observations, researchers are inevitably making prior assumptions about what are the relevant questions to ask, or what they are to observe and how to categorise these observations (see e.g. Laosa 1981). Although Newson and Newson at times suggest that their work has 'existential and phenomenological roots' (1978: 14), they offer no theoretical explanation for how they came to choose the topics for inclusion within their highly structured questionnaires.

Pearlin (1972) also used highly structured questionnaires for his cross-cultural study of childrearing. After administering his American-based questionnaire to Italian parents, he concluded that there was an absence of differences between the American and Italian data. However, his additional less structured interviews and qualitative discussions hint at other unexplored cross-cultural contrasts: 'The concept of personality is not relevant among Italians . . . the parents seem free from conflict or ambivalence concerning the way they raise their children' (1972: 50).

There is a striking absence of grounded theory (Glaser and Strauss 1968), and a lack of concern with the *conceptual roots of empirical work* in research that considers the part played by parents in childrearing. Ethnographers warn us that 'social scientists must take care not to become straitjacketed by the social circles in which they move' (Hammersley and Atkinson 1983: 21). Without such recognition, we find the third difficulty in this body of research is that it leads on, almost inevitably, to culturally based evaluations about good and bad parenting that are presented as objective descriptions.

Sometimes such evaluations are contained in the language used for apparently 'scientific' descriptions of children's 'needs', but the result all too often is that the childrearing of groups lower in the social hierarchy comes to be seen as both stupid and morally degenerate. As Yuen (1985) discusses, a significant aspect of power is to be able to discredit others' versions of reality. This can be seen clearly in the various typologies that have been developed to describe parenting behaviours. Waters and Crandall (1964 – discussed in Laosa 1981) described differences in maternal behaviour in terms of higher class mothers being 'less dictatorial', 'less severe' and less 'restrictive'. Shaffer and Brody (1981 – discussed in Laosa 1981) classify different styles of parental discipline as power-assertion, love-withdrawal and induction (that is, reasoning), and then examine the effects of different styles on moral development. Is it any surprise that they found that induction best facilitated moral development and was found most often in the middle class, while power-assertion was least associated with moral maturity and was found most often in the working class?

Newson and Newson describe permissive, and later authoritarian/democratic, dimensions (1965, 1978), and Raphael-Leff (1983) describes mothers as facilitators or regulators. In Maccoby and Martin's two-dimensional typology (1983), one dimension classifies parental characteristics as parent-centred, i.e. 'rejecting and unresponsive'. This leads on, not surprisingly, to a discussion of 'parental failures', which describes what is 'lacking' in such parenting – 'The frequent occurrence of situations calling for firm control implies that socialisation is already off to a bad start' (1983: 70). Such valuations implicit in the words used to describe parenting and parenting typologies transform and distance them from the ways in which mothers themselves construe their own behaviour, thus alienating women from their own common-sense understandings. In this sense, these expert typologies are more heavily based on second order constructs, rather than being grounded in social actors' own constructs (chapter 2). Baumrind (1967, 1972, 1975) describes permissive, authoritarian and authoritative types, a typology which is both implicitly and explicitly evaluative. It is not expressed in terms which women/parents themselves might use, precisely because the methodology does not seek to consider the meanings that behaviours hold for mothers/parents themselves. Furthermore, her discussion takes no account of variable social contexts,[3] rather assuming *a single set of valuable qualities* for children to develop within a monolithic American society. Hammersley (1979) discusses in more general terms how ethnographic analytic concepts may differ from traditional concepts in precisely these ways.

Sylva and Lunt (1982) offer descriptions of 'good mothering'. Relying heavily on naturalistic observations, they describe good mothering as requiring sensitivity, consistency, stimulation and responsiveness. Walkerdine and Lucey (1989) discuss how notions of 'sensitive mothering' have been promoted since the 1940s on a conceptual basis of 'attachment' which ignores the political and theoretical issues underlying such a concept, while women who fail to devote themselves to the baby's 'need for attachment' are pathologised as egocentric (Phoenix and Woollett 1991).

Childrearing may also be judged by reference to what contributes to 'success' within the existing institutional arrangements of Western societies, particularly educational success. Educational institutions are themselves built upon the cultural assumptions of some groups in society rather than others (Henderson 1981, Keddie 1971), and yet it is these particular educational evaluations that are used as the basis for measuring children's mental abilities (Henderson 1981). The power to define what is good childrearing may constitute part of the 'cultural capital' which the middle classes can pass on to their children (Bourdieu 1973, Tulkin 1975).

It is very clear that Newson and Newson (1978) regard working class parenting as inferior when it comes to relative advantages in wider social life. However, their discussion does not question what counts as education and cultural capital, or how *their own construction* of childrearing may inter-relate with constructions of educational pedagogy to create a neat but apparently 'objective' package of working class inability to profit from the educational system. It is particularly apparent in their discussion of home and school (Newson and Newson 1977) how they are constrained within both psychological and educational concepts. They do not consider that educational goals may themselves reflect middle class cultural values – that written culture is more highly valued than oral culture, that intellectual ability is more highly valued than practical ability, and that abstract knowledge is regarded as distinct from concrete knowledge (Walkerdine and Lucey 1989).[4] Contrast the following discussion of what counts as 'brains', given during the course of my own study:

> Sharon wasn't much of a scholar, she couldn't add two and two and she couldn't really write very much, but in fact she was much brainier than what Janet was, 'cos Janet couldn't use her hands all that much, but Sharon could. She had brains for working. She could put anything together . . . I think I'm actually the same, could *do* it in the practical but can't do it in the verbal. (Grandmother)

Laosa (1981) points out that much observational work on mother–child interactions has been directed at explaining differences in school performance among different social groups, so that their implicit agenda is to discover how lower class socialisation is deficient. The cultural circles between middle class/better educated mothers, middle class researchers and middle class educational institutions may all *reinforce each other* in their implicit evaluations and understandings of what childrearing is all about. Walkerdine and Lucey suggest that: 'Science claims to tell the truth about natural mothering but it is founded upon a set of fantasies and fears of what is to be found in the working class' (1989: 29). Furthermore, Gans (1962, discussed by Tulkin 1975) suggests that middle class researchers pathologise working class childrearing because they cannot accept the idea that working class life concerns an active rejection of middle class culture.

The problems in psychological discussions of childrearing differences have been increasingly recognised by psychologists themselves (e.g. Laosa 1981, Tulkin 1975, Walkerdine and Lucey 1989, White 1981). Laosa points to the necessity in research on socio-cultural diversity to: '. . . recognise and accept that human behaviour may be perceived as competent or incompetent only in the context of specific roles and value judgements' (1981: 134). Woollett and Phoenix (1991) discuss the limitations within developmental psychology resulting from the lack of attention paid to mothers' own experiences. Yet such psychological discourses of childrearing have been highly influential in a number of professions that deal with childrearing in families, such as the legal profession (Poulter 1982, discussed by Morgan 1985), social workers (Nice 1988), health visitors (Abbott and Sapsford 1990) and family therapists (Morgan 1985). Social policy issues have also been debated on the basis of assumptions embedded within psychological research, for instance in relation to daycare facilities (Bone 1977) or childminding (Bruner 1980, Bryant et al. 1980).

Much research on family lives is rooted in the concerns of professionals, or publicly defined social policy issues, rather than the concerns of family members themselves. Health care is also a matter of professional and social policy interest, but this is one area where children's needs are still met very much within the home rather than within a public institution (such as schools). While these health needs are of central interest to health workers, the involvement of such professionals has to be mediated through mothers. It is perhaps not coincidental, then, that it is here that some of the most interpretivist research work has been carried out in relation to maternal childrearing. These studies (e.g. Cornwell 1985, Graham 1985, Locker 1981) seek to understand issues of children's health care by starting from the perspective of mothers (although Cornwell's work has a wider focus than children alone). In Graham's writing, much of women's work as mothers is seen as health work, such that the family may be described as a health-care institution by professional researchers. Yet mothers themselves may not necessarily define their family lives in such all-embracing health terms at all. Thus while these studies provide a clear body of literature that examines women's lives with their children from a broadly 'grounded' or 'interactionist' perspective, they are still rooted primarily within issues that arise within public domains of social policy.

Sociology and childrearing: 'socialisation', 'reproduction' and social class

When students first begin to learn about sociology, one of the first topics they are likely to encounter is 'socialisation'. This is the concept by which traditional sociology has considered issues of childrearing, referring to the processes by which children learn to become members of society, gradually acquiring all the skills, knowledge and all aspects of learned behaviours that are part of the culture into which they are born. Since sociologists generally argue that almost all behaviours include an element of social learning, socialisation is a concept that includes virtually all aspects of becoming a human being. Yet, once students have been introduced to some of these ideas, they are unlikely to encounter issues of socialisation again as they progress within sociology. This is part of the overall tendency for both children and family life to be marginalised from the core concerns of sociology (Morgan 1985) in favour of more publicly based and male-centred social contexts.

'Socialisation' itself is a broad-ranging, umbrella notion, so much so that Waksler (1991) doubts that it can be a useful concept at all without considerable revision. The lack of sustained attention it receives within sociology means that it is not translated into an analysis of concrete daily interactions that might, for example, take account of maternal behaviour as it is experienced within specific settings. Sociology has neglected to relate macro-structuralist theories of socialisation to the experiences of real mothers and children. Childcare occurs very largely within gendered social worlds that seem to have been largely unrecognised by sociologists, or at best treated as marginal to 'society'. In this respect, sociologists are once again reproducing wider social attitudes in their own work.

The domestic unit occupies a key position in the lives of individuals, constituting a primary group of central importance to most family members, and mediating between individuals and more generalised social influences. Yet sociologists have tended to overlook the potential of family study not just as a site for the *application* of sociological theory, but as a site for the *development* of such theory. On the other hand, writers on family life have returned the compliment, since such writing is often quite unsociological and untheorised (Morgan 1975, 1985), and couched in highly evaluative terms (see e.g. Fletcher 1966).

The areas of family study that have received the most sustained sociological attention are marital relationships and wider kinship ties. Sociologists have shown very little interest in parent–child relationships. The lives of children in their own right are now receiving increasing, and long overdue, attention from the new sociology of childhood (Harré 1986, James and Prout 1990, Morrow 1992, Qvortrup et al. 1994, Waksler 1991) – although much of the older work in this area has concentrated on children within educational settings (see review by Davies 1982). This important new approach seeks to recognise children as independent social actors, with childhood viewed as a social construction rather than a natural and inevitable phenomenon rooted in biology. However, in seeking to gain a perspective on children as full members of society apart from their parents, there may be a danger of again neglecting and marginalising the significance of parent–child relationships.

Structuralist theories of socialisation
One of the only leading social theorists to pay attention to parent–child relationships is Parsons, writing within his overall func-tionalist analysis of society. Within this view, mothering activities are bound to occur in response to societal needs, contributing to the smooth running of the social system. This functionalist explanatory framework has been seriously and effectively critiqued (see e.g. Lessnoff 1973, Ribbens 1979), but it may be useful to distinguish this overall explanatory model from Parsons' more descriptive work (Goldthorpe 1983, Morgan 1975). While the latter is highly ethnocentric, I have been quite startled at times by the similarities between some of Parsons' writings and some of my own analysis of women's family lives – particularly their position as the centre-pin of the emotional life of the family (chapter 8). On the other hand, his description of men as the main link between the family and the wider social system is seriously flawed, overlooking the crucial ways in which women mediate between their children and other people in a variety of settings (see e.g. Graham 1985, O'Donnell 1985, Mayall 1988, and chapters 4 and 9 of this book).

Marxist writers (Morgan 1975, 1985) do not see socialisation in the same harmonious light as functionalist theorists, but they share the functionalist view of mothering activities as a response to *forces from outside* the family, in this case, the needs of the capitalist system for the 'reproduction' of a docile labour force (the term 'reproduction' being favoured in place of 'socialisation'). Marxist and functionalist approaches also therefore share the tendency towards explaining too much socialisation/reproduction, in the sense that: '. . . they would seem to be less satisfactory in explaining how individuals might come to challenge, question or seek to change these perceived roles' (Morgan 1985: 234).

Most Marxist feminist writing on family life has been concerned with an analysis of domestic labour and gender roles, rather than a detailed analysis of the care of children. While Smith (1983) is a notable exception, her explicit aim is to consider how family economic dependencies are determined by wider class relations, rather than to consider the domestic group as a social psychological unit where 'other things are going on' (1983: 7). Rapp argues that the relationship between family and social world is seen as problematic because we *conceptualise* it separately: '. . . it is this acceptance of 'the family' as a natural unit existing in separation from the total social formation which *creates* the problem of its insertion into that world, at least at the level of theory' (1979: 175, original emphasis). What these macro sociological analyses lead to, then, is a view of family interactions as determined by social forces arising elsewhere, such that they do not require sustained analysis in their own right in order to develop a satisfactory approach to social theory. The effects of this form of analysis can be clearly seen in sociological debates about social class patterns of childrearing. These debates build upon psychological descriptions of childrearing differences (which are themselves seriously flawed, as discussed earlier), to seek explanations of how variabilities in childrearing seem to be systematically related to social structure in the form of social class.

Sociological explanations of why different social classes appear to hold different childrearing values and practices overwhelmingly tend to see social structure (either in terms of social class or employment) as determining family interactions (e.g. Bronfenbrenner 1979, Daniels and Moos 1989, Kohn 1959, 1963, 1969, Pearlin 1972). Women's domestic lives with their children are seen as dependent variables, with the determining, independent variables based within the more male-oriented worlds of paid employment. There is only a limited amount of work that considers the possibility of an opposite flow of influence (reviewed by Lambert 1990). Yet alternative explanations are clearly possible for the data that these writers themselves present. Pearlin, for example, argues that Italian parents seek to retain great control over and solidarity within their families because family networks and family reputations are vital to obtaining work within employment institutions which operate particularistically. However, an alternative explanation that would seem equally plausible is that Italian employment institutions are particularistic *because* Italian families are very cohesive and maintain strong networks of influence.

Kohn makes his theoretical position clear at the outset: '. . . we take as given the existing social structure of class, religion, national background and the like and trace its probable impact on parental values and behaviour' (1969: 4). He argues that social classes develop different values because they experience contrasting conditions of life related to their different occupational experiences, leading to differences in childrearing, particularly as regards discipline orientations: 'This supposition does not necessarily assume that parents consciously train their children to meet future occupational requirements, it may simply be that their own occupational experiences have significantly affected parents' conceptions of what is desirable behaviour, on or off the job, for adults or for children' (in Bronfenbrenner and Mahoney 1975: 432).

Kohn's work has been significant, being reprinted in various collections of readings (e.g. Anderson 1971, Bronfenbrenner and Mahoney 1975), and leading on to other work which still continues (Ellis et al. 1978, Luster et al. 1989, Peterson et al. 1982). As Steinkamp (1983) suggests, Kohn has done much original empirical work to examine the connections between personality, family and social structure. However, his explanations must be seen as seriously flawed in a number of ways.

First, the most glaring difficulty with Kohn's work is his almost total disregard for the *gendered nature of parenting activities* (Ribbens 1979, Steinkamp 1983), while social class is defined simply in relation to men's occupations. Not only does this render his explanations seriously deficient theoretically, there is also evidence that women do indeed act as independent social actors within their family lives. A considerable body of research reveals the significance of women's own characteristics and experiences for socialisation processes (e.g. Douglas 1967, Hayes and Miller 1989, Jackson and Marsden 1966, Kerchoff 1972, Luster et al. 1989, Osborne and Morris 1979).

Secondly, Kohn's discussion of social class is a very simplistic one that dichotomises social class without paying attention to the upper class, or to the fragmentary nature of the middle class, or to sections within the working class. Indeed, in a review of Kohn's work, Steinkamp (1983) suggests that the intricacies of the relationships between men's occupational experiences and the values they hold are so complex as to render obsolete Kohn's narrow view of personality as simply derived from class position, even in relation to men's lives.

Thirdly, in developing this simplistic dichotomy, Kohn *conflates a number of different variables* such as education, income and political orientation as well as occupation. He then slips between these variables in discussing the reasons for social class childrearing patterns. Even more seriously, at times he also seems to be including different values as part of the *definition* of the differences in the conditions of life in the social classes, which are then said to account for the differences of parental values, rendering his explanations tautologous.

Fourthly, by relying on large scale surveys, Kohn's work suffers the difficulty of presenting a cross-sectional picture in time, so that he is unable to consider processes that occur *across time*, for instance, that the values a man holds may affect his selection of a particular occupation in the first place (Steinkamp 1983). Kohn's explanations rely entirely on current position in social structure, so that there is no consideration of how values may be *re*produced over generations. Together, these difficulties mean that Kohn does not pay attention to the possibility of *interactions between different variables* as these occur as real processes over time in people's lives.

Bernstein's work is primarily concerned with links between education, social class and family, and is rather more sophisticated and gender-aware than Kohn's. On the other hand, like Kohn, he is inclined to see the division of labour as determining childrearing patterns (1971). Yet this aspect of his analysis shifts somewhat between different sections of his work, so that he sometimes seems to suggest that some changes in childrearing may originate within the family, to be incorporated later within educational pedagogy, and may shape the division of labour (1975). Generally, however, Bernstein is most interested in educational systems and neglects to pay sustained attention to socialisation within family life.

Overall, then, sociological explanations of social class patterns in childrearing are heavily structuralist in orientation. As a result, they take a deterministic view of family interaction patterns. They fail to demonstrate the mechanisms that might operate with respect to mothers as distinct from fathers, in other words to show what social structure might mean in relation to women's lives and how this might impinge on the experiences of mothers with their children.[5] They also show the common tendency in such explanations to make assumptions about the direction of causal flow. This is compounded by a neglect of social processes over time, operating at the level both of broad historical changes and of individual histories and experiences. The overall effect is to remove this key area of women's lives from the concerns of sociological theory.

If we relate these criticisms to each other we can produce quite different explanations for the social class patterns found in the traditional work on childrearing. We could suppose that it is women's own childhood and young adult experiences that shape their later attitudes and values. As a result middle class women are more likely to marry men who are now in, or are likely shortly to enter, middle class occupations. Also as a result of these attitudes and values formed in their earlier experiences they are more likely to adopt certain styles of childrearing (see chapter 9). This quite different possible interpretation of causal flows would also result in a correlation being found between current social class, as measured by husband's occupation, and childrearing patterns – the very same patterns for which Kohn and his associates have produced such different explanations.

Historical sociology and interactionist approaches to socialisation

Writers whose ideas are less rooted in a macro sociological analysis have more scope for considering different sorts of reciprocal and interactive flows of influence between socio-economic circumstances and childrearing values. In reviewing historical work on family life in general, Morgan concludes: 'The point perhaps is not that we need to choose between either the family or industrialisation as causal or independent variables but that the whole attempt to frame the problem in these terms is one fraught with difficulties and should be abandoned' (1985: 175).

One researcher who has sought to *reconsider the causal assumptions* of macro theorising is Thompson. Thompson's oral history methodology and Weberian theoretical orientation lead him to consider links between social structure and family life in rather different terms: 'I have come increasingly to believe that the more important question . . . is the reverse of what almost everyone has studied: it is how far can differences in family life and values explain variations in economic success?' (1984: 515). Thompson's innovative research compared two Scottish communities of similar economic base but with different socialisation practices, leading to the suggestion that differences in childrearing (among other factors) have led to different levels of economic prosperity in the two communities.

It is perhaps no surprise that it is those writers who are closest to a *micro, phenomenological view* of social life who are most likely to view socialisation as an *active process* between children and adults within specific social contexts. Berger and Luckmann (1971) describe socialisation in terms of the individual 'taking over' the world in which others live, in a creative process by which people come to occupy the same world. As a result: 'We now not only understand each other's definitions of shared situations, we define them reciprocally. . . . We not only live in the same world, we participate in each other's being. Only when he [sic] has achieved this degree of internalisation is an individual a member of society' (1971: 150). The socialisation process is 'mediated' by the child's significant others, who not only occupy a particular position within objective social structure, but also have their own 'individual biographically rooted idiosyncrasies' (p. 151).

While children may actively participate in the socialisation process, this participation occurs on rather unequal terms: 'it is the adults who set the rules of the game. . . . The child can play the game with enthusiasm or with sullen resistance. But alas, there is no other game around' (1971: 154). Consequently, the individual child's particular social reality comes to be seen as inevitable, such that even if s/he encounters later in life the possibilities of other realities, this will remain the child's 'home world' and will have a stronger sense of reality than any other subsequent ones: 'Primary socialisation thus accomplishes what (in hindsight of course) may be seen as the most important confidence trick that society plays on the individual – to make appear as necessity what is in fact a bundle of contingencies, and thus to make meaningful the accident of his [sic] birth' (p. 155).

While Berger and Luckmann's analysis probably represents the most significant sociological account of socialisation to date, since it was written there has been a resounding lack of interest from sociologists in the processes of family socialisation in general.[6] A major piece of follow-up work that utilises the phenomenological approach to analyse childrearing is the research carried out by Backett (1982), which offers an 'ideal typical construction of family processes based upon the parents' own understanding of their world' (Morgan 1985: 201). However, as Morgan points out, there is a presumption within Backett's approach that parenting is constituted between mothers and fathers, without reference to structural or historical factors – 'we cannot let our analysis stop at the domestic walls' (Morgan 1985: 203). Nevertheless, Backett's work was an important point of departure for my own study, with its goal of deconstructing the taken-for-granted aspects of parenting and of 'ordinary family life' by listening to parents' own voices.

Many sociological accounts of socialisation, whatever their orientation, owe a significant debt to the work of Mead, who is often considered to be a founding father of symbolic interactionism within sociology. His analysis of socialisation treats humans as *intrinsically* social beings, such that we cannot become recognisably human without social interaction, and this approach has been developed more recently by Burkitt (1991). At this point, we start to see common ground between sociological and psychological analyses of socialisation that seek to develop a constructionist perspective (Harré 1986), overcoming the individual/social dichotomy. Nevertheless, Mead's own work is criticised by Ingleby (1986) for replacing the duality of individual/social with the internal duality of 'me' and 'I'.[7]

Furthermore, all this work (largely by male writers) tends to depend upon highly abstract theorising, with little reference to how the issues relate to the lives of real mothers, fathers and children. In this sense, it somewhat replicates the longstanding tendency to theorise processes of 'socialisation' while failing to demonstrate the relevance of these sociological insights to everyday concrete situations. Indeed, it is striking how far empirical work on the lives of mothers and children has been carried out instead by female researchers.

Postmodernist accounts of socialisation, on the other hand, tend to view maternal childrearing as increasingly irrelevant, or unsuccessful. From this point of view, parental childrearing has either been replaced by the pervasive influence of the mass media (Denzin 1987), or has become unstable. This latter argument suggests that social realities have become so multitudinous, contradictory and changeable that parents have no basis on which to develop confident ideas about childrearing. As a result, people may panic, using simplified ideas that create a temporary order but with a constant instability (Dencik 1989, discussed by Cheal 1991). Here postmodernists seem to share the pessimism of anti-modernist accounts of contemporary Western family living that long for a return to a supposed golden era of stable traditional family life. Yet such analyses replicate the longstanding tendency of traditional sociology to marginalise and underestimate the significance of women's experiences, perspectives and direct daily interactions with their children. While expert discourses propounded within the public domain may have become multitudinous and contradictory, I suspect that many women have a longstanding capacity for dealing with contradiction and complexity in their lives, as much feminist analysis would argue, and as later chapters reveal.

Conclusions for the feminist sociological study of childrearing

In interactionist terms, socialisation is crucially concerned with children's internalisation and *interpretation* of shared meanings: '. . . the immediate apprehension or interpretation of an objective event as expressing meaning, that is, as a manifestation of another's subjective processes which thereby becomes subjectively meaningful to myself' (Berger and Luckmann 1971: 149). From this point of view, a key aspect of children's socialisation concerns the stock of social knowledge held by the significant others with whom they interact during primary socialisation.

Critical psychology and a phenomenological sociology of family life converge in their mutual concern with meanings, questioning the assumption that the realm of *action* is separate from the realm of *meaning* (e.g. Adlam et al. 1977). Ingleby describes how critical psychologists have fundamentally reassessed the conceptual split between thought and action, and have sought to break down

> . . . the individual/society dichotomy via the following two-stage argu-
> ment. First, human thought, perception and action must be approached
> in terms of *meanings*: secondly, the vehicles of 'meanings' are codes
> (especially language) whose nature is inherently intersubjective.
> Therefore, mind is an intrinsically social phenomenon. And if
> psychology is the science of mind, then the object of psychology is not
> individuals, but (to put it rather ineptly) *what goes on in the space
> between them*: that is, the codes which structure action. (1986: 305,
> original emphasis).

In the present study, then, I am primarily concerned with meanings, but I do not apologise for thereby failing to give an account of 'real relationships' and 'actual behaviour' between parents and children, since such a failing is only possible if we presuppose a dichotomy between meanings and actions. When mothers/parents described their lives with their children in my research interviews, my concern was not with how far they were giving a 'true' picture of what they 'really' *did* – or even how they 'really' *thought* about what they *did* – with their children, but with how far we can discern parental philosophies, ideologies or meanings within their accounts of their concrete practices with their children, because such meanings are themselves central to socialisation. There was no question of treating women's accounts of their lives as distortions or ideologically unsound constructions of their concrete realities.

At the same time, it is crucial that we do not reify meanings themselves, or treat them as if they have a reality of their own which research is somehow seeking to describe. Meanings are always socially constructed within particular contexts, and are manifested in a variety of ways. The research process is one such context, of which the researcher her/himself is clearly an important feature. Part of the fascination of research is that in this very undertaking you help to constitute the object of study.

Yet if we view socialisation as the child's internalisation and active interpretation of meanings,[8] we approach a position where it almost does not matter what a mother 'actually does' with her children, as long as both mother and children understand what she does as signifying love, caring and positive valuation. In discussing work on different family cultures, Tulkin suggests that a middle class observer might view some behaviour as 'extremely strict', but 'the torrents of threat and cajolery neither impinge on the feelings of parental affection, nor are meant as signs of rejection. As one mother explained to her child, "We hit you because we love you"' (Gans 1962, quoted by Tulkin 1975: 310).

Poster suggests that we may indeed regard children's 'needs' as constituted for them by parents, because 'they label and give meaning to the child's actions . . . The child has no needs, properly speaking, until it interacts with its parents, and in this interaction the parents, by responding to the child's behaviour, determine the existence and character of the child's needs' (1978: 5).

Such a view opens up almost unspeakable questions, however. For instance, current child sexual abuse concerns lead to some very highly charged debates about what are regarded as such evils, in what could be seen as a contemporary 'moral panic' (Cohen 1973). However, such highly evaluative public debates may also shift the meanings attached to particular private adult/child interactions, and such shifts may close off certain discussions. Thus it may be more difficult openly to discuss physical contact between parents and children, or to consider the possibility of sexual feelings between mothers and their children, let alone fathers and their children, or other adult males who work with children.

In such processes, the meanings of particular behaviours between parents and children may be changed, such that an act which has previously been seen as quite desirable or normal may come to be charged with guilt and ambiguity. This then raises difficult questions about the inter-relationship between public discourse and private (intimate?) understandings. Mothers/parents and their children are not islands, of course, able to develop their own particular shared understandings of the meanings of their interactions, without regard to the wider social meanings (see e.g. Statham 1986). There may be complex negotiations of meanings within and across different 'families' and other settings. Jamieson and Toynbee's adult interviewees suggested the opposite process was at work in recalling their childhoods in the early twentieth century:

It appears that the right of parents to children's services and obedience was so universally accepted, that our most compliant respondents reacted with some puzzlement when we asked questions about how their parents got them to carry out their chores. Some people said they had no other expectations. Other children in their neighbourhood were similarly involved in chores and had the same standards of behaviour expected of them by *their* parents: '*We were all doing the same thing*'. (1990: 91, original emphasis)

Diversity of understandings may thus be particularly difficult to deal with in the area of childrearing since it may be much easier to induct a child into a particular maternal definition of reality if the child does not encounter alternative definitions in settings outside the home. There is the further significant possibility/likelihood that children may in addition spontaneously generate their own particular meanings by which to understand their lives (Walkser 1991). From this point of view, perhaps we are mistaken to seek a *general* theory of children's development or needs, since different children may *assert* different needs (as parents themselves will often say), as well as encountering their parents' particular constructions of their needs.

Those who work directly with practical issues of childrearing, particularly issues of child abuse and neglect, may feel that my present discussion is not much help when faced with distressing circumstances. Nevertheless, it is a legitimate and important academic contribution to stand a little apart, and analyse issues from a slight distance. Furthermore, unless we do consider the meanings which parents and children attach to their own interactions, any interventions may be unhelpful at best, while the imposition of our own meanings and unconsidered evaluations of childrearing may at times be positively damaging.[9]

In seeking to explore and discuss mothers' own understandings of their childrearing, how does my present discussion relate to these interactions between public and private meanings? I am seeking to understand quite private meanings, while discussing them within the public context of a research publication. I have sought to explore variabilities of meanings as empathetically as possible, but as Morgan points out, even the documentation of diversity constitutes 'a reflection of a fundamental ethical and political orientation' (1985: 121).

While 'choice' and diversity have been increasingly celebrated within contemporary Western cultures, choices are not made in a vacuum. It is a powerful negotiating device to be able to suggest that a personal preference is underpinned by a wider morality or ideology. An even stronger position can be maintained if a personal preference can be presented as if it is not a choice at all, but rather an inevitable part of the way things are, rooted perhaps in nature or biology. For these reasons, it may be difficult for us to tolerate diversity, including differences in childrearing perspectives, because such diversity may undermine our own position.

Childrearing, psychology and sociology 25

I have also sought to stay close to an 'insider perspective', hoping to avoid evaluative judgements. It is possible (inevitable?) that readers will discern such evaluations in my discussions (and see the Introduction to Part II for some discussion of how the interviewees felt about this). What an emphasis on meanings does do, however, is to put mothers' own voices centre-stage. In this sense, it has an important contribution to make to a feminist sociological study of childrearing.

Notes

1. Exploring Parenthood is a national British charity started by a child psychotherapist and a family therapist, to provide workshops led by 'a team of experts ... to promote a dialogue and partnership between parents and professionals' (Exploring Parenthood Trust 1982, Latimer Education Centre, Freston Road, London W10 6TT, ph. 081 960 1678). I am aware of mothers in various locations in Britain who have been introduced by church organisations to the Dobson tapes from America (discussed by Judith Stacey 1990). I was informed of the movement based on the book by Dreikurs (1972) (an American psychiatrist) by a mother in the research, Kate. She was unsure of its origins, having been introduced to it by a personal acquaintance. Nevertheless, we must also be aware of the limitations of the impact of expert advice books on mothers' childrearing ideas. Advice books seemed to be used mainly by those women who were unsure of their own childrearing ideas, and turned to advice books to find confirmation for childrearing ideas which they already held but for which they wanted validation (as other studies have also suggested, e.g. Jamieson and Toynbee 1990, Stolz 1967, Urwin 1985, and see also Ribbens 1990a).

2. In the following discussion, I present a critique of the work of Newson and Newson. Nevertheless, their work was a vital reference point for my own study. In many ways it was highly innovative at the time their longitudinal work commenced. I was also personally very grateful as a mother to find some account of childrearing that tried to listen to what mothers had to say, rather than telling me in any overt way what I ought to be doing with my children. It seems Newson and Newson have become more inclined over the years to move towards prescriptive writings – see e.g. Newson and Newson (1989).

3. For a more detailed discussion of Baumrind's typology, see Ribbens (1990a), chapter 6.

4. Some feminist writers have similarly noted the priority given to masculinist publicly based knowledge over more female-oriented, domestically based knowledge (e.g. Belenky et al. 1986, Edwards 1993a).

5. All of these issues relate to difficulties in the sociological treatment of the social class position of women, as well as children. I shall return to this question in chapter 9.

6. Although a few notable exceptions have built on the symbolic interactionist approach (e.g. Denzin 1977, Dreitzel 1973).

7. These terms are difficult to define concisely. They both refer to social aspects of the self, but the 'I' is the individual object which has consciousness and can be a stimulus to others, while the 'me' refers to the reflective identity developed as a result of others' reactions to the 'I'. For a fuller discussion see Burkitt (1991).

8. Alanen (1990) suggests that we should describe socialisation as 'construction' rather than 'internalisation', as a way of emphasising both its social and its interactive character.

9. For a study of child abuse which particularly brings mothers' own voices into focus, see Hooper (1993).

2

The Feminist Study of Childrearing

Many feminist writers have been aware of the significance of motherhood for women's lives, but have not paid attention to the *content* of everyday mothering activities. In this chapter, I consider feminist debates on motherhood, explaining the particular feminist position adopted within this book and some of its methodological implications. This is a position which seeks to use both 'insider' and 'outsider' perspectives on women's lives with their children, while prioritising the importance of listening to what mothers have to say about their own childrearing.

Feminist analyses of motherhood and childrearing

> The history and fate of feminism are intimately tied to the history of the family. (Judith Stacey 1986: 237)

> . . . feminism and motherhood have often seemed to be fighting one another, pulling women in two different directions, interposing a theme of divided loyalties instead of permitting a political unity and sense of individual wholeness.
>
> (Oakley 1986b: 74)

Feminism, motherhood and childrearing

One of the most important – if not *the* most important – contributions that feminists have made to discussions about family life is to question how far it is rooted in biology and nature, and to open up for investigation how far motherhood in particular is indeed socially constructed. This has enabled certain questions to be raised that previously could not be expressed, concerning the social construction of what is described as a maternal instinct (e.g. Badinter 1981, MacIntyre 1976), whether or not children need to be cared for by their biological mothers, and whether children's interests and mothers' interests necessarily coincide.

Since motherhood is so crucial to women's lives and identities, it is perhaps not surprising that it constitutes a highly contentious and sensitive topic within feminist writings (for reviews, see Segal 1985, Judith Stacey 1986, Tong 1989). At times feminism has been seen as so anti-motherhood that ordinary women with children have felt quite alienated from feminism (Friedan 1981, Richardson 1993), while feminists who have children have sought to reconcile this with their political orientations (Gordon 1990). This is not just a matter, however, of feminist anti-maternal writing versus women's everyday choice to become mothers, since there are sharp differences of view among different feminist writers themselves. Chodorow and Contratto (1982) suggest that the extreme divergences in feminist writings on motherhood may themselves be a reproduction of the more extreme feelings we have experienced towards our own mothers when we were ourselves small dependent children. Judith Stacey, in contrast, suggests that the complexities of (American) feminist attitudes to motherhood and family cannot simply be described as oppositional, but as being in tension: 'contemporary feminist visions are actually characterized by unresolved tension between advocating androgyny and celebrating traditionally female, and especially maternal, values' (1986: 237).

What the feminist debates have perhaps shown us is that motherhood is likely to be a crucial but sensitive part of women's lives, involving *deep ambivalence* in a central part of our self-identities, an ambivalence which may be reflected and perpetuated in our relationships with our daughters (Flax 1978, Rich 1977). Thus while motherhood may at times be analysed as the cornerstone of women's oppression (e.g. Firestone 1971, Mitchell 1971), recent feminist writers have been concerned to point out the ways in which it may also sometimes offer women scope for an experience of power and active agency (e.g. Gordon 1986, Johnson 1988, New and David 1985, Ribbens 1993a). Oakley comments that 'people who mother are women who in any event represent a threat to the social order' (1986b: 83, referring to Douglas 1970) – such that the interests of capitalism and patriarchy require that 'women should not find in motherhood a sense of their own active power to change the world' (p. 87). Rich also refers to women's experience of authority and control in relation to children, power in its patriarchal sense. However, she suggests that this power is turned against women through its domestication: 'In transfiguring and enslaving women, the womb – the ultimate source of this power – has historically been turned against us, and itself made into a source of powerlessness' (1977: 68).

These illustrations demonstrate how the experience of motherhood has been the subject of extended and heated feminist debates. Women writers have indeed been preponderant in considering changes in women's roles in twentieth-century Western societies, including the extent, nature and explanations for any such changes. However, whether explicitly feminist or not, such writers have been more concerned with the institution and experience of *being a mother*. They have paid very little attention to the *content of childrearing* (Gordon 1986).

Yet issues of childcare, presumptions about the needs of children, and decision-making about how to deal with and relate to children are major preoccupations in women's everyday lives. Furthermore, a consideration of how women perceive, understand and resolve some of these issues around childrearing is essential to any analysis of gender relationships, divisions of labour and distributions of resources within households.

This gap in feminist writing has been partly acknowledged by some writers, who call for the development of feminist theories of children's needs and child development, and how these relate to the needs of mothers and fathers (Hodges 1981, Judith Stacey 1986). However, unless we start by listening closely to what women themselves have to say about their childrearing, there is a danger that a feminist theory of 'child development' might be unable to undertake the necessary fundamental reconceptualisation.

Private/public debates
A further potential input from feminist writings to the study of childrearing concerns the theoretical rethinking that is possible by paying attention to notions of public and private in social life, concepts which have themselves been the subject of sustained feminist debates (for a review see Edwards 1993b).

One concern is that the concept of the 'private sphere', like the concept of the 'family', may in itself be used *ideologically*, such that in using the concept we may implicitly be giving a sense of reality to what is in fact an ideological device (Eisenstein 1984, Ross 1979). There is therefore the suggestion that it is academic discourse which constitutes the boundary between public and private. However, if *social actors themselves* regard the family as a naturally private unit, then it will indeed have such an effect in terms of their actions, and thus have significance for people in their everyday lives. Examples of how people may use notions of private settings in their lives may be found in discussions of working class families and families living in poverty (Allan 1989a, Allan and Crow 1990), and Edwards' (1993a) discussion of mature mother-students. If social actors themselves use such notions in their everyday lives, these concepts must be regarded as relevant to our understanding of social life. This is how these concepts have been used within the present study.

Any application of these concepts must, however, take account of their broader historical and social construction. It is thus clear that the division between public and private settings has particular relevance and meaning in post-industrial Western societies, where 'work' has become ideologically separated off from 'family', and domestic life has been idealised as a 'haven in a heartless world' (Davidoff et al. 1976).

Feminist writers have also been at pains to point out that this ideological separation of public from private spheres is illusory in the sense that the State has taken a longstanding and increasing interest in regulating and supervising family life. This has been analysed both historically (e.g. Davin 1978, Rapp 1979, Riley 1981), and contemporaneously in relation to family law (Brophy 1987, Carol Smart 1984), social security systems (Land 1976, Ungerson 1983), policies on childcare provisions and facilities (New and David 1985), the work of health visitors (Abbott and Sapsford 1990, Oakley 1981) and policies on community care (Sassoon 1987, Ungerson 1990).

Nevertheless, the contradictions in the relationship between women and the Welfare State have also been debated by feminist writers, who have pointed out the ways in which the State may both constrain and enable women's domestic lives (Jane Lewis 1986, Riley 1981). There is also a danger that such analyses, demonstrating how the State helps to shape private lives, may replicate traditional sociological tendencies to see women's family lives as passively subject to, and shaped by, large scale forces from without.

The post-war years have seen the increasing significance of 'the home' for modern family life (Crow 1989), both as a physical space and as a psychological experience of private territory. At the same time, notions of privacy may not be simply coterminous with the physical space of the home. The view of 'the family' and 'the home' as historically situated, ideological devices opens the door for us to deconstruct the family as a natural unit by examining *how its boundaries are socially constructed* in such a way as to become real for social actors, and this has been a very important consideration for the present study: 'As a social (and not a natural) construction, the family's boundaries are always decomposing and recomposing in continuous interaction with larger domains' (Rapp 1979: 175). Rapp suggests that 'the family' is to be distinguished by the element of normative commitment required from its members, and it is this commitment that leads to people's recruitment to the material relations of household. Rapp further argues that the normative commitment of 'family' may or may not overlap with household membership, and may also occur differently for different household members, so that in effect they may share a household but belong to different families. These issues are all explored within the present study.

Beyond the debates about the private home, there is also the question of the continuing importance of *significant informal networks* beyond the home:

> Philip Abrams (1978) pointed out the difficulty of 'crossing the frontier between formal social action and informal social relationships' when he was investigating the possibility of developing neighbourhood care programmes which would link bureaucratic and private domain relationships. He was so impressed with the differences he referred to them as 'alien worlds'. (Stacey and Davies 1983: 14)

Where there are informal links between women as mothers, do these constitute significant networks and *gendered social worlds*? While such issues have been discussed most clearly within the work of feminist historians (e.g. Smith-Rosenberg 1975), they may also have relevance to contemporary mothers. Accounts of women's lives as mothers may underestimate the continuing significance of women's social contacts outside the home, and thus overstate the isolation of 'housewives' within the private home (Bell and Ribbens 1994). The exclusive picture of housewives as isolated may thus neglect an extremely significant aspect of some women's experiences as mothers, not least because such networks imply the possibility that, beyond the private sphere of the home, there may also be a female social world that is not part of male public worlds.

It becomes apparent therefore that there are a number of different possible meanings for the 'private sphere' in women's lives:

1 as referring to women's lives as mothers living in *domestic households* often equated with the concept of 'the family';
2 as referring to mothers' involvements in *gendered networks* and communities beyond the household, which may or may not represent a source of alternative values that challenge the views of male partners (discussed in Bell and Ribbens 1994);
3 as referring to a specifically *female culture* (Dubois et al. 1980), based upon women's shared domestic and child-oriented experiences and possibly relating to a specifically female psychology (Edwards 1993b).

At this point, we can see that the public/private distinction may not be a matter of specific physical locations at all, although it clearly has a particular relationship with socially defined physical space. Cheal (1991) suggests that what is referred to by the terms public and private should rather be regarded as 'contrasting principles of organisation', of moral economy and political economy. Ferree (1985, 1987) discusses how women may lead a 'divided life', between two different systems of values. In reviewing

German research on the work and family lives of working class women, she describes how the women move between a use value orientation, where work is personally produced towards the satisfaction of the needs of others, and an exchange value orientation, where work is governed by the instrumental and abstract nature of market relations. Moving between these two creates deep ambivalences for women, even while they may value both. Each value orientation requires a psychological shift of gear, while the capacities developed in each type of labour are often devalued by those for whom women work in their other life.

This discussion resonates strongly with Edwards' work (1993b) on the ways in which mature mother-students may seek to accommodate the very different experiences of being a mother in the private domain, and being a student in the public domain. Furthermore, Ruddick (1982) suggests that there are specific ways of thinking that are related particularly to maternal experiences, and O'Brien describes the 'cultural cohesiveness of femininity and the universality of maternal consciousness' (1981: 50). Nelson's work (1989) concerning daycare providers who are non-employed mothers reveals how the deep ambiguities they experience, caught between the expectations of mothering relationships and the expectations of contractual relationships, lead women to withdraw from this employment.

There are therefore various aspects to what we mean by the public/private distinction which, I suggest, together amount to different 'ways of being' in the world (Edwards, 1993b). But whatever the private/public division actually refers to, what these terms are seeking to elucidate is that women's lives are different from men's in socially patterned ways, raising the central feminist concern as to whether we value our differences from men, or seek to equalise our relationships with men. If a 'private' – as distinct from 'public' – 'way of being' refers to a particularly woman-centred experience, is this a source of oppression for women, or something to be valued that may be subversive of more masculinist, public ways of being? More specifically, does a domestic sphere have value, or is it the primary site for women's oppression? And if women's experiences within private settings do give rise to a female culture and way of being, what should be the relationship between this culture and a more explicitly political feminism based within the public sphere (particularly if the two then disagree)?

A number of writers have suggested that we have to stop thinking in such either/or categories and recognise the contradictions at the heart of women's lives, particularly in relation to our domestic lives. The division between public and private settings may thus be both constraining and enabling for women (Allan and Crow 1990), such that women may be both powerful and powerless with regard to their children (New and David 1985), creating a mix of freedom and unfreedom (Morgan 1985). Furthermore, these varying tensions and ambivalences will also be substantially cross-cut by issues of class (Ferree 1985) and race (Bhavnani and Coulson 1986, hooks 1982).

> When paid work and housework are both examined critically, they emerge as different, but neither separate nor equal, modes of social relationship that carry distinct meanings. To be true to women's experience, scholars must recognise both the values and costs of each . . . when a theoretical or political focus on the rewards to be gained in either type of work obscures the rewards renounced in the other, the resolutions suggested will necessarily be insufficient and temporary. (Ferree 1985: 534)

One of the difficulties in discussing these contradictions is how to find an appropriate language. If we use terms from public settings, we may automatically start to devalue women's private ways of being by describing them through concepts that are rooted within men's lives (Edwards and Ribbens 1991). If such devaluing becomes part of women's own understandings, we ourselves help to create the experience of the private sphere as oppressive (Sharistanian 1987). But if we use a language based within private settings, we may also risk obscuring the ways in which women's lives are disadvantaged in respect of public lives, overlooking the resulting constraints. Judith Stacey thus calls for us 'to recognise contradiction and to apply a critical perspective that distinguishes between giving value to traditionally female qualities and celebrating the female in a universalistic and essentialist manner' (1986: 237).

Insider/outsider analyses

The concepts of public and private, rather than the traditional sociological notions of macro and micro social levels, do much to bring women's lives into focus within social analysis. Yet the difficulties with these concepts pose a dilemma: how are we to situate our feminist academic perspectives? How are we to conceptualise women's lives in ways that both value women's perspectives within the private sphere yet also allow for critical insights from outside? This 'catch 22' for feminism is similar to that of the ethnographer who seeks both insider insight and outsider analysis without importing outsider misinterpretations.

In her widely cited article (1981), Margaret Stacey discusses how sociology has been conceptualised from the outset from male concerns within the public sphere, using masculinist concepts that arise from publicly defined issues. Stacey calls for a fundamental reconceptualisation *starting from women's concerns* within the domestic sphere. Yet this is a highly difficult project, since the concepts we use express aspects of what phenomenologists would describe as the taken-for-granted nature of social life.

Kelly-Gadol (1976) draws our attention to the significance of women's parenting roles for our *active agency in the reproduction of society*. She explores some of the ways in which public worlds may determine private ones, and patriarchy and property relations may operate in both spheres. However, she also goes on to say:

> The most novel and exciting task of the study of the social relation of the sexes is still before us: to appreciate how we are all, women and men, initially humanised, turned into social creatures by the work of the domestic order to which women have been primarily attached. Its character and the structure of its relations order our consciousness, and it is through this consciousness that we first view and construe our world. To understand the historical impact of women, family and the relation of the sexes upon society serves a less evident political end, but perhaps a more strictly feminist one. (1976: 323)

The feminist position taken within this book depends upon the following arguments:

o   We must not treat family life as 'natural', but must seek to deconstruct its taken-for-granted assumptions.
o   We must not take the boundaries of public/private ways of being, or of different cultures, as given, but look to see how they are experienced, constructed and negotiated by women themselves under circumstances which may be both constraining and enabling.
o   We must recognise that childrearing is a crucial area of women's lives, which deserves to be brought to the centre of the analysis and valued in its own right.
o   We must as far as possible reconsider these key issues for women's lives without evaluation, and without the imposition of professional/expert agenda or prescriptions, which have been largely developed by white middle class men.
o   We must take women's experiences and cultures seriously, using an 'insider' perspective to understand women's experiences on their own terms. By understanding women's cultures we can both value women's own lives and ideas, and also become more self-conscious about them.
o   We also need to take an 'outsider' perspective to approach this task reflectively and analytically within the context of a wider social analysis.

o We have to be conscious of the multiplicity of women's cultures, and the circumstances in which they are situated. We must always remain sensitive to issues of significant social identities such as race and class, that inter-relate with gender consciousness and its expression (Hewitt 1985).

Some limitations of an insider analysis
The emphasis within the present book is upon the exploration of women's own perspectives on their childrearing, prioritising the insider perspective and placing less emphasis upon an outsider perspective. It is important to recognise the limitations of this approach. First, this approach rules out *certain forms of explanation*, i.e. those based upon statistical correlations and causal modelling. It must be recognised, however, that while ideas about linear causality are predominant within the social sciences, other forms of explanation are also possible – psychoanalytic interpretations for example, or non-linear explanations allowing more scope for the dynamic and interactive nature of social action within historical processes.

Secondly, some feminist writers on family lives may well feel that my emphasis upon women's own accounts has led to the muting of any critique and analysis of *the socio-historic framework* for family life and childcare in contemporary Western societies. As I discussed earlier, feminist writers have done substantial work to deconstruct some of the circumstances of life in 'private families', in terms of ideologies that present family life as both inevitable and desirable, and in terms of social policies and processes that make alternative household arrangements more difficult to sustain or even to conceptualise. Yet the women interviewed in my own study generally showed little awareness of such debates (other than the issue of maternal employment), raising again the question of the relationship between some forms of feminist analysis/politics and the views of women themselves.

While such feminist socio-historical analyses have been concerned to show the constraints within which women's lives occur, the women interviewed in this study were more inclined to focus on those aspects of their lives where some sense of choice was felt to operate. The overall pattern or structures of constraints/opportunities were generally taken as given, although women might at times negotiate and resist around these structures. Thus most of the women believed in the importance of maternal childcare and made very few references to the absence of public childcare provisions. They were indeed more inclined to question the ways in which public/work lives are organised than to question prevailing domestic arrangements. There was also no discussion about the ways in which childcare arrangements may be assumed, under-pinned and shaped by social policies. To incorporate such analyses, then, the methodological emphasis upon the women's own meanings must be supplemented by discussions from other sources. Within this book, this particular sort of outsider perspective will be found primarily in the opening and concluding chapters.

Thirdly, an exclusive reliance on insider perspectives may make it more difficult to perceive issues of *gender* within childrearing (although see discussions of gender in chapter 3). In the accounts given in my own study, gender issues could be discerned to be operating in a number of ways, some of these much more prevalent than others:

1   An *explicit* discussion of (in)appropriate gender behaviour, generally considered in relation to children who are behaving out of role such as Mary's unladylike daughter, Susan's son who enjoys dancing.
2   Descriptions of children's *characters* that are *implicitly* in line with gender roles; while these are apparent in some accounts, there are also other accounts where children's characters are not described in ways appropriate to their gender stereotypes.
3   *Expectations of differences* about the general *development* of boys and girls, often with the implication that this is rooted in biology.
4   References to children's *leisure activities* in ways that are *implicitly* consistent with gender roles, often mapped onto the sharing of such interests with the parent of the appropriate sex such as girls shopping with mothers, boys involved with fathers' sporting activities. The latter appeared to be a particularly frequent pattern, with sport as a common focus for the father–son relationship.
5   *Implicit* cultural assumptions that *'individuals' are always gendered* – that it is impossible to conceptualise individuals without also considering them as female or male individuals.

While all of these gender expectations could be discerned in the accounts of some women, gender appeared to be more significant in the accounts given by fathers rather than mothers. Other studies also suggest that fathers are more likely than mothers to emphasise the sex of children and treat them differently (reviewed by Huston 1983). Other researchers, using different methodologies, also suggest that it may hard to discern sex-related differences in parenting behaviour (Statham 1986), but an outside observer of parental behaviour may see differences of treatment that parents themselves may not acknowledge (McGuire 1991).

My final concern about the emphasis upon insider perspectives is rather different, because it concerns the translation of such perspectives into an academic format. In particular, how can we write for an academic audience without losing the emotional content of mothering experiences? The feelings mothers have for their children may be as deep and powerful as any emotions women know. I have sometimes wondered at the temerity I have shown in this research project – I wanted to write about mothering, and what is important to mothers about their childrearing. But where are all the incredibly deep feelings in all this? And where are my feelings too? I have strong emotions about this research, and yet it appears to have been such an intellectual project.

In their review of various feminist works on motherhood, Chodorow and Contratto (1982) caution us against being carried away with our emotions about motherhood. They suggest the need for primary *and* secondary process thinking in our discussions of motherhood, but how we can incorporate both? This problem is akin to the ethnographer's difficulty in making the move from first to second order constructs (Schutz 1954) – such a move may be necessary, but how do we accomplish it without losing sight of the first? By writing about motherhood for academic research, I have been taking experiences from within the private sphere and writing about them for an audience in the public sphere. While I have sought to use a methodology and a language that stay close to women's own perspectives, I am also concerned that somewhere along the line the emotion has not been expressed, and has become obscured by the requirement of a rational discussion for a more public audience. There have been growing moves within sociology to consider how we incorporate emotions within our subject matter (Duncombe and Marsden 1993, Stevi Jackson 1993). Within my own research, however, I fear that this is one goal I have not been able to achieve satisfactorily.

Methodological issues in the feminist study of childrearing

So far I have argued that a feminist approach to childrearing must pay attention to certain theoretical and political considerations. These concerns meant it was crucial that my own research should give priority to mothers' own multifarious voices, using concepts and analysis rooted within the concrete everyday experiences of women's lives as mothers. Schutz (1954) argues that we must pay attention to the relationship between sociological concepts and everyday concepts. Such considerations have particular relevance to the study of women's lives, since much existing sociological and psychological work quite literally renders women's perspectives and experiences invisible. Furthermore, I would endorse Bernardes' (1988) call for a methodology that enables us to study people's lives as 'unities'. This does not, however, assume that people do experience their lives as unitary, since this is itself a key question within the sociological enterprise (see chapter 9).

The importance of paying systematic attention to the sources of our concepts, and their relation to people's own understandings, leads to an exploration of *meanings*, including their emotional import as well as their cognitive organisation and interactional contexts (Locker 1981). Furthermore, I believe that such an attention to concepts and meanings is an extremely powerful activity for sociologists – the terms of sociological agenda and descriptions can have a major impact on the whole meaning of everyday reality within which people are operating, although this may rarely be recognised as sociology (Bernardes 1987, 1988). In tackling problems in society, sometimes we need to consider whether we should redefine the problem, rather than look for solutions within the assumptions of the present definitions (Bernardes 1985b, Dawe 1973, Finch 1985, 1986). Furthermore, attention to topical concepts and insider perspectives may be especially significant in understanding issues such as family life, 'child development' and childrearing (Henderson 1981, Hess 1981). As I discussed in the previous chapter, meanings must be central to any analysis of childrearing.

The two methodologies that I found appropriate for dealing with these concerns were ethnography and life histories, using a grounded theory approach (Atkinson 1979, Glaser and Strauss 1968, Hammersley and Atkinson 1983, Smith 1988). A significant methodological principle of ethnography is naturalism, but this raises particular difficulties in the study of the 'private' arena of 'the family', where participant observation is a disruption on whatever terms it is conducted (see e.g. Tizard and Hughes 1984, and Vetere and Gale 1987). There is thus *no body of ethnographic work on family life* (and/or parent–child interactions in whatever setting), in the way that there is on schools and other educational settings, or on deviant groups. Ethnography is not only about observation, however, as Agar (1980) makes very clear. The life history interview in particular can incorporate ethnographic methodological principles in a way that is close to how people 'naturally' do think of their family lives – as histories of individual life spans and generations over time (see e.g. Cunningham-Burley 1985, 1986 on the significance of grandparenthood). For the purposes of the present study in particular, with the focus upon the women's own meanings, open-ended talk was the most appropriate method to use. Furthermore, the ethnographic principle of holism meant that I did not arbitrarily narrow the study to particular predetermined areas of childrearing, and sought to consider childrearing across a variety of different settings.

Ethnography is also concerned with processes over time. There are links here with the concerns of historical sociologists such as Philip Abrams:

> Process is the link between action and structure . . . . But history is not a force in its own right, any more than society is . . . . We can construct new worlds but only on the basis and within the framework of what our predecessors have constructed for us . . . . This shaping of action by structure and transforming of structure by actions both occur as processes in time. (1982: 3)

By using a quasi-life history method for my interviews, I was given accounts of women's lives with their children over time 'in which flux, emergence, precariousness and change are persistent facts at all levels of analysis' (Thompson 1981: 55). I was also in contact with a subgroup of the women interviewed over a period of some years.

The interviews that are used as a basis for discussion in subsequent chapters took place over more than four years altogether (the first pilot interview was conducted in December 1985 and the last full contact with the case-study families occurred in February 1990, although they were contacted again briefly in Winter 1993/4). While the study was broad-ranging in content, it was focused in terms of the social circumstances of the women included. The research thus concentrated on 24 white women living in middle income households in the South East of England outside London, all with an eldest child aged 7 at the time of our first meeting. Not all the women were currently living with the father of the child/ren, but all had been married to the father previously if not currently. Eight of these women were interviewed several times, and in these families interviews were also conducted with seven fathers and six maternal grandmothers. (For more details of the samples, see Appendix.)

I thus made quite specific decisions about who to include in this research. The choice of who we study carries many potential political values, since those studied may be chosen as representing people in particular need, or alternatively as representing something desirable. I did not focus my sample by either of these considerations, but by reference to a number of other concerns.

In several respects, my interviewees would appear to be women living within stereotyped 'traditional' families. There are widespread assumptions that we all 'know' what such 'traditional families' are and how children are brought up in them. Looking behind this stereotype and listening to the women's own voices may help us to reflect on some of the assumptions generally taken for granted about apparently 'ordinary' families. By providing detailed pictures of childrearing from within such families, the aim was to uncover some of our basic assumptions about them. Such assumptions are the basis for dominant ideologies that affect all mothers (see chapter 1), whatever their own circumstances, household formations, class or race. The research included in this book aimed to question such stereotypes by considering childrearing in a number of 'families' that had not been labelled as 'problematic' (by themselves or others) and considering just how much variability occurred between them. By looking at the variability behind the stereotype, I hoped to tease open our understandings of 'normality'. If we do not listen to women living in these circumstances, we fail to look behind the ideology to explore how women themselves experience and understand 'conventional' family life. Indeed, it is striking how Judith Stacey (1990) found that her search for a stereotypical 'traditional' working class American family was unsuccessful, leading her instead to study a household that had its own variations and idiosyncrasies.

Secondly, I was particularly concerned with issues of class in relation to women's and children's lives, since it was clear that this was problematic (see chapter 1). Indeed, since the time I made the original research decisions, the issue of women and social class has become a major debate within sociology. Another stereotype that tends to occur within the sociology of family life concerns the contrasts drawn between middle and working class families (Walkerdine and Lucey 1989), some studies even defining *out* households falling in the middle ranges of class hierarchies in order to present clearer contrasts between different class groups. I decided instead to focus on the variability between women living in broadly similar economic circumstances within the middle ranges of income, since it is precisely within the middle range of social class classifications that ambiguities are greatest about class contrasts in childrearing (Newson and Newson 1976). The emphasis upon household income rather than social class was one way of dealing with the difficulties in classifying women's class position. Indeed, it should be clearly noted that the sample included women from both working and middle class households by conventional classifications.

Thirdly, I was concerned about the difficulties researchers have had in describing childrearing in terms that are non-evaluative. The childrearing of various social groups has been extensively studied by white middle class researchers, who have evaluated it, found much of it wanting, and presented it as deprived – even despite their intentions to do otherwise (see chapter 1). I hoped that I might introduce fewer unconscious evaluations if I were studying mothers in circumstances close to my own, in terms of their class, income and ethnic group.

Paradoxically, one of my own experiences during the course of the research was a growing and painful awareness of the sources of my own *differences* from the women I was studying (discussed further in Ribbens 1990a). Furthermore, I believe that the research process itself marginalised me from these social worlds more forcibly than might otherwise have happened, by requiring me to distance myself and intellectualise encounters that I had previously engaged with as more directly emotional experiences. I was working under circumstances that look very close to the situation which Lynn Davies describes as good ground for a 'truly participative' feminist ethnography (1985: 94), a sort of everywoman's ethnography carried out from within women's social worlds. Yet the research process in itself set me apart, moving between public and private ways of being, and I have to take responsibility for the project within the institutional constraints of its production.

The first part of each interview used a quasi-life history approach, asking mothers, fathers and grandmothers to talk about their lives since they first had children. The only significant source of predetermined structure in a life history interview is that it contains some sense of chronology, and in the present research this embodied the notion of childhood as time passing, incorporating certain 'phases' (Backett 1982) such as early babyhood, toddlerhood, entry into school.[1]

Researchers of intimate personal/family lives have been concerned with the distinction between public and private accounts (Cornwell 1985) and with the level of self-disclosure that may or may not be occurring (Duncombe and Marsden 1993). The ways in which women talk about their childrearing are bound to be affected by who they are talking with/to, and some accounts will be regarded as more or less socially acceptable or 'risky' than others. Furthermore, this is not just a matter of Goffmanesque impression management. People do have a right to their personal privacy, and some matters are difficult to discuss. Speaking aloud about serious weaknesses in their family lives might give these a reality the women did not want to create (Berger and Luckman 1971). Negative feelings towards their own children might be particularly difficult to speak. Nevertheless, in many respects, my impression was that women were being fairly open about their own failings and anxieties – 'It's quite difficult admitting all this but it's true.' Other women joked about the potentially discreditable nature of what they said to me – 'You'll be able to use these tapes as blackmail!' Overall, in Masserik's terminology, with some women I seemed to stay close to the interaction found in the depth interview, while with others we moved close to his description of the phenomenal interview, where there is a 'joint search for shared understanding' (1981: 203).

Even if women were giving me socially acceptable accounts, there were variations in what they considered to be acceptable. Furthermore, those features which they most took for granted and did not therefore seek to 'manage' could in themselves be revealing. Indeed, I found myself listening to mothers talking in the research interviews in ways that took me quite by surprise. Interviewees were often extremely reflective and elaborated at length on issues that concerned them about their children, expressing strong recurrent themes that varied greatly between individual women. Where they were not using explicit rationales and ideologies to explain their childrearing, most would still explore in great detail the intricacies of daily life with their children. While some women (particularly those who felt most comfortable about their own mothering) clearly enjoyed talking about their childrearing more than others, strong individual themes emerged as I listened to all the women. The work of George Kelly (1955) came to mind, and the notion of *core constructs* being used to organise the meanings by which they understood their lives with their children (discussed further below). Furthermore, as I shall argue in later chapters, these core constructs relate to very fundamental issues about how we view the social world and the place of individuals within that.

As I reflected on the sorts of talk about children I was used to hearing amongst mothers in my everyday life, I began to realise just how much is generally left out of conversations. Just as people in general, and women in particular, steer clear of the contentious topics of religion and politics, so I began to wonder whether mothers, in their everyday conversations with each other, generally steer clear of the deeper underlying ideologies of childrearing, focusing instead on the apparently more superficial – but safer – issues of the 'trivia' of daily life with children.

Furthermore, mothers are also likely to seek out others with similar childrearing views to their own (Bell 1994). Not only are differences of view perceived as threatening (representing an Otherness that carries the potential for refuting our own beliefs), but also they are counter-productive to our endeavours to construct a coherent and useful framework by which to live our lives, and to bring up our children. If we are seeking such a framework, we will instead need to interact and develop our ideas in conjunction with those who will help us to confirm and elaborate those ideas, rather than those who present us with a completely different set of core constructs from which to start.

When it came to the analysis, I initially sought to become immersed in each transcript, seeking to understand each account on its own terms, and developing the sort of constant comparative approach described by Glaser (1969). Later I also brought to the analysis my growing interest in the meaning and significance of public and private divisions in women's lives, paying attention to the setting that was concerned in any particular description of mother–child interaction. I thus made a broad distinction between:

1   issues of childrearing that only concerned members of the immediate household, and that occurred within the physical space of the home, and
2   issues of childrearing that arose when other people were present within the home, or that involved children moving outside the home.

When I first began the analysis of the childrearing accounts the women gave me, I intended to start from the nitty-gritty details of everyday childrearing issues, such as food, sleep, clothing and cleanliness. However, once I began the analysis it became apparent that for some reason there were considerable difficulties in this, and I realised I needed to change my analytic approach around.

It was not that the everyday details were not important as elements of the childrearing accounts. They were indeed profoundly important. Christine was particularly explicit in valuing the trivia of everyday life (and see also Diane Bell 1990 on this issue):

> . . . it's all the little things that are important, not any of the big things, children accept big things without question, but it all comes down to the quality of everyday life, doesn't it? . . . it's all the little things you can actually change. So that's, I think, how you really show children that you love them, by all the little ways, all the little things.

I came to realise, however, that the significance of the details for my analysis concerned what they revealed about the *underlying* frameworks of meaning and images which shaped how women dealt with any particular issue. The understandings and images underlying the concrete trivia of everyday life were intricately interlaced by the women to create particular sorts of frameworks of meaning which they used to make sense of their concerns in bringing up their children. In this way, they developed their own 'family portraits' in their lives with their children (see Part II).

For example, a key construct in Susan's account centred on her need 'to get on' (with household or other tasks) and whether or not children enabled her to do so. This theme underlay her discussion of the substantive topics of children's sleep, family size, children's relationships, activities and characters, feelings of guilt at apparent problems with a child's school progress, children's behaviour in social gatherings, and children dressing themselves. Kate had apparently similar substantive concerns in her account, but they were discussed in different terms using the construct of 'attention' (see chapter 8). In Margaret's account it was 'being your own person' (see chapter 8) that operated as a leitmotif for her discussion of such topics as bedtimes, dressing and choice of what to wear, homework, and goals in future life. Thus each woman's childrearing account was developed around these more underlying constructs, which constituted her particular framework of meaning, rather than being organised around the substantive topics of daily life with children. The latter acted instead as the grounded sites on which her more underlying constructs were worked out.

It was therefore apparent that women might appear to adopt the same position on any particular issue but this could be for quite different reasons. Conversely, they might appear to be doing different things, but the underlying rationales might be very similar. Thus, to understand what the women were saying on any particular topic, it was crucial to include *a consideration of the meanings* that particular actions held for the women themselves. For example, whether or not a mother allowed her children to have sweets every day, or frequently bought the child presents, might have very different implications according to the meaning those actions had for the woman as a mother. To withhold sweets or to provide sweets could *both* be construed by different women as acts of love and caring, and unless we know the significance of the action for the mother we cannot understand what is going on in her childrearing.

As I struggled to discern *any* basis for making comparisons between the different childrearing accounts, I therefore came to refocus my analysis, to put the nitty-gritty issues of childrearing into the wider framework of the women's family lives (see chapters 3, 4 and 7). In a sense, this is absolutely proper within an ethnographic analysis, where what is said should always be under-stood in relation to the social context and cultural understandings of the individual who is speaking. The difficulty in relation to family life is that such understandings are so very much taken for granted that it is extremely hard to discern them at all (Morgan 1985), let alone consider their implications for the accounts being given. The various ways in which women dealt with these cultural assumptions helped to illuminate their different discussions of substantive topical problems of childrearing (see chapter 8). However, in exploring these assumptions, I have been concerned both by what was shared and by what was variable between the different accounts.

Writing from more academic concerns, Walkerdine and Lucey (1989) are also explicit about the significance of childrearing trivia, not only for children but for wider political issues (a topic to which I shall return in chapter 9): 'by examining the most boring details of domestic and child-rearing practices, we are not simply engaging in a debate about education and development, but uncovering the most fundamental political questions about the production of democracy, about freedom and about women's oppression' (1989: 33).

Note

1. For further details of the interview designs and details see Ribbens 1990a.

3

Individuals, Families and Children

There is no such thing as society, there are individuals and there
are families.

(Margaret Thatcher)

While the idea of 'society' may be questioned, the existence of 'the
family' and of 'individuals' tends to be accepted uncritically. Within
contemporary Western culture, such notions are central to our
understandings of the world. These concepts are core cultural
elements, and as such, generally taken for granted to the extent that
we do not even realise their existence. This social construction of
'the family' obscures the amount of effort that goes into its
creation. Indeed, the invisibility of its creation is also part of the
imagery, since 'the family' is supposed to be a natural unit, that
occurs inevitably by itself.

Such notions are crucial to the ways in which women understand
and make sense of their lives with their children. Specifically here, I
shall consider how the core notions of 'the individual' and 'family'
can be seen as both polarised and intertwined, and how the notion
of 'child' stands in relation to these constructs. These are crucial
elements also within elaborated ideologies, such that even to raise
queries about the concepts may be regarded as quite radical and
almost immoral. Yet a key feminist concern has been to demonstrate that 'families' are not natural and inevitable units, but are
constructed within particular cultural, historical and political
contexts (chapter 2). Indeed, legal definitions of 'the family' have
provoked passionate contests in the USA (Judith Stacey 1990).
Sociologists working broadly within a phenomenological perspective have also been concerned to question the concept, and to show
how its usage is highly political, being a powerful moral resource
that can be invoked to particular purposes by institutions and
within inter-personal relationships (Bernardes 1985a, 1985b, 1987,
Gubrium and Holstein 1990).

Besides unquestioned assumptions about 'families', contemporary
Western culture also takes it for granted that we can be regarded,
and can regard ourselves, as 'individuals', even though there may be
particular categories of individuals such as children (James and
Prout 1990). Yet all of these notions are culturally and historically

specific. Once we start to examine these notions or concepts we open up a whole new set of questions, which we may regard as a dangerous minefield or as a fascinating array of subtle and shifting meanings to be explored.

Uncovering the assumptions that lie behind cultural notions of 'the family' or 'the individual' can involve paying close attention to the ways in which the words are used within particular contexts, including 'casual remarks, stories, proverbs, myth and non-verbal behaviour' (La Fontaine 1986: 27). The examination of differences and contradictions of meanings is also crucial in enabling social observers or social actors to discern the existence of taken-for-granted cultural and personal assumptions – as phenomenological sociologists and psychologists working with personal construct theory have discussed for many years.

In examining these concepts here, I shall try to explore some of the ambiguities and contradictions that arise with regard to the relationship between individuality and family life, and how the mothers dealt with some of these issues as they talked to me about their children. Mothers varied a great deal in how they incorporated these different cultural threads of family and individuality within their own particular frameworks of understanding. Furthermore, while different women emphasised some elements more than others, within individual accounts there could be tensions between the different elements, and these tensions might appear at times as inconsistencies and contradictions. Indeed, Bronwyn Davies (1982) suggests that inconsistency in talk may be essential if it is to be able to deal with the complexities of action. Thus each woman might seek to incorporate the different strands of meanings to make an overall harmonious tapestry that is pleasing to the eye (whether her own or someone else's), but might well find loose threads that were left dangling, or threads that could not be included easily to make one complete design.

We are all individuals

'The individual' within contemporary Western culture
Various writers (e.g. Dumont 1972, Mann 1986) have noted for some time now that contemporary Western culture operates with a particular notion of 'the individual' that is crucial to our political and ideological systems, as well as to expert and professional discourses, and to everyday understandings of the world. In examining 'the category of the person' in historical and anthropological perspective, Lukes (1985) suggests we can discern both a

narrow usage of the word and a broader meaning. Drawing on the work of Mauss and of Strawson, Lukes defines the narrower sense as the use of the personal reflexive pronoun, referring to an entity that has both states of consciousness and bodily characteristics. Lukes suggests that this notion of the person is universal, and without it social life as we recognise it would be impossible. The broader notion of 'the person' however, varies culturally and historically, and comprises inter-personal attitudes, or a 'structure of sentiments' (1985: 298).

Thus Triandis writes that 'in Africa, and most of Asia, people think of the self as a component of an ingroup, rather than as an independent entity' (1987: 81). Similarly, Dumont discusses a particular version of 'the individual' in relation to caste society: 'As opposed to modern society, traditional societies, which know nothing of equality and liberty as values, which know nothing, in short, of the individual, have basically a *collective idea of man* [sic] (1972: 42, added emphasis). Dumont suggests that in 'traditional society' stress is placed on society as a whole. Ideals are concerned with social ends of order and hierarchy, so that particular people ideally contribute towards a global order.

By contrast, the contemporary Western notion of 'the individual' is of 'an autonomous, self-directing, independent agent' (Lukes 1985: 298). Dumont suggests that in 'modern society' each particular person is regarded as incarnating the whole of humankind. Ideals are concerned with individual ends, towards which social life is the means. 'Society' is thus regarded as a collective individual, and reified. Such ideals focused on 'the individual' have, within Western culture, developed into the deep-rooted ideological value of 'individualism', although a number of different versions of individualism may be discerned (Bellah et al. 1985, Dizard and Gadlin 1990). The overall valuation of the individual is sometimes traced to particular religious belief systems (Mann 1986) and to a market-based economy (Hockey and James 1993), with the more recent historical events of the Second World War fuelling this ideology further (Newson and Newson 1974, Walkerdine and Lucey 1989).

This cultural construct of 'the individual' is of course quite fundamental to psychology (see chapter 1), but has also been at the heart of sociological theorising, including that of Durkheim and Weber. Yet this abstract vision of 'the individual' is, in much public life, fundamentally both male (Lukes 1985), white middle class (Bellah et al. 1985), adult (Alanen 1994) and independent (Hockey and James 1993). Furthermore, this individuality is fundamentally perceived in Western culture as *rational*, which Weber and Foucault regarded as central to modern societies (Barry Smart 1985). Recent theoretical concern with overcoming dualistic notions of 'individual' and 'society' has at times called into question our construction of 'the individual' (see chapter 1). However, notions of individuality have also been fundamental to much feminist writing, particularly liberal feminism which is focused around notions of rights and equality (Midgley and Hughes 1983).

Some approaches to family studies also seek to extricate 'the individual' from social constructions of 'the family' (see e.g. Cheal's discussion of the life course approach within family studies 1991, and Bernardes 1986b), although 'the individual' may be argued to be as much a social construction as 'the family'. How we are to regard the nature of this 'individual' is itself a complex terrain that can be hotly contested: 'This individual may be understood as a system of biological processes, of psychological processes, as a moral entity or as the sum total of a complex set of interactions with other individuals' (Morgan 1985: 276). Different understandings of the nature of 'the individual' can lead to different professional claims to expertise, while some therapeutic approaches may assert the importance of 'the individual' becoming self-determining about her/his own development (Birch 1993, Giddens 1992).

The significance of 'the individual' in contemporary Western culture seems to be increasing, particularly around concerns about the nature of 'the self', and of 'self-development' as a personal responsibility (Giddens 1992, Lasch 1980).[1] If there is increasing 'individualisation' of modern life, writers vary as to how they evaluate this. Some see it as a key to the ills of contemporary Western living: 'American cultural traditions define personality, achievement and the purpose of human life in ways that leave the individual suspended in glorious, but terrifying, isolation' (Bellah et al. 1985). Thus Bellah and his co-authors (1985) and Dizard and Gadlin (1990) all regard the excessive pursuit of individualism in American culture as in urgent need of moderation, and argue for a fundamental questioning of the values of *public life*. Giddens (1992), on the other hand, sees the search for the autonomous self as holding the potential for the democratisation of *personal life*.

If 'the individual' is a basic Western value, 'the family' is undoubtedly another one, and the links between them are by no means clear-cut. Are they necessarily antagonistic or can they be reconciled? Does 'the individual' occur most clearly within 'the family' or outside it, in the public domain? Does the pursuit of 'individualism' undermine the more collectivist orientation of 'family' values, and if so, how can modern life preserve both values without doing so at the expense of women? Such questions have been raised by a few writers (e.g. Bellah et al. 1985, Bjornberg 1992, Cheal 1991, Dizard and Gadlin 1990, Yeatman 1986), but attention is generally directed either towards general 'family' values, or to ideas about romantic love and attachment between adults. Giddens' discussion is particularly remarkable for the absence of any extended discussion in relation to 'family' values, and while he makes some references to parent–child relationships, these arguments are left undeveloped and unspecified. This lack of interest in parent–child relationships with regard to our cultural valuation of 'the individual' perhaps reflects the adultism of sociology, which in turn reflects the wider cultural exclusion of 'the child' from the notion of 'the individual' (Hockey and James 1993). There is, furthermore, a lack of empirical referents for much of this discussion (Bellah et al. 1985, Bjornberg 1992, and Hallden, 1991, constituting notable exceptions).

A proper examination of such issues, however, must first recognise some of the deep ambiguities about how being 'an individual' is understood in relation to public and private life. Most discussion of the Western idea of 'the individual' (who is implicitly male) locates him within the public sphere, for example via notions of 'the citizen' within political theory, or 'the wage labourer' within economic theory. Furthermore, the notion of 'rights' is attached to the figure of the individual, and laid down in national constitutions and international charters (O'Neill and Ruddick 1979). It is in this sense that Bellah et al. (1985) suggest that primary goals for the socialisation of American children concern processes of separation, individuation and 'leaving home', since it is only through leaving home and family behind that 'the individual' can become himself. Similarly, Bjornberg (1992) assumes that the process of individualisation is concerned with individual achievement in relation to political and work life, departing from the family. It is perhaps for this reason that Giddens' (1992) main discussion of childhood is in terms of issues that must be worked out in therapy and left behind, for the autonomous self to emerge.

Yet, without entering complex debates about the nature of 'the self', the position of 'the individual' in relation to 'the family' unit is clearly more complex and paradoxical than this. Indeed, Yeatman argues that it is the identification of 'the individual' with the public sphere that has led to the neglect of domestic life within sociology. She argues, instead, that it is precisely the development of unique personalities that lies at the heart of family life, which is *defined* as 'the world of love relations and of parenting, a world which includes all forms of social interaction which have as their primary reason for being the constitution, by way of social evocation and recognition, of the individual as a unique personality' (1986: 163). While this definition has the disadvantage of obscuring the potential for conflict between collectivist family values and the valuation of unique individuality, Yeatman is able to make a very clear differentiation between contrasting versions of 'the individual' as these occur within public and private lives:

> If individuality in all its aspects lies within social life, then society itself must be differentiated into those arenas of social interaction which speak to and express the *unique or particularistic aspects of individuality* and those which speak to and express *the universalistic or public aspects of individuality*. I refer to these as domestic and public aspects of social life respectively. (1986: 166, emphasis added)

Yeatman is then able to argue forcefully for the inclusion of *both* spheres within the proper domain of sociological enquiry, an inclusion which she suggests holds the potential for transcending the individual/society dichotomy. In the discussion that follows, we need to keep in mind both meanings of individuality in Western cultures, the particularistic and the universalistic, as well as discerning the continuing relevance of the pre-industrial, or non-Western, collectivist idea of the person.

'The individual' within accounts of childrearing

So far I have argued that 'the family' and 'the individual' are key elements of Western cultures and value systems. Since these are culturally and historically located concepts, it is possible to examine their construction not only within public discourses but also by social actors within their everyday lives. Is it, then, possible to discern how parents use and create these social constructs as they bring up their children, and how some of these complexities are manifested?

While individuality may be an underlying theme in the socialisation of children, it is one which is hard to disentangle precisely because it is so very fundamental to our culture. As Bernardes puts it: '"Family ideology" supports a child rearing process that *creates* individuals, and which simultaneously closes off any potential alternative paths of human development. The rearing of children in a non-individualistic manner is simply *unthinkable*' (Bernardes 1985a: 282, emphasis added). And yet for women, part of the shock of giving birth seems to lie in the difficulty of simply 'taking in' the expulsion and arrival of a new individual or 'person': 'I just really couldn't believe it. It was really difficult to believe . . . . I really felt she was a stranger . . . . It's such a funny thing, that suddenly you've got this person that you've got to get to know . . .' (Sue Johnson, quoted by Oakley 1986a: 117).

Backett comments on the significance attached to 'understanding' children as individuals, which she suggests was experienced as a primary responsibility by the middle class Scottish parents she interviewed: 'Other children were taken very much at "face-value" and less effort was made continuously to interpret their behaviour, that is "understand" it. The parental bond was perceived not just as a blood tie but also as a continuous responsibility to *make sense of that particular child*' (1982: 103, added emphasis). This process of 'making sense' of children in effect is one of creating their individuality. Within my own analysis, I first really became conscious of the relevance of notions of 'the individual' in considering the long descriptions women sometimes gave of their children's individual characteristics, descriptions which they might ponder and puzzle over:

> The eldest . . . is responsible, very caring and very perceptive, very tuned into other people's feelings, and if I'm not well she will sense it immediately and she'll help . . . . She is not very strong academically, that's not her interest . . . . Number two, she's totally the opposite, she's slightly bored at school . . . . She's a very quick child . . . she is a perfectionist. If anything I think probably the first one will be full of wisdom and the second one will develop intelligence . . . and the third one is very musical . . . (Ellen)

Through such reflections, women actively construct their children's distinctive individuality. This is 'the individual', not as an abstract principle, but as the owner of a distinctive set of characteristics, creating a specific and irreplaceable person.

Using rather different language, Newson and Newson (1978) similarly suggest that the recognition of unique and idiosyncratic individuality is specifically located in children's experiences within family life, for instance through the acceptance of 7-year-old children's common desire for particular bedtime rituals. Note here, though, that the second part of this quote hints at the relevance of a collectivist sense of self, in other words, who you are is defined by your relations to others:

> That parents are in a unique position both to know about such idiosyncrasies and to indulge them must be of enormous importance in the development of a child's personality. By knowing about them, they establish the child as an individual . . . . In a not dissimilar way, the child is dependent on his [sic] parents' role as a memory bank to which he can continually refer for evidence of himself as an individual with a history . . . (1978: 442–3).

The family in general – and parental care in particular – is thus seen as the setting for the recognition of our idiosyncratic individuality particularly with regard to our sources of dependency and *vulnerability*. Ideals concerning 'the family' stress family life as an important setting for a collectivist orientation towards co-operative sharing and mutual self-help, and it is within this overall collective framework that individuality is constructed within the family. It is noteworthy that this example given by the Newsons, concerning children's idiosyncratic bedtime rituals, centres on the recognition of children's individual dependencies, not their individual achievements. An assertive, achievement-oriented individuality may be seen as more appropriately occurring outside the family. There are thus some crucial ambiguities about the nature of individuality and its relevance to private/public settings, not only in terms of unique versus universal individuality, but also in terms of dependent versus assertive individuality.

Interestingly, in the present study, the two women who seemed to give the greatest priority to the child *as an assertive 'individual'* within the family unit were the two who were furthest apart in social class terms. Margaret is a university administrator, from a prosperous background. Margaret's construction of her daughter's individuality related to the person as rational and self-determining, and the creation of this individual was a central goal of her childrearing. For Margaret, then, it was crucial for her daughter to learn to be 'her own person':

> I would hope that all the decisions about what was right or wrong to do she would actually make herself and . . . that she could set her own standards. I mean obviously I would hope that they would be like my own, but I hope that she will end up being her own person.

Janet does not have Margaret's educational qualifications or her middle class family background. Unlike Margaret, Janet did not put the emphasis on rationality and being able to argue a particular point of view, but she did value self-direction, energy and independence. While Margaret's notion of individuality was of an emergent quality, for Janet individuality seemed to be inherent. An underlying assumption in her account was that it was impossible to stop her son from being himself. This theme united a number of disparate topics, from the right age to introduce mixed feeding, to the prevention of accidents, to the ineffectiveness of smacking him.

While other women did not put quite the same emphasis on individual autonomy and self-direction, there was a common belief that prescriptions of what is right or wrong in childrearing always have to take into account the specific nature of the child (Stolz 1967), because needs as well as strengths are individual:

> I don't think there is a right way or a wrong way, it's just what applies to your child, its own particular make-up, its genes or whatever. (Amy)

Not only is the individual character something that has to be considered, but several women referred to ways in which they felt it should be respected and nurtured:

> . . . every child has got a gift in a particular area, a particular brightness, every child . . . but it's up to the parents and the teachers and the child, between you, to find out where that is. . . (Ellen)

Hallden (1991) has also described the nurturing of individuality as a key value for parents of 4-year-olds living in rural working class households in Sweden.

Recognition of the child as an autonomous being may thus be considered to be part of what counts as caring for children. As such, in the present study, it was the basis for criticisms of any view of the child as the possession and extension of the parents.

> I think my husband thought of them as possessions, they weren't people. . . . They were little girls who should look pretty. But he'd never talk to them. . . . He'd no real feeling for finding out or caring [about their feelings] . . . He's not really interested in *them*. (Lindsay)

By contrast, Janet spoke approvingly of her husband – 'he does take an interest in Russell as a person'.

Thus, in important ways, the sense of children's individuality is *created* by those around them. One of the ways in which mothers accomplish this creation is through the perception of the child as having *in-built* qualities and characteristics that are seen as part of her/his nature. The body is a very immediate manifestation of this unique individuality after birth, and both birth weight (Oakley 1986a) and physical attractiveness may be regarded as highly significant:

> Instead of saying, 'Is the baby alright?' I said, 'Has the baby got any hair?' . . . She had loads of jet black pretty hair and she was a beautiful baby. And the funny thing was, I thought I hope I don't have an ugly child . . . (Marie)

Babies are perceived to have more than just a physical appearance that is 'given'. Mary suggested that a mother should seek to love her children as 'they are', even if they had characteristics the mother found hard to accept – 'It's very important to love them for what they are. You see people trying to change people and you shouldn't.' Such acceptance is more difficult, of course, if a new baby does not live up to a woman's expectations, whether in terms of gender, physical attractiveness, or dis/ability.

Nevertheless, while mothers are thus actively creating their children as unique individuals, this uniqueness is also compromised and contingent, being qualified by ascribed characteristics, particularly social understandings of age, gender and family history. Such ascribed characteristics set limits on the notions of unique individuality as discussed by the mothers, just as they do with more abstract notions of the needs and rights of universal individualism.

Biological sex is the very first piece of information that is generally given on the delivery of a baby (Oakley 1986a). Mead's commentary on American births is still relevant: 'The sex of the child, marked by a name, is the way in which the fact of birth is fixed in the minds of friends, family and relatives who have not seen the child. . . only after birth does the child move, and *at once*, from 'it' to a named, fully sexed individual' (Mead 1962: 247, added emphasis). Thus individuality cannot be conceptualised without reference to gender – it is ungendered individuality that is 'unthinkable'.

However, explicit discussions of gender roles occurred very infrequently in the interviews (see chapter 2). Over time, a child's gender becomes a fact of life that is so taken for granted it may merit only a passing comment – 'he's a proper boy' (Shirley). As Garfinkel (1967) has discussed, however, taken-for-granted expectations may not be made explicit until a situation arises where they are *not* met. Susan discussed her husband's feelings about inappropriate activities according to gender, in relation to her son's desire to learn modern dancing alongside his sister – 'My husband's more into football and golf and all that and to have his son doing – but he would never stop him.' Mary explicitly discussed other parents' concerns about future sexual orientation, and how appropriate behaviours are therefore implicitly sex-linked:

> . . . mothers of boys who are gentle and quiet, they worry themselves sick. . . . And my husband said, 'It's only natural, they don't want their boys to be a cissy.' The number of mothers who've said that to me, 'If John turned out to be a queer I'd –.' They want their boys to be aggressive and they don't want to tell them off. It's funny that.

On the other hand, Hilary was unusual in expressing *approval* of gender-inappropriate behaviour in her daughter (although she also anticipated its modification in teenage years):

> *Hilary:* She's quite wilful, and he's very placid . . . she's got much more character.

Jane: Is that a good or a bad thing?
Hilary: Good in some ways. I think it's good for a girl particularly . . . I
    think girls tend to get trampled down in life a bit . . .

The reference to 'having more character' raises the possibility that
notions of 'individuality' are *themselves* stronger in relation to boys,
and seen to be more of a masculine trait (as Gilligan's 1982 work
would suggest).

Gender might also be relevant to the construction of individuality
through its use as an explanatory device for particular
characteristics.

. . . he's just boisterous but I think boys probably are. (Susan)
    I keep mentioning Paul [as troublesome] more than I do Mary-Rose,
it must be boys. (Shirley)

Turning to age status, this constitutes an ascribed but transitional
position which defines the individual within the more general status
of 'child', which is absolutely crucial to the ways in which mothers
in Western societies understand their relationship with their
offspring. Backett (1982) stressed the centrality of the notion of
'phases' for the ways in which parents are able to make sense of
their children's changeable behaviour. Yet, while specific ages are
regarded as carrying different implications for how to deal with
children, parents may vary considerably in what they expect of
children at particular ages (Backett 1982).

There is also variability in how age is used to define the limits of
babyhood, but there is a common tendency for babies to be
described as not quite 'human',[2] or not having their own
personalities (Backett 1982). Part of the difficulty of toddlerhood is
that the child has mobility but may be quite unpredictable, without
the stability of behaviour patterns that express personality – 'It was
very much a feeling of – probably until she was two and a half or
three, of taking her out and not knowing what she would do, she
could do anything' (David). In some versions of individuality, then,
it is only gradually over the years that children become defined as
persons, with their own unique emerging individualities and
predictable characteristics.

Besides age status, individuality is also defined in terms of *birth
order*. Ellen referred to her daughters throughout her account by
reference to their position in the family – 'number one . . . my
number two . . . my number three'. In this regard, individuality is
implicitly contingent upon family patterns. Paradoxically, then,
while *unique* individuality may receive its clearest recognition within
family life, individuality is also bounded and intrinsically understood by reference to membership and continuity of 'the family' – a

collectivist notion of the person again. The naming of a child may reflect this, sometimes naming the new individual as a person in his/ her own right, but sometimes perpetuating a 'family name' (Lieberman 1987). The child is seen as the production of a union between members of two particular families of origin, so that some of the individual's uniqueness may be derived from the *combination* of characteristics from two different families. In this way, the arrival of the child 'makes the family' by acting as *a symbol of the union* of two families, creating a new 'family' which is itself both unique and yet also derived from past generations. Besides physical appearance, as the child grows older, particular behaviour patterns may also be regarded as characteristic family traits. In these ways, individuality is understood to be relative.

So far I have argued that individuality is actively constructed by mothers in the process of making sense of their lives with their children, and this individuality is sometimes seen as given and sometimes as emergent. Yet unique individuality is also compromised by age, gender and family history. Such contingencies can be seen to be aspects of ascription to specific roles, a form of social learning that is seen as antithetical to modern notions of individualism. Such ascribed roles may, however, be relevant to the alternative notion of 'the individual' as a collective entity, as discussed earlier. The collectivist orientation and traditional authority of the family are features which are also sometimes seen as representing a continuation of pre-modern values and understandings. I shall turn next to the ways in which the women could be seen to be creating 'the family' as a cohesive and clearly demarcated unit, but we shall see that this concept too is cross-cut and compromised by age and gender divisions.

Becoming 'a family'

'The family' in contemporary Western culture

'The family', as an element of contemporary Western culture, is conceptualised as an entity that exists as a concrete and natural unit. Furthermore, this concept of 'the family' generally is taken to refer to a very particular form of household, and such assumptions underpin much Western social policy (Bernardes 1987, Van Every 1992). This entity may be valued in itself – 'I think the family is very important' (Christine Woodley-Mason, see pp. 138–44) – even if such valuation varies between different cultural groups within Western societies (Brodbar-Nemzer 1986).

Working within an approach which they term 'social constructionism', Gubrium and Holstein (1990) have particularly elaborated
the argument that 'family' is not an object but a feature of
discourse: 'family is as much a way of thinking and talking about
relationships as it is a concrete set of social ties' (1990: ix–x). Thus
to refer to 'the family' is argued to imply solidity, referring to an
object-like thing with boundaries, although what 'it' refers to shifts
according to who is speaking. Using examples from a variety of
practical settings and expert discourses, Gubrium and Holstein
demonstrate how the meanings and practices of 'family' are
generated and signified through discourse. In their discussion of
family therapy, they launch a detailed critique of the notion of
'family' as a 'superpersonality', in which families appear as entities
which are separate from their members. Nevertheless, while
Gubrium and Holstein make some very important points about the
dangers of reifying 'the family', and demonstrate clearly how this
happens in expert writings, this argument raises a very fundamental
sociological issue, namely, is the group ever greater than the sum of
its parts? They thus fail to consider how regular interactions
between family members over time may generate particular family
cultures that those same members may then experience as very
powerful (and at times constraining). While 'family' is clearly very
importantly constructed through discourse, family members
themselves *experience* family life as a real and powerful force in
their lives that cannot just be reduced to the influence of
individuals.

For households in circumstances similar to those of my own
study, it is largely the mother's task to create 'the family'. There are
two very important processes in this:

1   internal cohesion, welding the individual members together into
    a meaningful unit, and
2   external demarcation, drawing clear boundaries and separating
    the family clearly from other social units.

In the remainder of this chapter I shall consider the internal
processes of family creation as a cohesive whole, and how 'being a
family' creates tensions for 'being an individual'. The external
demarcation of 'the family' will be dealt with in the next chapter.

If 'the family' is indeed impossible to identify at a concrete level
(as Gubrium and Holstein argue), in what ways is its unity signified
and symbolised and made to appear concrete? A number of
powerful symbols appeared in the women's accounts, including the
home, spending time together (whether meals, playing board games,

or family outings) and pictorial representations such as photo-graphic collections. Yet in all these cases, it is the presence of children that is crucial to 'family' symbolism.

When the first child is born to a married couple, this is expected to produce a different sort of social unit – the baby is not seen as a simple addition to a 'household', but an essential ingredient in the creation of 'a family'.[3] The household is thus expected to be more than a collection of individuals who have to learn to live together. There is the additional central expectation that they constitute a social unit that can be demarcated from those around, and that is made special by the presence of children. So when the baby arrives, the woman is in the position of being confronted with this new being, for whom she is responsible *as an individual*, but at the same time, the arrival of this baby is expected (by her and by others) to lead to the establishment of a *new social unit*, which is 'the family'. In common parlance, the question, 'Have you got a family?' is taken as asking whether or not you have children – a married couple does not constitute 'a family'. Furthermore, providing this 'family' may be construed as the essence of loving children:

Jane: Could you say in what ways you think perhaps you make a good
   job of being a mother yourself?
Susan: . . . Giving them loving I think is the main thing.
Jane: And loving involves all the things you mentioned?
Susan: Yeah, giving them a good family life, I think.

'The family' within childrearing accounts

There was considerable variation in how far mothers understood their lives with their children through this notion of constituting 'a family', but there were common references in the present study to activities that related to doing things together 'as a family'. This whole process of creating the family was very much taken for granted, another *invisible production*, as with 'coping' (Graham 1982). However, the production/creation of the family unit involved the women in a great deal of effort, as the centre-pin in securing family cohesion. Indeed, as they were talking to me about their lives as mothers, they were actively constructing the family as a particular sort of social unit. It may indeed be the case that 'the family' requires constant attention towards its creation, suggesting that its achievement may for some be quite fragile.

One of the ways in which 'the family' is taken as given and unquestionable is to see it as a 'natural unit' – rooted in nature, in biological processes, and therefore inevitable and unalterable (a view which feminist writers have argued against for some time – see chapter 2). In the present study, both fathers and mothers referred to the conception of the first child as 'a natural progression' – 'it wasn't a big step, natural progression, didn't think twice about it . . . it just seemed very natural' (David). Some were ambiguous about describing the first conception as a 'decision', almost suggesting that 'starting a family' was not a 'decision' at all, but an inevitable event.

It may also undermine the construction of the family as 'natural' and inevitable, if babies arrive according to the timing and planning of the parents. Yet the 'natural' time for the first pregnancy may be considered to be quite a clear-cut period in the woman's life (Berryman 1991, Phoenix 1991). To ask, 'Did you plan to have your first child?' is to ask something women might not wish to answer unambiguously:

> It wasn't really sort of a decision, right today will be the day when we start, it just sort of happened I suppose really, and my son came along and that was it. (Angela)

Rational planning and calculation may not be considered the appropriate discourse for discussions of 'family' life, being more the language of work life and the 'public' sphere. Interestingly, then, pregnancies were more often described as 'planned', part of a rational decision-making process, if there were considerations involved about the woman's ideas of 'career'. The timing of the first pregnancy also was described as a clear decision-making process where there had been some differences of attitude between husband and wife.

Making a home, making a family   If starting a family was seen as a natural progression in life, for all these women the home was the central site for its establishment. Imagery of the private home is crucial to notions of 'family' (Allan and Crow 1990), but the notion of 'family' is also crucial to notions of 'home'. The two images of 'home' and 'family' thus stand in a reciprocal relationship (Gubrium and Holstein 1990). The physical space of the house is important for the very fact that it is a most potent symbol of the boundary of the family unit. Its comfort and attractiveness hold family members together within its physical boundaries (Young and Willmott 1973). At the same time, those same boundaries demarcate the family unit clearly from 'the world outside', and establish the family as having its own authority. The demarcation of the family home was largely taken for granted by these home-owning families (although see chapter 6 for Sandra's discussion of living with a family business on the premises), but several of the grandmothers described the great significance of the moment when they had achieved a 'home of their own' after lengthy periods of shared accommodation, and were able to establish their own 'private' space for their families. Penny's parents, for example, lived with her aunt for their first eighteen months of married life, before moving out – 'We thought we were on cloud nine really, didn't we? Our own little – well it was only a council house, but it was ours.'

For the contemporary families, the home can be in itself a major source of activity for both spouses, in terms of housework and house maintenance. Several writers (Backett 1982, Boulton 1983, Oakley 1976) have described housework and childcare as tasks that are in competition for a woman's time, constituting separate roles pulling women in different directions. For Rosemary, 'work' referred to household domestic chores, not childcare – 'I do try and spend time with them, but at the same time, I do still like to get my work done.'

However, this analysis of conflict between childcare and housework tasks may overlook some subtle *inter-connections* between the two activities, such that ideas of motherhood may be *bound up with* attitudes towards the house as a physical space. This is not just a matter of giving priority to children's activities over a tidy house, or vice versa, but that a woman's attitude to a tidy house may run parallel to her childrearing attitudes, such that housework and mothering attitudes are revealed by the same indicators. 'Letting children *make a mess*' was described by some women as an important issue in good mothering – 'To me, mess is irrelevant, it'll all wash off. I'd rather they enjoy themselves' (Shirley).

> My health visitor came round once when I was in an absolute awful mess when they were younger, and I said, 'Oh gosh, I'm in an awful mess'. She said, 'My dear, the time I go to a house where there's children and there's no toys around, I'll worry.' She said, 'Never, ever worry about toys because it's a clean mess.' And I feel like that, her saying that went a long way, and if I go to a house where there's no toys around and they've got children, I always think of that, and I think, that's strange, because they should feel at home, they should be allowed to, within reason, do what they want. (Rosemary)

By contrast, *an orderly house* was important to others as an indication of a good mother:

> I know somebody who I think is pretty lousy as a mother, she doesn't do anything for her children, she doesn't really spend time with them. In fact she doesn't spend time doing anything, she doesn't look after the house, she doesn't really look after herself. She's pretty lethargic and lazy in everything, and just leaves her kids sitting watching the television . . . . (Penny)

Pauline described issues to do with children's activities disturbing the house – jumping on the furniture, or playing with the telephone – as a source of conflict between herself and her husband. I found Pauline's house very neat, comfortable and well-decorated, but on reading the write-up of her case study, (Ribbens 1990a), Pauline felt that my account of the tensions in her family life inevitably implied that she keeps 'a dirty house, going round all day with rollers in my hair, throwing beer bottles at my husband'. Thus for Pauline, a clean home was seen as a key indicator of her family life and relationships.

Family togetherness at home and abroad   Thus part of the meaning of work on the house as a physical entity may be the creation of a particular sort of space where the family may spend leisure time together, away from work time, which for most families occurs in physically separate areas. While the existence and meaning of leisure time itself raises gender issues, it is generally considered to be time under our own control, so how we spend it signifies important choices about how relationships are prioritised. Leisure time can be a potent representation of the ideal family image:

> I would like to see us doing more together as a family than we do . . . we don't really go out much together, we don't do much game-playing together. (Pauline)

Board games were mentioned quite often in the accounts, and might indeed seem like a trivial pursuit, but some women revealed a very striking evaluative feeling around the issue.

> Jane: . . . what about the ways in which you're not such a good mother?
> Susan: Well, the fact that I don't really enjoy board games and I'm not one for puzzles and things like that, which I wish I did enjoy but I just don't! I wish in a way I had more time to sit with them and do things with them, but I just don't have the time.

Mary regarded playing board games as an important maternal responsibility, one which she did not initially appreciate:

> I made myself enjoy it and now I really do enjoy it. Because I thought, it's no good unless I enjoy it, so I forced myself to enjoy the games.

Some of this feeling may be attributed to the perceived educational value in sitting and doing puzzles with young children – Jo, for example, felt she ought to play games with her son to encourage his concentration level. However, such perceived benefits only partially explain the significance attached to such activities, which Margaret described as 'silly games':

Jane: What constitutes family life do you think? You mentioned about having meals together.

Margaret: I think that's quite important. I think playing kind of games. We play quite a lot of silly games like the London Game, Scrabble, Cluedo, and things like that, and I suppose that's quite fun.

Playing board games may thus signify freely chosen leisure time spent with 'the family', in pursuit of childish fun. Furthermore, it is time spent not with any particular child but all together, on an equal basis, in direct interaction within the physical space of the home. When the husband in particular plays board games with the children, he can be seen to be fulfilling the ideal of the 'involved father', 'at home' with 'the family', in a way that *does not threaten* the woman's own authority with the children. It is thus a potent representation of desirable family imagery.

So why did Susan express such guilt over not enjoying board games herself? I believe it is partly to do with her own ambivalence towards her family life *en masse*, finding it difficult to achieve a harmonious family image with three quarrelsome children:

> . . . that's not that I don't enjoy the kids because I do, but to be honest I enjoy them one at a time rather than all three together. All three together is just really hard work . . .

A failure to 'sit and play' board games thus signified a failure to spend time creating and sustaining 'the family'. Furthermore, by not *enjoying* such games, Susan suggested she was guilty of admitting a failure to have the right *positive feelings* about 'her family' – a serious failure in her motherhood.

In her study of suburban Australian households, Lynn Richards (1990) found that 'togetherness' was overwhelmingly seen as the defining feature of 'a good family life'. Several of the women in my study had photographs of the children, and sometimes of 'the family' (particularly on holidays and outings) displayed in the house. Such displays represent powerful images of family togetherness. Outings from the home can also act as potent representations of happy 'family life' if undertaken all together. In such contexts, women can confirm that they are indeed part of a successful family unit, like others. Holidays, visits to London, to 'theme parks', and swimming at leisure centres, were all discussed by many women as providing happy family memories, and Margaret also referred to visits with her husband and daughter to the theatre and opera as a focus of 'family life'.[4]

Penny gave considerable emphasis to such family togetherness:

> I suppose at the moment what I admire about other families is when they do things together as a family, and I think, now that's nice, they all

> do things together as a family . . . they all go swimming or something like that.

She described her own happiness as realised when her experiences live up to such imagery:

> We went off on Sunday, we went into London for the day, and those are the things I really enjoy, when we all do things together as a family. Those are the times I'm at my happiest.
>
> I just like the whole thing of being a family. Happiness for me is going out together as a family, down to the pub for a drink, or just a walk round the village, it doesn't have to be anything spectacular, that's happiness to me . . .

Nevertheless, Penny was also aware of potential disjunctions between such imagery and lived realities:

> . . . there's a family who don't live a hundred miles away from here, who appeared to be all hunky-dory and wonderful . . . And then one night she ran off with another man. And things like that make me realise that things aren't always what they appear to be . . .

There were indeed considerable strains and tensions apparent in the women's discussions of 'family togetherness', centring particularly on ambiguities about the relevance of fathers, and age and gender divisions within the household.

'Families' include fathers? A parent and child may be argued to constitute the most fundamental basis of 'the family' – hence the feasibility of the concept of 'lone-parent families' (Wilson and Pahl 1988). But lone-parent families are in fact generally female – 'It's only natural really' (Angela) – and it is generally seen as 'natural' that mothers are the primary childcarers. Indeed, I have argued elsewhere that mothers in contemporary Western cultures are always seen as carrying the ultimate moral responsibility for their children, while the possible significance of fathers is becoming generally more ambiguous and diverse, even polarised (Bjornberg 1992, Ribbens 1993a).

Within the apparently 'conventional' families in my own study, images of family togetherness did not always correspond to how things worked out in everyday interactions. While the women living with their husbands were quick to tell me their good qualities as fathers, in the details of their accounts strains could also become apparent in constructing 'the family' with an involved father. Much of the care of pre-school children occurs in women's worlds, either within or outside the home (see chapter 4, and Bell and Ribbens 1994), and men are marginal to these worlds.

Of the seven men interviewed for the present study, only one expressed views suggesting that he constructed 'the family' in terms similar to the women's. This was Jack, who ran a 'family shop' in the front part of the house, so that 'work' and 'family' became overlaid in significant ways. In discussing the build-up of the business, he said:

I like to feel that we are doing it, not just me. As the kids get older obviously I try and involve them more and more in different things in the family, and more responsible things to do with the family, and hopefully keep them as a family.

Indeed, most of the fathers themselves spontaneously described themselves as marginal, outsiders to the 'family life' at home – 'I'm only sort of visiting when I'm here' (Tom).

David: You come home and the kids say, 'Mum, who is that strange man in the house?' That sort of syndrome . . .
Jane: So what would you say are the most important ways that a father can show his children that he really cares about them?
David: Arriving home at five o'clock!

At the time of the research, a series of British Telecom television and newspaper advertisements (see Figure 3.1) strikingly represented this feeling, depicting images of the husband returning home to find himself a stranger to his own family, or of a man going to church to marry his boss.

Rather than themselves expressing regrets at being marginal to the worlds of paid work, the women expressed resentment at how far the worlds of work took their husbands away from 'the family'. O'Donnell reports a similar view among the American women she interviewed:

I think they would agree that men's patterns of workplace involvements need to be reorganised and reconsidered every bit as much, if not more so, than those of women. Indeed, having witnessed how much women feel they gain from parenting, it becomes clear how much men, perhaps even more than women, are confined and limited by their roles (1985: 165).

Husbands' separate sporting activities were even more heavily criticised by some women. These symbolised an assertion of men's separate individuality, and often involved them in exclusively male networks which undermined 'family togetherness' (discussed further in Ribbens 1989a).

However, at the same time, when the man *is* at home, there is potential for disagreements about childcare which may threaten the woman's authority with her children. Women may therefore also

Figure 3.1 *British Telecom advertisement illustrating the idea of the isolated father*

If your five-year-old son were asked to draw a picture of his family, would you be in it?

'I WAS really choked. He gave it to me at breakfast one Saturday. Really proud of it, he was. There was his mother, his big sister and him. I just wasn't in the picture.'

Most people would agree that time is the one thing we could all do with more of.

What most people don't realise is that the right communications package is one of the shorter routes to saving time at work.

I unfortunately, given the complexity of business communication today, getting one's hands on the right package isn't exactly easy, is it?

Here, on the business side of British Telecom, we have literally thousands of a complex of the latest in time-saving systems, equipment and services.

Everything, in fact, from simple radio pagers to fax machines to the technology that allows complex data to be sent across the country in seconds.

Our problem was how to get the items relevant to you into your hands without wasting your time with the rest.

We were serious enough to call in a leading management consultant and, together, we think we've found a solution.

It's called Workplan and this is how it works.

You phone and ask for Workplan. In a day or so, you'll receive the first stage which is a business-orientated questionnaire designed to help you evaluate where improved communications across might help.

(Even if you decide not to return this, you'll benefit from what you'll learn about yourself as you respond to its questions.)

If you do return a completed questionnaire we'll use your answers and a bank of computers to analyse your particular business needs.

Then we'll make up and send off your personally compiled Workplan handbook.

This is a ring binder containing information and advice on the communications options we believe would be most likely to save you time.

If at that moment, or indeed anytime in the future, you'd like to discuss specific items with one of our people, you only have to call and say so.

Ah, we hear, but I'm too busy to get into all this.

All we can do by way of persuasion is reiterate the words on the introduction to Workplan. 'If you haven't got time to fill this in, you need to fill this in.'

In business, time is money. In your personal life, it can be priceless.

Call us free on 0800 800 846 and ask for your copy of Workplan. Our lines are open 24 hours a day, seven days a week. **CALL US FREE ON 0800 800 846**

British **TELECOM**

seek to circumscribe their partners' family role, whilst at the same time complaining of their non-involvement. As one woman said:

> I'll tell you what annoys me, at weekends or when he's home in the evenings, and I've allowed the kids to do something new, he'll say, 'I don't think they should be doing that' . . . and I say to him, 'What do you think I do when I'm here all day on my own?' You know, he's telling me what to do, and how to look after them, and I say, 'Look, I manage on my own all day, just keep your nose out.'[5]

In the process of establishing their own maternal authority, women may limit their husbands' involvement in childcare from the earliest days after the first birth (Brian Jackson 1983). There may thus be some ambivalence about how far mothers *want* their husbands to be part of the childcare unit when it is an important basis for their own experience of authority (an issue that may extend beyond Western culture – Bernard Van der Leer Foundation 1992).

Thus while the father as an involved parental figure may be an important part of family imagery, there may be some ambiguity about how this works out. Perhaps the minimum goal for most of the women interviewed was that at least fathers should show that they valued these 'families' which their wives had created – that they were applauding this significant maternal production, appreciating its benefits and the effort necessary to produce these: 'A supportive husband enhanced a woman's enjoyment of looking after her children through both his respect and appreciation for her efforts as a mother, and his recognition and acceptance of her inevitable feelings of frustration and irritation in child care' (Boulton 1983: 177).

Nevertheless, while ambivalence was apparent, many women did express considerable disquiet at their husbands' marginality. Jo, whose husband is a farmer, described how their marriage nearly broke up because he put 'work before family'. After some counselling help they decided to make themselves into 'more of a family' by having a second child – 'it made a family having the second one'. Similarly, Ellen had very directly sought to involve her GP husband more fully in her concept of how 'family' life should be:

> I remember when we had the first one, he was quite involved, but then he had a very busy job so there was always an excuse to not be around . . . . I think he only gave the children a bath because I insisted . . . . I think if I hadn't made him do that he wouldn't have done it, I think he would have been totally work-absorbed, worse than his father. Although he said before, he said he would not let it go like that, it's still some sort of pull to be like your parents. There is nothing much

you can do about it yourself, you need a partner to pull you out of that . . . [I] made it clear in no uncertain terms what I expected him to do, and he did rebel against that now and again of course, quite often we had troubles through that. Then we had our au pairs and he wasn't needed at the centre of the family . . . certainly in those days he was very much an outsider. So after three au pairs and the kids out of nappies and we then moved into this house, I refused to have another au pair, and he didn't like that at all, he really wanted to carry on with it, quite comfortable thank you . . . . I just could see that we would drift apart if I had an au pair, and since then just very gradually he's been doing more and more and it's wonderful now . . .

In contrast with the women, none of the men expressed any sense that they regard their spouses as too marginal to family life, (though one did describe his wife as 'selfish' within the family). However, some expressed the reverse concern, that they would have liked their wives to share more in the responsibility of the breadwinner role (which O'Donnell 1985 also found in her North American study). In this sense, the women and the men did indeed seem to experience different *'family'* lives, much as Bernard (1982) suggests that they experience different *married* lives.

Before they became fathers, the men had previously been long-term cohabiting partners, and generally husbands. A further issue, then, is how far the *'marriage' relationship* may be regarded as a separate construction requiring its own work within the family unit, or how far it is subsumed under 'the family' once children arrive. In the present study, the marital relationship was more often described as part of 'family' life, part of the taken-for-granted backdrop of childrearing. With an eldest child of 7, time alone with husbands was only likely to occur in the evenings, and this would depend on children's 'bedtimes'. A few women referred to the desirability of some holiday time without the children, generally in the form of an extended weekend, while most saw the marital relationship as set somewhat to one side, put on 'the back burner' until a future time when the children leave home.

. . . perhaps by then [in ten years' time] he won't be so involved with cricket and he might realise that I'm still around. (Shirley)

Maintaining a united front   While women may strive to create their 'family' as a cohesive whole, ascribed characteristics of age and gender may interweave with this central notion, creating a complex balance of structured inter-personal dynamics within the 'family' unit. Age status underlies the construction of a very fundamental division between adults/parents and children. Many parents took this entirely for granted, establishing differences of power and authority. Most parents felt that children must be taught to respect adults, with 'cheekiness' cited many times as the commonest reason for reprimanding children. This status division between adults and children was underwritten by the normative expectation that parents should maintain a 'united front', so as to avoid creating opportunities for children to question the authority of adult decisions and directions within the family. To maintain the fundamental hierarchical division between the two statuses, of parent and child, there is thus a strong expectation that parents should present children with a *single united authority*, rather than with two individuals with different points of view. However, this is also implicitly recognised to be a 'front', that may well fall apart into discord out of sight of the children. For example, in her North American study, Stolz (1967) found that in over half the families involved mothers and fathers held different ideas about the type of control over children that was desirable.

The term, 'united front', signifies the ideology that *parental authority is shared*, rather than either father or mother taking over-riding control. Indeed, this underlies recent legislation and policy development, as seen in the Children Act 1989 in Britain, which is based upon the ideal that mothers and fathers will continue to co-parent and share authority even if separated or divorced. While in practice one parent may take more authority with the children even when they are both present, the ideology of the 'united front' suggests that this authority is not based on unilateral decision-making, but is underpinned by shared parental agreements. The achievement of such a 'united front' can thus be a common basis for negotiation between the parents – 'We do always talk things through because if you don't present a united front children very quickly pick up the difference' (Christine) – and there may be considerable concern if the united front is not realised.

While parents were supposed to achieve unity, so too were children. Many of the mothers' accounts paid considerable attention to the topic of sibling relationships. Quarrels between children are a fundamental threat to family unity, undermining the ideal of the harmonious whole.

It's lovely, Antony and Grant were just cuddling each other this morning out there. I think Grant had fallen off the stool . . . he sort of went up to Antony and put his arm round him and I sort of said, 'Oh are you going to cuddle your brother?', and so they both did, Antony stopped what he was doing and he stood there and he cuddled him and he gave him lots of kisses, which I thought, oh, that's lovely. [*laughs*] They're probably beating the daylights out of each other ten minutes later, but it's nice to have those moments, to know that they are there for them. (Sally)

Amy described sibling conflict as the result of children's different stages of development. In this sense, she described it by reference to notions of individuality that cannot be altered and must therefore be lived with. She made sense of and accommodated the threat to 'the family' as a cohesive whole by reference to her notion of 'individuality' as given. Other mothers, however, sought to foster good sibling relationships more actively, and found it difficult to accept children's quarrels. Shirley had no siblings herself and was distressed by her children's quarrels, which she tried to explain in various ways:

> They argue quite a lot, bicker. I don't think they mean it, but I'm sure they just do it to wind me up. And they certainly succeed sometimes. But I think deep down they like each other really!
> . . . I don't know, maybe if I had two of the same sex.
> . . . mind you, I don't know if I had a boy first whether that would have made any difference. It really depends on the type of children, doesn't it? And their temperament. There's so many facts to consider . . .

Gender as an aspect of internal 'family' unity   As with age divisions, gender cross-cuts family unity in ways that are generally completely taken for granted. In the women's accounts, gender lines were particularly clearly drawn in 'leisure' activities. Shopping was an activity that was frequently shared between mothers and daughters, while sport was frequently described as a shared activity between fathers and sons, as the Newsons also found – 'often to the exclusion of females' (1978: 289). The Newsons also stress the pleasure women reported in the companionship of their daughters at age 7, often centred on 'feminine' activities, almost amounting to 'a feminine conspiracy which deliberately excludes men and boys' (p. 288), especially in working class homes.

While sharing the same gender was thus thought to provide the basis for companionship between parent and child, there was also at times the suggestion of something special between parent and child of opposite sexes. However, what this special tie consists of was left unstated. The Newsons suggest it may be a particularly private aspect of the relationship, often being concerned with a particular warmth and protectiveness, for both mothers and sons, and also fathers and daughters: 'there seems to be a tendency for children to turn to the opposite-sexed parent to express dependency or to solicit indulgence, and to the like-sexed to enjoy more grown-up companionship on a equal level, sometimes

with a spice of almost conspiratorial adventure for both the pair'
(1978: 292).

Motherhood and individuality While men's 'family' responsibilities
are largely seen in terms of financial support, women act to secure
the family's cohesiveness. Yet while a woman may strive to create a
sense of individuality for her children as well as a sense of family,
'starting a family' may be the very moment at which she loses her
own sense of individuality. The 'mother' is the heart of 'the family',
and in herself its most potent representation. Hence concerns that,
if mothers 'go out to work', 'family life' is threatened. Various
feminist writers have discussed this identification of motherhood
and family, and its historical construction (e.g. Rose 1986, Scott
and Tilly 1980), with women themselves operating with familial
values rather than individualistic ones.

In the present study, while experiences varied considerably and
strains might be apparent in a number of ways, the women largely
subscribed to this construction of 'family' imagery, centred on
childrearing. Various writers have at times discussed the domestic
sphere as constituting the one social setting where women may
benefit from a female power structure (e.g. Ribbens 1993a, Stacey
and Price 1981, Stolz 1967). The women in the present study
expended a great deal of energy towards the construction of their
'families', and its achievement could be regarded as a source of
considerable happiness and enjoyment. Rather than wishing to
reduce their own 'family' responsibilities, they were inclined to
express a desire to incorporate their husbands more closely within
the family unit. Worlds of work were thus seen as threatening to
the family life which the women had created and which they
valued.

The ambiguities about family togetherness and individuality
discussed here are not only highly relevant to childrearing issues,
they are central to some of the difficulties for women's identities as
mothers within contemporary Western culture, because these
paradoxes are played out not only within childrearing, but also
within mothers themselves. Women as mothers embody and
internalise some of these contradictions. While the child's unique
individuality was emphasised and valued in some accounts more
than others, there was also variability in how far *parents themselves*
were seen to have *individual identities* and rights apart from their
family and work roles.

> You get to find out for yourself, you've got to have time for yourself,
> that's something else that I've learned. That you've got to have your

own time, you've got to have space. And your child isn't absolutely
everything, because *you* count as well . . . . (Kate)

Some women took a different view, that '. . . you can't really
have a life of your own' with children. Pauline expressed this view
more starkly:

In some ways I think your life is over as soon as you've had them,
because you become someone else, you become a mother, and that is
your role . . . It is frightening once they grow up and they leave home,
you're not really going to have anything . . .

It is thus significant that Janet and Margaret (discussed above),
whose accounts gave strong priority to the individuality of their
children, also expressed a strong sense of their *own* individuality
outside their motherhood role – Margaret through her full-time job
and political activities, and Janet through her longstanding and
consuming interest in horse-riding. Again, however, cultural
assumptions are difficult to uncover. Alibhai suggests that in her
experience as a Ugandan Asian woman motherhood could be
experienced as an extension of a woman's individuality, rather than
a threat: 'For my mother . . . there was never a sense of conflict, or
a feeling of being drained of her selfhood . . . it was a vital
addition, an extension of her strength . . .' (1989: 3).

Conclusions

I have argued that 'the individual' as well as 'the family' can be
seen to be a social construction. The mothers interviewed in the
present study varied in their *emphasis on individuality and family* in
relation to their children's lives. While all the women sought to
incorporate and balance out both of these notions in their
childrearing, a major source of diversity concerned how they sought
to accomplish this balance. Some women placed more emphasis
upon the creation of 'individuality', and paid minimal attention to
ideas of 'family' togetherness, while others were more concerned to
give priority to the creation of 'the family' as a unit, and paid less
attention to ideas of individuality for their children.

The balance between the view of the child as a member of a
collective family unit, and as an individual apart from the family, is
a delicate one. Susan expressed both perspectives in her account,
suggesting that her children could be seen both as a collectivity that
could be described as a whole, and as separate individuals:

Jane: If you were to tell somebody about them now, how would you
    actually describe them?
Susan: What, all three? All together, or separately?

Jane: Separate people.
Susan: . . . I mean all three have got their own little characters really.
    They're all lovely in their own ways.

'The individual' and 'the family' are constructs that are in an inter-dependent but contradictory relationship. The family is the site for both the construction and the expression of unique individuality, but both individuality and family are compromised by age and gender, and individuality is also understood by reference to nuclear family position and extended family membership.

There are fundamental ambiguities about the recognition of the child by the parents as a unique but dependent individual, as a gendered individual of a certain age, and as *family member*. Hence the central dilemma as to whether unique individuality is seen to be closely tied into family life and receiving its clearest expression and recognition within the family, or whether it is seen to require 'the individual' to leave the family behind.

Notes

1. The exact relationship between concepts of 'the individual' and 'the self' is itself a further issue that potentially leads us into complex philosophical and social theoretical debates. Their exact specification is not, however, necessary for the present discussion of their relevance as cultural notions to issues of childrearing.

2. The 1950 US Census used the word 'persons' to ask how many individuals lived in each household – as a result many babies were not recorded.

3. For a review of the debate about concepts of 'family' and 'household' see Doucet (1991).

4. Not all outings taken together constitute images of happy family life however – see the discussion of shopping in chapter 4.

5. This quote is left unattributed as it led to some discussion between the woman and her husband when they read their write-up together.

4

Friends and Relations

Women's engagement with the construction of 'family' does not only involve issues of internal cohesion and family togetherness, as discussed in the previous chapter. In discussing groups in general, Amos Rapaport (1981) refers to the ways in which both internal and external processes are significant in creating a sense of identity within any specific group. In addition, then, the notion of 'family' raises issues about how boundaries are drawn, demarcating 'our family' from other social units:

> They was the time when we was on the lan'. They was a boundary to us then. Ol' folks died off an' little fellas come an' we was always one thing – we was the fambly – kinda whole and clear. An' now we ain't clear no more. I can't get straight. They ain't nothing keeps us clear. . . . There ain't no fambly now. (Ma, in *Grapes of Wrath*, John Steinbeck)

In this chapter, then, I will look at how and when such boundaries are constructed and negotiated in relation to a range of informal relationships with friends and relations. These contexts raise further issues for the concepts of individuality and family, which I will explore throughout the chapter. In particular, I will discuss on the one hand issues about family boundaries, and on the other hand issues about children's individuality/sociability.

The concept of 'boundary' is not one the women themselves used in their accounts, and I am here applying it as an anthropological concept rather than a family therapy term (see David et al. 1993). An examination of boundaries also raises issues of public and private divisions and how these are constituted (see chapter 2). The boundaries described by the women interviewed were flexible and contingent creations they might use in varying ways, either assertively or defensively with regard to their own maternal authority.[1]

One of the ways in which the family may be demarcated from other sources of authority is by being *self-sufficient*. A mother who cannot meet her family's needs alone has been unsuccessful in creating 'the family' by failing to keep the boundaries clear in terms of self-sufficiency: 'About a third of the respondents actually indicated that to resort to outside advice was somehow an admission of failure to cope with something that they should have been able to manage themselves. Thus . . . the couples in this study tried to contain their difficulties within the group . . .' (Backett 1982: 102). There are very major issues at stake for a mother when outsiders become involved with her family, which may vary according to who initiates the involvement and on whose terms. Thus if a woman can create and cope with this family unit alone she also correspondingly keeps control of these processes within clearly demarcated boundaries.

Bernardes suggests that it is a general feature of the ways in which the concept of 'family' is used that we can hold conflicting images of family simultaneously – a generalised notion of 'The Family' and an idiosyncratic notion of 'my family': 'individuals feel no discomfort about describing their own family life as "unusual", and yet believing that they are seen by other people as having a "usual" family life, and finally asserting that most families conform to a pattern or "type"' (1985a: 203). An important resource towards the establishment of clear family-based authority is thus for the woman to accomplish her own production of 'an ordinary family', which is accepted as such not only by its members but also by those around her and the world at large.

Yet the notion of a bounded family unit may sometimes be invoked by women and at other times held in abeyance, being used within particular contexts, at particular times, for particular purposes. The notion of 'family' may be muted during working hours, when men are away from the home and the locality, while women and their children spend their time in networks of other women and children (Bell and Ribbens 1994). 'The family' may thus be a notion that is particularly appropriate to specific sections of time, namely evenings and weekends, while also acting as an assumed backdrop to the daytime networks. Similarly, women may invoke the concept of 'family' in the establishment of their own authority, and some social settings may be experienced as a threat to maternal authority while others may be experienced as respecting that authority: 'By outside help I mean essentially medical or other professional help. Informal exchanges with friends or relatives were seen by respondents as qualitatively different. Such exchanges seemed to be perceived more as gathering wider personal experiences on which to base decisions . . .' (Backett 1982: 102).

Furthermore, women varied in their *assertiveness* of maternal authority outside the home. This is a highly sensitive issue for women, because their children's behaviour is often felt to reflect on their adequacies as mothers: 'At all ages in childhood, in an ongoing and more specific study of incidents of conflict between mother and child, we are finding a complication and exacerbation of the mother's feelings wherever an onlooker is involved' (Newson and Newson 1978: 439). There was considerable variation in how far the women seemed to regard spaces outside the household as being under their control, in the sense that they expected their own childrearing rules and assumptions to be relevant, rather than someone else's. There was thus variability as to how far expectations that operate in one social space (the family) might be seen as irrelevant (or perhaps heavily modified) in another social space (such as visiting other people's houses, or in public places). This is explored further in chapter 9. This is another important aspect of the ways in which boundaries could be seen to occur.

The ways in which 'the family' is inter-connected with other social settings is largely women's concern – as with childrearing within the home and the family's internal cohesion. But even more than with women's activities inside the home, this other aspect of 'family' creation has been treated by social researchers as quite invisible. O'Donnell (1985) refers to mothers as 'social agents' in performing this external mediation for 'the family'. O'Donnell points out that, not only do we lack basic descriptions of these activities in their own right, but we also have no understanding of their implications for children, 'families' and neighbourhoods. Graham (1985) has described mothers as mediators on behalf of their children with regard to health authorities. The notion of mothers as mediators can be extended to a great deal of mothering activities, both with regard to children's relationships with fathers and siblings and with regard to children's social relationships more generally.[2]

In the first part of this chapter I will discuss issues of boundaries, and mediations across these, with regard to the position of maternal grandmothers. I will then turn to other informal social relationships the women discussed as key parts of their children's lives. With regard to the post-industrial, Western notion of the individual, much of the material presented here will demonstrate how this concept was *not* seen as relevant within these significant areas of children's lives. An important concern, discussed by all the women, was their children's lives outside the family, their *acceptability to others*, and the achievement of harmonious social relationships in various informal settings. Rather than invoking the concept of the individual in such contexts, the mothers took a view of children as social beings, and this represented a crucial childrearing concern. In this regard, the concept of the individual as a unique, idiosyncratic and potentially dependent being had relevance to family contexts (as discussed in chapter 3), while the concept of the individual as universalistic, assertive and achievement-oriented was relevant to formal public contexts such as education and future employment. The concept of the individual did not, however, seem to be invoked with regard to informal social contexts. Instead, a more *collectivist understanding of 'the person'* as socially defined (as discussed in chapter 3) seemed to be more relevant.

This aspect of childrearing has been almost entirely overlooked within established expert discourses, which focus instead on social *skills* as part of children's development *as individuals*. Indeed, we have virtually no empirical work which examines young children's social lives as part of childrearing.[3] Yet the view of children as *social beings*, enmeshed within a complex network of informal relationships, was a very important part of the childrearing accounts women gave me. In widening the discussion, then, we can see how individuality is a concept that is also in tension with notions of sociability in broad terms. Indeed, we have seen in the previous chapter how individuality within the household was compromised by children's social membership of the family. Furthermore, for many women, entry into school was regarded in significant ways as a continuation and extension of children's lives as social beings, as well as signalling the commencement of their educational development and careers as individuals (Ribbens 1993a). These informal social contexts carried considerable significance for the lives of the women themselves, for other family/ household members, and for aspects of local communities, as well as for theoretical issues of sociology and social policy (Bell and Ribbens 1994).

Close-knit families – grandmothers and other kin

While family boundaries may be strongly invoked in certain contexts, notions of 'family' are not always clearly demarcated in their usage. So far, I have discussed the concept of 'family' as if it can be taken fairly unambiguously to refer to the immediate domestic unit. Its usage in reality is clearly, however, much more flexible than this (Gubrium and Holstein 1990). The variable and slippery nature of the concept of 'family' could be seen in the various ways it was used in both the women's and the men's accounts. Sometimes 'family' could refer to the new nuclear family, and sometimes it referred to a much wider network of relationships and sense of identity. Rapp also discusses these *two 'levels of meaning'* (1982: 170) in relation to the United States, and refers to the nuclear usage as the 'normative' family. In the parents' own accounts, these different meanings were not made explicit, helping to blur any ambiguity apparent concerning the place of wider kin (especially the grandmother) in relation to the new nuclear 'family'.

It is now widely recognised in sociology that premature conclusions have been drawn about the demise of the 'extended family'. Nevertheless, I was surprised by *the significance of maternal grandmothers* in the lives of the women interviewed, and the frequency of contact between the two women (highly reminiscent at times of Young and Wilmott 1962). In drawing their spatial maps of people significant in their lives (see Introduction to Part II), all the case-study women included their families of origin immediately after their current nuclear family members – sometimes putting them alongside the latter, and sometimes just one step further out. Where grandmothers were still living, all the mothers were in regular contact, and for the majority this occurred at least weekly. Sandra however, did not regard this level of contact as frequent:

> Jane: . . . all the little things (the children) do from day to day, who would you tend to talk to about those things?
> Sandra: Mum.
> Jane: Do you see a lot of her?
> Sandra: No, once or twice a week, and we sit down and chat for an hour.

At least half the mothers were living within ten miles of their families of origin, and for some, this proximity had been very consciously sought:

> I was born in Midworth . . . when we got married we moved to Shenwood. No way would any building society give us a mortgage around here, so we had to move to Shenwood . . . and we've slowly gradually come back, step by step. (Rosemary)

More permanent moves away from parents might be made within very clear limits – 'this is the furthest North I'd go . . . it seemed such a long way to drive back to our parents you see' (Hilary, who had moved about 15 miles from her parents). In a larger scale English study, Warnes (1986) found that 40 per cent of mothers were living within five kilometres of their own parents. Similarly, Finch (1989) found that 72 per cent of adults in Britain live within an hour's journey of their mothers, 50 per cent of people with a mother still living visit at least once a week, while 40 per cent of women with a sister are likely to visit them also at least once a week. Gerstel and Gross (1987) also describe the widespread continuation of extended kinship ties in the United States, even among middle class households.

Maternal grandmothers could be important to the women as

mothers in a variety of ways. Firstly, they were seen as the most appropriate substitute carers if husbands were not available (Brannen and Moss 1988, Daniels 1980). The use of friends as substitute carers on a regular basis was generally seen as an imposition, while paid childminders were often not seen as a satisfactory form of care at all. This may be because childminders are not expected to feel the same sense of responsibility as the mother, or a relative.

Secondly, grandmothers could be an important source of female company, sometimes leading into complex networks of cousins. Susan had her mother, grandmother, mother-in-law and sister all living nearby and available for company during the day. Susan was clear about the benefits:

> It does make a difference . . . people would pop in, and you can just walk down the road and see somebody . . . . I mean I can understand people beating their children, because if you're stuck in a house with loads of kids, it drives you spare . . . when I've got to that point I'll just go out or call my mother.

Even though Penny was living hundreds of miles from her 'home town', she still had regular contact with a wider circle of relatives, as well as her parents and sister, with regular extended visits 'home'. Women's contacts with their own mothers, and with other female relatives, at times occurred along with their husbands on 'family visits' at weekends, but at other times they saw them during weekdays, *without male company* being present, especially during the early years of babyhood when the mothers were least involved in paid employment (Devine 1990).

Thirdly, then, grandmothers could be a resource (often only mentioned in passing) available during the day when things were going wrong. Rosemary went to see her mother when she left her eldest child crying on his first day at school – 'I just remember wheeling Helen round to my mum's and crying.'

Fourthly, grandmothers could also be important people with whom to share childrearing concerns. The case-study women were asked who they would expect *to talk to most about the children*, about things that happen from day to day. Sandra and Shirley both immediately referred to their mothers, who lived close by – 'Well, I see my mother usually every day, she usually calls in for a chat' (Shirley).

Nevertheless, there were significant tensions with regard to grandmothers' involvements, and many women expressed some reservations in this regard (Blaxter and Paterson 1982, Cunningham-Burley 1985, 1986). Sometimes this would be attributed to concerns about grandmothers' health, and a desire not to 'impose' too much. Issues of maternal authority were also involved, however, since grandmothers' involvements might prevent mothers from developing their own independent judgement and expertise.

Emily and Christine had both developed their own particular philosophies of childrearing and had reservations about their own childhoods. They were both in frequent contact with their mothers, but suggested that talking to their mothers about childrearing risked unwelcome reactions – 'I talk to [mum] quite a lot . . . . I talk to her because I want her approval and she doesn't give it' (Emily) – 'I talk to my mother actually a little bit reservedly because I know she's slightly judgemental. . .' (Christine). Emily and Christine discussed this source of tension precisely because they wanted to develop their own attitudes to their childrearing, apart from their mothers.

The childrearing influence of grandmothers can be felt, of course, not only in the form of suggestions or effects in the present, but also in terms of experiences from the past – the mothers' own childhoods and upbringing. With the follow-up families I was able to listen directly to the fathers and maternal grandmothers who agreed to talk to me, so that in my original study (Ribbens 1990a, chapter 7) I was able to compare the childrearing accounts given to me by these different individuals. A crucial element in the analysis that emerged was how far mothers defined the home as a particular setting with clear boundaries, and consequently a unique set of relevant expectations. My comparisons suggested that in dealing with the children *within the home*, these women had stronger parallels with their own mothers' views than with the perspectives of their husbands, even though all concerned subscribed to the ideology that mothers-in-law should keep their distance in deference to the primacy of the nuclear family. Where women (such as Emily and Christine) had developed different childrearing ideas from their own mothers, they had incorporated their mother's ideas rather than rejecting them. Furthermore, the seeds of such *changes* appeared to be rooted in other aspects of their childhoods, and not with the influence of husbands. Within the private sphere of the home, these women were all happy for their own mothers to look after their children because they felt they would basically take a similar approach to themselves.

Outside the home the women appeared to have developed more variable and independent ideas about how children should relate to the outside world, often reflecting their own experiences as adults. What happens between parents and children outside the home is, of course, openly visible to others, and is in this sense more available as a source of common knowledge and shared norms and expectations. By contrast, none of us can ever *directly* know what happens between another parent and child as an intimate dyad without others present. Our childhood experiences of being mothered within the home are both unique and private, and my analysis suggested that these childhood experiences inevitably constituted the starting points for the mothers' perspectives on their intimate and private relationships with their own children. Thus, within the family home, they might want to recreate their own childhoods, or to do things differently (Byng-Hall 1985), but any difference always had to be defined by reference to what they knew, which was their own childhood experiences.

By contrast, despite ideologies of unity between parents (see chapter 3), it was *within* the home that the women all expressed the strongest conflicts with their husbands about how to deal with their children. If ideas of childrearing within the home are largely built upon childhood experiences, there may be considerable need for negotiation when a couple have children and 'start a family of their own'.

> I think also if you're trying to bring up children with a partner, if you've been brought up similarly then you're going to have less problems, because you're going to agree about how to bring them up. Well, my ex-husband was brought up so differently, and I hadn't bargained for how difficult it would be trying to bring up children when you both come from such totally different backgrounds. We disagreed all the time . . . . (Lindsay)

It may thus require considerable negotiation to come anywhere close to ideological expectations of 'a united front' and of 'involved fathers'. Indeed, some of the women had clear ideas – based on their experiences with their own fathers – as to how they expected their husbands to behave as fathers, and were unpleasantly surprised when their husbands did not share these ideas.

Some of these issues were discussed by Jack. Continuity within the family was a strong theme for Jack in how you bring up the children – 'I think a lot of it is down to how you were brought up yourself anyway' – and this continuity could stretch backwards over generations. Such influences were however seen to be modified within a marriage – 'I think as you get older, married and have a family, we influence each other . . . and between us it ends up to be different.' Such issues will be exacerbated considerably if parents divorce and set up new families again with other partners. In such step-family settings, ideas of childrearing will potentially be negotiated across two new family cultures, involving four adults with varying family backgrounds. Indeed, step-families may be explicitly advised to abandon notions of 'the united front' altogether (Cox 1990).

Thus while the arrival of the first grandchild might be a time of drawing closer together between the new grandmother and mother, boundaries might at times have to be drawn quite firmly and symbolically, to create the new 'family' that commences with the arrival of the baby, and to establish the woman's maternal authority. As new mothers, then, women might seek to keep their own mothers at a slight distance until they had established their confidence – their 'own way of doing things'. If such boundaries were not drawn, not only might this undermine the woman's own authority as a mother, but it could also create additional difficulties in the way of negotiating a 'united front' with her husband. However, once maternal authority was established, women could allow the family boundaries to become more blurred (although for some, it could be that independent maternal authority might never be fully established, and perhaps might not necessarily be desired). Thus, over time, for many of the women interviewed, their own mothers were almost as involved as their husbands with childcare – either practically, or as a source of everyday discussion about children. In this sense, Backett's study (1982) of fathers' and mothers' joint negotiation of parenthood may have omitted important aspects of the processes of childrearing constructions.

Beyond home and family

Encouraging their friends is important, they've got loads of friends. (Susan)

Paul was always very shy, painfully shy, and lacking in confidence . . . he has a lot of friends now that he meets out of school, so we're particularly pleased with that. (Kate)

The friendships, social contacts and leisure activities of children formed key themes in many women's accounts, and were a very important part of the women's own daily activities and pre-occupations. In this sense, women described how they actively shaped and mediated their children's experiences with other children and adults in informal social worlds beyond the family unit. At the same time, the nature of these social worlds acted as both an opportunity and a constraint for women in developing their ideas about their children's upbringing. Kellerhals and Montandon (1992) also write of the importance of local friendships, for all social strata, for the ways in which parents relate to their children, while parents emphasise both autonomy and the capacity to relate to other people as values for their children's development.

Freedom of movement and association – *'You always know where they are'*

Martine Segalen (1986) describes a long-term historical trend for participation in unrestricted peer groups to be progressively less important as a source of socialisation for children. In the present study, many women had childhood memories of greater freedom of movement in peer groups outside the home than they allowed their children, and described this as a significant source of difference for childhood experiences – 'It was a lot more freer, I mean my mother never used to know where we were . . .' (Kay) – 'Nowadays you have to be so careful' (Susan). Nearly all the women spontaneously discussed *worries about letting children go out* of the home alone. Among those few who did not mention such a concern, there was often an assumption that children simply did not move unaccompanied outside the home. Worries about children's movement centred on perceived dangers from traffic and from 'strangers'.[4] In the Newsons' research (1978), a statistically significant gender dimension was found in mothers' reports of children's movements outside the home, but a gender difference was not apparent in the present study (possibly a reflection of the small numbers involved).

In a survey concerning the *parents of teenagers*, carried out by *Good Housekeeping* magazine (Harvey 1989), it was reported that one in four of the respondents listed personal safety as their greatest concern for their teenage children. Subsequently, large headlines appeared in at least one popular newspaper – 'Parents in fear of attacks on young' (Sutton 1989). Pearson (1983) has pointed out the very longstanding tendency for each generation to believe that public order and safety is breaking down by comparison with their youth. What is striking in the present interviews is how often these women reported actual *differences in freedom of movement* outside the home, when comparing their children's experiences with their memories of their own childhood.

Nevertheless, mothers often described fresh air – 'getting out of the house' – as desirable for children – 'not staying in front of the television' (Hilary). Most of the women in the study dealt with their concern about movement by setting *strict limits* on where children might play outside the home.

> They go up and down here on their bikes now with Paul . . . There's quite a few kids just up and down here, so Gill, who's next-door-but-two, she sort of keeps an eye on them if they're at her end, and I keep an eye on them at my end . . . If they go into someone's house they

always come and tell me where they are, otherwise they don't go out for a week! So they're pretty good on that! If they touch the road they don't go out for a week. (Susan)

Hilary was explicit about the advantages of living in a cul-de-sac of 'family houses', in providing the possibility for communal 'safe play'.

While 'playing outside' might thus be restricted, it was taken for granted that play with other children is desirable, and that children's friendships are important. If children have friends '*round to play*' at home, their friendships can be monitored from a slight distance, within an environment that is expected to be safe, with another adult present. With pre-school children, play with friends often occurred during the day, in the company of both the mothers, who might meet for coffee or lunch while the children played. Over time there was a gradual expectation that this would be replaced by unaccompanied visits. Some women expressed concern when children hesitated about such invitations, and several women discussed the problem of how to deal with a child who is reluctant to go to a birthday party:

> Marie: She would never go to anybody's, she would go to her friend's house to play, but she wouldn't go to anybody else's house to play and wouldn't go to any parties or anything like that, she would have invites but wouldn't go unless I would stay with her.
>
> Jane: How did you handle that?
>
> Marie: Well she just didn't go . . . I didn't like to say, 'Well can I come?' . . . So in fact this year when it was her own birthday in November, a friend from playschool is six days older, and had her party, and she said, 'I don't know if I'll go', and I said, 'If you don't go now to this party, you don't have a birthday party of your own', so she went and enjoyed it . . .

Feeling confident about going alone to parties and to visit other houses was thus seen by the women as a significant step, a goal towards which they actively sought ways of assisting their children.

During the pre-school years, such social interaction might develop from various sources – from ante-natal contacts between women, mother and baby groups, toddler groups, playgroups and a complex and varied selection of children's activity groups (see Ribbens 1990a chapter 5, Bell and Ribbens 1994). It was particularly at playgroups that children might start to initiate their own choices of friendships. By the age of 7, informal social exchanges might involve frequent arrangements to have children 'home to tea' after school – 'she often has friends round for tea, and she goes there as well' (Mary). Angela expressed her regret that her son could not do this since she was in full-time employment, and

Shirley gave this as her main reason for still not wanting to work full-time.

Many mothers thus described ways in which they supervised their children's social contacts. Marie described high levels of intervention in her children's friendships, and such relationships formed a central theme in her account. While she believed children should learn to stand up for themselves – 'I always say, don't tell tales, go away and sort it out among yourselves' – there were limits to this, and she had intervened in her daughter's social relationships inside school:

> I thought, oh well, she's coming home crying, I'll go up and see, just to make sure it's not all Anna's fault, because I know Anna's no innocent when it comes to it, so I went up to see her teacher . . .

Informal visits to other houses thus allowed for maternal oversight in general terms, but such visits could also introduce children to *differences of everyday family life*, providing some unexpected and perhaps uncomfortable insights into how other families might be different from their own. Angela described how her son had some long-term friends he had known all his life, since she became friends with the women at a mothers' group. When she and her husband parted, it was the other children who expressed most concern at this difference of family life:

> It was his friends actually, his friends couldn't understand . . . 'Why doesn't your daddy live here then any more, where's your daddy?' And some of the children . . . actually asked their parents, 'Where's [Matthew's daddy] now then?' One little girl in particular . . . she cried . . . and said, 'I don't want daddy to go like Matthew's daddy went.'

Ellen described a particular occasion when her children were introduced to a different and unwelcome experience when visiting other children:

> They went to a little boy who lived on a farm . . . Some sort of butcher bloke came and prepared a pig for the dining room table, and the children were watching, and they were then three or four . . . I was absolutely furious . . .

The women varied as to how far they expected their children to encounter such differences or similarities in other families they visited. While Ellen believed that her children needed to learn about varying attitudes in different families – 'I don't want them brought up in isolation, they've got to see other points of view as well' – at times this could become somewhat problematic. The *concept of 'house-rules'* that some mothers used provided a basis for recognising such differences more explicitly, while accommodating them within a shared framework. The implication was that each house operated by its own system of rules, and children had to learn to defer to the rules of the house they were visiting:

> . . . very often it's easier to say that wherever we go has house rules, and if it's not acceptable for the child of the house, then it's not acceptable for my child to do it . . . You can't go dramatically against the sort of thing that is house rules for that house. I mean for example, there are a number of children that come in and sit down to a meal without washing their hands, and I will not accept that in my house even though it's not my child because then these rules are unreinforce-able for my children. So yes, we all, more or less, have house rules. (Christine)

In this way, each woman could allow room for differences in expectations of appropriate behaviour, clearly expressing an awareness of and accommodation to varying family cultures, while still upholding the general principle of a mother's authority in her own home despite such differences of view. However, the notion of house rules might only operate when a child's own mother was not present to assert her own authority. When Christine smacked a child in front of his mother, the incident ended the friendship – 'I'm afraid my hand shot out and I hit him before I even thought about it . . . we really did fall out.' On the other hand, Angela's group of close friends all agreed they could correct each other's children even when the other mother was present (although perhaps not paying attention), thus to some degree assuming a collective rather than a particularistic authority:

> I tried to be consistent with him, I wouldn't allow him to do anything in anybody else's home that he was not allowed to do in my home, and vice versa really . . . but it never bothered us either if one of them was doing something and the mother happened not to be looking at the time, one of us would correct them, but we didn't mind. I would never mind if another girlfriend of mine said, 'Matthew, don't do that'.

In these various ways, then, these women expressed strong concerns about their children's social relationships with other children. They actively mediated the establishment of friendships, and stepped in to provide encouragement if they felt the child needed help, or to define limits that might have been breached. Such friendships were likely to be first established within private homes in the company of adults, but were seen as the basis for the development of skills in establishing important peer relations in other contexts outside the home. Nevertheless, such relations were still supervised from a distance. Any differences of family lifestyle children encountered in their social interactions might be thought to need some management. The women in the playgroup samples generally anticipated few differences concerning expectations of children's behaviour in different families. Any differences that did exist might be managed within the notion of 'house rules'. However, where women had developed ideas of childrearing and family lifestyle that were not widely shared by families with whom they interacted, there might be more of a challenge to their own ideas, and greater potential for serious disruption to their socialisation of their children.

Social acceptability to other adults – 'dying' of embarrassment

While the notion of 'house rules' enabled women to teach their children to deal with differences between family cultures, it also taught children to defer to other adults. The acceptability of their children to other adults was a frequent concern among the women interviewed.

> Mary: I want her to be popular and I lay there worrying that people don't like her.
> Jane: You mean other children don't like her?
> Mary: No, no, she's very popular with other children. But other mothers don't like her . . .

Many writers (e.g. Newson and Newson 1978, Ruddick 1982) have pointed out how mothers in contemporary Western societies feel 'held to account' for their children's behaviour. If children do not follow the wider social rules they let the mother down – revealing that they do not have a 'proper family life' and upbringing. *The individual* is thus seen as crucially *representing the larger social unit*, or as an extension of the mother. One woman described an incident where several local children had attended a birthday party at the house of a doctor who lived in the village. When the mothers came to collect their children, the doctor publicly rebuked one mother for her son's behaviour, and then invited the other women into the house for a drink. This must surely come close to the ultimate social disgrace for many mothers!

The two most frequently cited guidelines for social acceptability were *manners* – saying 'please' and 'thank you' – and showing *respect for other people's belongings* – particularly their furniture. Amy was well aware of such widespread expectations, with which she explicitly disagreed:

> I don't know why there's this big hang up about manners because they become automatic . . . I don't really teach my children manners, I hope they will pick it up from me . . .

Exactly what behaviour is considered to constitute good manners is of course variable between social groups. Shared definitions of good manners can act as very important parameters of class cultures and networks, which depend upon their criteria being known only to those who belong to these shared networks. Such shared expectations can thus be used to identify 'insiders' and can be used as an exclusion device against 'outsiders'. In this sense, manners can almost act as a secret language of social acceptability. At the same time, there appeared to be more than just a form of cultural labelling involved in the women's discussion of manners.

Hilary particularly discussed manners in the context of her family of origin. Not only should children 'say please and thank you', they should also learn to defer to age status:

> . . . my mother would be horrified if the children did not say please and thank you . . .
> I think it's something they have to learn early on, and that sort of thing is quite important. And also that they, if some adults come in and they want to say something to you, that they should be quiet when they are told to do and that kind of thing . . . I think those kinds of things are quite important, but that's like social behaviour — just to be socially acceptable because you never know when you have to expect them to do something and do it properly.

For Hilary, then, manners revealed that you are a proper family as you think *others* would see it. Children were expected to learn to contain their individuality within social rules set from outside the family. Nuclear family patterns may thus be deferred to what is needed to be acceptable outside, and this is a process that several of the mothers said they had themselves been taught very clearly during their own childhoods.

Susan expressed very similar ideas, with the wider 'family' again constituting a significant audience:

> Susan: . . . If we're at a family 'do', he's the one that always seems — 'Simon do this, Simon do that, eat properly' or whatever . . .
> Jane: Is that particularly when you're out?
> Susan: Yes, just when we're out, for the attention . . .
> Jane: Is it ever bad enough to put you off going out?
> Susan: It could be if I let him I think . . . . In the end it just gets embarrassing . . .

Children could therefore be potentially disruptive of the rules of social interaction, with *embarrassment as a sign of breakdown*, almost leading to withdrawal.

Jo explicitly stressed the need to exert proper control *inside* the home if children are to behave properly when *outside* it:

> You want them to behave when they're out, so if you don't discipline at home how are they going to behave when you're out?

However, while part of Jo's concern was with her children's social acceptability as a reflection on the family, there was also a different implication in her account, since she suggested that learning the social graces could be a passport to having *greater power outside the home*. She felt unsure of herself in social gatherings, and wanted her children to feel confident. She believed that learning a socially acceptable manner would give them this confidence:

> Not to be bumptious or extrovert but then they wouldn't be because we're not. But if they're asked something at a social gathering to be able to answer and speak out and not to be afraid to speak out.

Social acceptability, and potentially also social confidence, could thus be seen to depend on knowing 'how to behave'. However, not all rules of acceptable behaviour are clear and unambiguous. Sandra regarded herself as stricter than other mothers but when I asked her what mothers should be strict over, she replied rather generally – 'Behaviour mostly'. I was puzzled at first as to why women might refer to 'badly behaved children', but could not always tell me what would constitute 'bad behaviour':

> *Sally:* . . . the main thing is being firm enough.
> *Jane:* About any particular issues?
> *Sally:* Behaviour really.

However, this ambiguity may arise because 'bad behaviour' may be *contingent on particular situations* (and see David et al. 1994). A 'badly behaved' child is one who does not follow the mother's lead even when she indicates the rules appropriate for the particular situation at hand.

Children may thus not always be taught specific behavioural guidelines, but may be expected to develop a social competence in *dealing with rules in specific contexts*. In this sense, they are learning the skills necessary for social encounters to occur smoothly, since, as symbolic interactionists point out, rules and norms are always negotiated within specific interactions. Goffman (1956) describes how the principal consequence, when social actors fail to agree appropriate norms in any particular social interaction, is likely to be *embarrassment* – and women were certainly well aware of the danger of such a consequence if their children behaved inappropriately – 'I'd die, I think' (Shirley). The significance of embarrassment in social interaction has been neglected by sociologists (Heath 1988), but the avoidance of embarrassment – as distinct from behaviour that is simply inappropriate – would seem to be a major issue for the socialisation of children among the women interviewed. For children to become competent social actors, they have to learn to avoid creating embarrassment, since this is a key indicator that interaction is not being managed smoothly and is at risk of breaking down.

Thus the significance of teaching children to 'say please and thank you', and 'don't jump on the furniture' is that these may be taken fairly widely as clear indicators of parents' *general intention* that children should learn to manage their social acceptability, even if children have not yet learned all the complex cues necessary for the accomplishment of good manners within particular settings.

Amy, however, resisted such ideas, and sought to prioritise her children's individuality above immediate social rules and smoothness of social interaction, while Susan and Hilary, on the other hand, believed their children should learn to defer to the social rules of others. Thus life inside the home might be defined at least partly by reference to the need to present yourselves as a proper family outside the house. However, for Jo, people familiar with the social rules in any setting could then be in a position to assert themselves. In these processes, there were quite different expectations about the nature of individuality and social life, alongside different expectations about how power and control are negotiated across the boundaries between family life and life outside the home.

These expectations might work differently in relation to various sorts of settings. In contexts outside the home, there can be subtle nuances which affect the extent to which children are seen as likely to cause embarrassment by disrupting shared expectations of interaction in unpredictable and unacceptable ways. Work settings and formal occasions such as weddings were discussed as particularly difficult places to take children, with shopping another area that could be fraught with a sense of being under scrutiny[5] (discussed further in Ribbens 1990a: chapter 5, and see Edwards and Ribbens 1991). I suggest that these nuances about the potential children have for causing embarrassment in different settings may be part of the definition of *what counts as 'public'* for these women. In industrialised Western societies, the gendered historical division between public and private spheres depended crucially on the removal of children from the public sphere, while their presence in the home constituted a major raison d'être for the creation of a particular sort of private sphere. Nevertheless, not all private households are regarded as equally able to cope with children's embarrassing disruptiveness. Several women described how motherhood had led to their withdrawal from social contacts which involved people living in households without children, because they found it too stressful to deal with the embarrassment caused by children in such settings. Women might thus describe varying levels of assertiveness in relation to other adults' expectations of children's behaviour in different settings outside the home.

Conclusions

In this chapter, I have described mothers' concerns with their children's lives beyond the immediate contexts of household and nuclear family. We have seen in this discussion how family boundaries might at times be strongly invoked and at times kept muted, with significant implications for power and authority. I have also suggested that these mothers helped their children move as individuals beyond the family/home, but the women were very concerned with their children as social beings, both as representatives of the family group from which they may be seen to have originated (involving a collectivist notion of personhood), and as people who have to learn to avoid causing embarrassment and to become socially acceptable both to other adults and to other children – to become socially competent actors in a variety of social settings, including informal friendship groups. Mothers varied in several key respects around these issues – whether they drew clear boundaries around the family as a separate and specific social space, whether they expected there to be some continuity between inside and outside the private home in terms of what could be regarded as appropriate behaviour from children, and whether they felt able to assert their own ideas about appropriate behaviour or felt an obligation to teach their children to defer to other people's social expectations. Such variability might occur between different women, but also the same woman might vary in these respects at different times or in different settings.

These are issues to which I shall return in chapter 9. In the next Part of the book I shall seek to bring some of the mothers to life as women in particular circumstances, developing their own ways of understanding their lives with their children. In the case studies which follow, I hope to present some insight as to how different women's childrearing accounts need to be understood as wholes, before going on in Part III to dissect the accounts of all the women around certain central maternal preoccupations and images of children.

Notes

1. For a fuller discussion of the concept of 'boundary' in relation to mothers' lives, see David et al. 1993.

2. For a discussion of mothers' mediation between their children and teachers, see Ribbens 1993a.

3. Indeed, it is only recently that sociological texts have started to pay sustained attention to the significance of the informal social relationships of adults (see e.g. Allan 1989b, O'Connor 1992, Swain 1989).

4. I am here only concerned with mothers' perceptions of dangers. It is of course very difficult to know whether British society today really is more dangerous for unsupervised children, or whether the danger is magnified by newspaper reporting – as some of the women themselves pondered.

5. Mothers may have had good reason to feel conscious of the public gaze in settings such as shopping: Warner (1989) based her anecdotal descriptions of 'family life' today entirely on incidents she had witnessed in public settings outside the home, such as shopping.

Part II

Portraits of Childrearing in Four Middle Income Households

Introduction to the Portraits

In this Part, four individual women's childrearing accounts are explored in some depth, and a further two considered more briefly. I see this process as one of portrait painting, presenting detailed pictures that seek to avoid caricaturing and distorting these women's individual perspectives. Only gradually, in subsequent chapters, will I move towards a clearer model of some of the issues. Furthermore, I believe that an approach that begins from the topical details of women's everyday lives with their children is more in keeping with women's own understanding of issues, and more in line with how the ethnographic work actually occurred.

After all the initial 24 interviews had been completed, I thus chose six women for more intense follow-up.[1] The six women were selected to provide a number of women and households, such that the group *as a whole* would include important aspects of variability. Such variability can be seen (a) in the childrearing perspectives the women themselves described, and (b) in terms of significant aspects of their lifestyles more generally. The group thus included:

o women whose own mothers lived very close-by or many hundreds of miles away;
o women whose husbands' work entailed very different implications for the household;
o women whose marital relationships varied considerably in terms of the women's expressed satisfaction;
o women whose own educational qualifications and occupational

experiences were quite varied, and whose current involvement in paid employment was also varied;

o women whose enjoyment of motherhood had also been very varied in terms of expressed satisfaction.

Four of the women were drawn from the playgroup samples, and two were part of the theoretical sample (see Appendix), included because their children did not attend State schools.

Only in considering childrearing accounts as wholes can we understand what particular concrete issues meant to each woman. For each woman, with her particular set of meanings and relevances, topical childrearing concerns might carry quite different sorts of significance according to her larger understanding and perspective of how she brought up her children. The present discussion is, however, structured by the basic analytic categorisation I introduced as a result of my growing interest in public/private differences (see chapter 2). The case studies therefore distinguish between (a) childrearing and motherhood experience within the immediacy of the private household, and (b) being out and about with the children in more public social settings. I also include here the spatial representations or maps I asked participants to draw of the people who were important to them in their current lives[2] (Thrower, Bruce and Walton 1982).

In presenting the case studies I have sought to stay as close as possible to the women's own descriptions. I have therefore included long direct quotations in places, while at other times I have tried to summarise the interviewees' own discussions, in terms that remain as close as possible to their own words. I have tried to indicate through my own choice of language (for example, 'it appeared that . . .') where I am aware of moving further away from the women's own accounts to incorporate more of my own perceptions and understandings and analytic shifts of focus.

To a degree, then, I sought to enable the women to draw their own pictures, so that the results would be a series of self-portraits. This was a major reason[3] for my decision to return to the women with the portraits once I had drawn them, to allow them to read and comment upon the accounts I had written of their talk with me. After all, if they did not recognise themselves in these verbal pictures then I certainly had no basis for describing them as self-portraits (a form of 'respondent validation' in Reason and Rowan's terms 1981). Some participants were more enthusiastic than others in their endorsement of the portraits – 'It very accurately sums me up' – and some sought to elaborate further on some aspects of the pictures.

The clearest *reservations about the portraits* in the original study

(Ribbens 1990a) were expressed by Penny Barton and Richard Woodley-Mason. While both fully endorsed them as accurate representations of what they had said, they both voiced some concern as to whether or not they had expressed their own views adequately in the interviews. This seemed to centre on a concern that they 'came over' as rather strict, placing over-much emphasis on discipline. I cannot judge whether this is because of some unintended distortion on my part, or whether it reflects a difference between verbal and written discourses of childrearing. Written discourses, for example, in advice books are perhaps more inclined to advocate 'permissive' parenting styles – indeed, it is often on the (shaky) basis of what is written in advice books that assumptions are made about the rise of permissive parenting in actual child-rearing practices. An emphasis upon parental discipline is perhaps more often found in spoken discourses, both in terms of everyday conversation and in terms of political rhetoric. In writing up the childrearing accounts given by parents in the research interviews, I was translating an oral account into a written one.

There may also, of course, have simply been a shift in their views over time. Penny Barton expressed this particularly clearly after re-reading her account for this book in 1994:

> I remember I cringed when I read it a year later, but I found it makes sense again now. I must have been going through a funny phase I think! But it isn't until you do something like that that you realise how much you've changed.

However, I must also clearly acknowledge that, in practice, even where portraits were enthusiastically and fully endorsed by participants, they cannot be regarded as self-portraits. I have made numerous decisions about how to select, structure and present the material, and I am writing them for particular audiences (Morgan 1985, Ribbens 1989b). Perhaps my role is therefore closer to that of the portrait-painter who nevertheless allows people to decide for themselves how to dress for the portrait, and what objects to include.

The six women will be discussed in three pairs, to make it easier to draw out some broad features of comparison and illustrate certain central themes:

Chapter 5: Penny Barton and Sandra Hopkins both took an overall orientation to childrearing which gave priority to the idea that children have to learn to fit in with adult beliefs and patterns within the household, but had quite marked contrasts in how they interpreted this overall idea. Both of these women were drawn from the playgroup samples.

Chapter 6: Shirley Wootton and Emily Warren both gave priority to childhood as a special, almost magical time, such that children have special needs to which adults should respond and adapt their own expectations of household patterns. Emily was one of the theoretically sampled women, whose children were being educated outside the school system.

In the Overview of the portraits, I also discuss Pauline Davis and Christine Woodley-Mason, who both expressed some ambivalence and mixed views about their childrearing ideas. While they both clearly suggested that children should fit in with adult ideas, they also appeared uneasy about this at times. Christine was also drawn from the theoretical sample, since her eldest child was being educated privately.

While the portraits have been organised in this way to aid the reader's general orientation to the details of the case studies, this organisation is very much a heuristic device, not a clear-cut classification of the women. Thus all the women, not just Pauline and Christine, expressed degrees of ambivalence and mixed views.

Notes

1. Two families had already been interviewed several times during the course of the first phase of interviewing, including fathers and maternal grandmothers. These families were not, however, included as part of my case studies, although their interviews have been used in other ways throughout the analysis.

2. I am indebted to Elizabeth Murphy for this suggestion.

3. The other major reason was one of ethical considerations – see Ribbens 1990a, chapter 2.

5

Fitting Children into Adult Frameworks

Both the women introduced in this chapter took an approach to childrearing that assumes that children have to learn to fit in with adult beliefs and patterns in the household, and also in society more generally. Furthermore, they both stressed the importance of discipline in achieving this. If children are not controlled they may take every opportunity to assert their own control and may become 'little monsters' (as one child was repeatedly described). There was thus the image of the possible unleashing of all sorts of dangerous and inhuman forces if children are not disciplined. Nevertheless, there were also some quite marked contrasts between the women as to how they interpreted this overall idea.

Penny Barton

Date of first interview – 1988. Source of contact – playgroup. Aged 31, one younger sister. Primary and comprehensive school in Northern home town, moved to Newcastle upon Tyne to undertake teacher training. Taught till birth of first child; no paid employment up until time of first interview. Married while a student.

Husband – David Barton aged 33, building society manager, earning around £18,000, with cheap mortgage and company car.

Children – Zoe aged 7, local primary school; Adam aged 5, local primary school; Samantha aged 2½, about to start playgroup. Ectopic pregnancy occurred between Adam and Samantha.

Housing – bought their first house in Newcastle, moved South to modern spacious end-terrace house four years previously, in village on edge of urban area.

Of the various case-study women, Penny Barton came closest to the stereotype of the happy and successful traditional family, of children and non-earning mother supported by the male bread-winner. In drawing her spatial map of people important to her (Figure 5.1), Penny unproblematically portrayed herself encircled

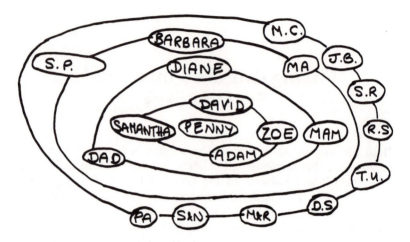

Figure 5.1 *Penny Barton's spatial map of people important to her*

by her husband and children, with a series of other concentric circles radiating outward, to signify her relations and friends. Both Penny and David were brought up in a small town in a beautiful part of Northern England. The move South was necessary for David to secure his managerial position, and Penny was acutely conscious of employment problems in their area of origin. Unlike David, Penny has been socially as well as geographically mobile, since her father was a miner for over twenty years, and her mother was a factory worker. David's father is a medical doctor.

'I think I've changed a lot since we moved down here really.'

Penny and David left home to go into higher education and have never returned to their town of origin. After two years of teaching, she 'fell pregnant' with Zoe and gave up her job, with Adam born two years later. The move South when Zoe was three felt like quite a risk, but it was a risk that has worked out.

Penny described how the relocation involved moving between quite different sorts of regional cultures. While educational provisions were in some ways better in Newcastle, in her new area Penny felt that all schools would be good because of the children's home backgrounds. She also believed her children would have better prospects in the South. She described less pressure to conformity in her new area, and children were more involved in activities outside school. Some of her own attitudes had changed since the move, particularly as regards their diet.

> Well, the move has made a big difference to me . . . I mean, just things like this diet thing I was telling you about . . . I think I've changed a lot since we moved down here really.

'I was so ecstatic at becoming a mother.'

Penny hesitated to describe her first two pregnancies as 'planned', and felt she started her family at a young age for 'professional people'. Having children had always been a very important part of her expectations:

> *Penny:* I was always going to be a mother. It would have been dreadful if I'd found out we couldn't have had children. I probably would have been suicidal. I mean that's how important it was to me. Although I always wanted to be a teacher, it was always something I just did until I decided to be a mother . . .
> *Jane:* So were you sorry to give up work at all?
> *Penny:* Well, not really, because I was so ecstatic at becoming a mother.

Furthermore, Penny enjoyed her pregnancies and giving birth (apart from a rather traumatic ectopic pregnancy):

> . . . the whole three pregnancies have been very, very easy . . . I love being pregnant and bringing them up. I love the whole thing about it.

'Breast is best, but only if it's best for mum as well': learning to do what is right for you.

Looking back, Penny regretted not following her own feelings about feeding Zoe. She decided to breastfeed because she felt this was right, but found it a struggle:

> I breastfed Zoe because I thought that was very important at the time, but I struggled, not in terms of — I mean I had plenty of milk — but I'm a very busy type of person, and I couldn't sit and breastfeed and think that the house needs dusting and hoovering . . . I was pushing myself to the absolute limit, and I was just so exhausted . . .
> I always felt as if I was undressed with boobs hanging out all over the place, I don't know, perhaps I'm too fussy.

Penny chose to bottle-feed the subsequent children straightaway:

> My motto is — breast is best, but only if it's best for mum as well. And it wasn't best for me, although I had plenty of milk . . .

Penny had come to believe that a mother should make her own decisions, and do what feels right for her as a person, despite any sense of pressure from outside. She had concluded that trouble comes if your ideas are one way, but the way you feel about things is different. What matters is to work out what is right for you, and then you can expect your children to learn to live with that — 'The trouble is when your ideas are over here, and *you* are over there.' This was one of the strongest lessons she had felt about motherhood, that she should have 'listened to herself'.

Order and routine, or relaxed mothering?

Penny regretted not being more relaxed as a mother but she was clear that she needed order and routines, both in her house and with her children. While feeling that this was the only way she could 'function', she also wondered whether it had made motherhood more difficult at times:

> I'm very routine, as you can see, I'm very particular. My cousin [says] . . . she's never seen such a neat fridge, everything jumps to attention when you open the door. I'm just very orderly, I have to have things in their right place, or I just can't function . . . And I suppose I'm a bit the same with the kids really.
>
> I can tell you now what I'll be doing every Tuesday for the next so many years, because Tuesday is my shopping day . . . and the kids are very routine . . . Zoe always went to sleep at the same time every day, and I'd wake her up at the same time every day, and Adam and Samantha were the same . . . I'm a very routine person, so perhaps that's what made it difficult as well, I wasn't flexible enough.

Establishing sleep routines had been difficult with Zoe, but Penny had definite ideas about how to respond in the middle of the night:

> I was quite determined I was not going to give in to her, and she never got out of the cot . . . I used to take my knitting up and sit in the bathroom knitting, or reading a book . . . I'd go back in and rock her bottom, give her her dummy, sneak out, close the door, wait another fifteen minutes, back in, do the whole palaver again, until eventually after two hours she would go back to sleep.

Eventually Penny decided she would have to 'put her foot down' to 'crack this really bad habit':

> I let her carry on for an hour, just crying and screaming and carrying on. And then I went to her, and it took me an hour to calm her down, but I got her back to sleep and I left her. And then the next night she woke up and cried again, and I left her, and she only cried about fifteen minutes and I calmed her down. And the next night she never woke up and that was it, that was it cracked, she slept right through from then on.

Discipline: 'If I think something is important, I'll enforce it.'

While Penny felt a need to live by routines, she also made distinctions between routines that centre on work and career, and routines that centre on children. Life for a new mother was much easier when the former had given way to the latter. Such routines had to be imposed, and she emphasised the importance of discipline:

> I know from experience if you don't have discipline in the classroom, you can't achieve anything else, so perhaps that's how I feel at home.

If necessary, discipline must be enforced by a smack:

> . . . it's got to hurt . . . So if I smack mine they get a good smack, they know they've done something wrong, and it doesn't happen again. But it isn't very often I have to smack them . . . I am quite a strict disciplinarian, if I'm cross about something they know about it.

Nevertheless, it was in relation to this section that Penny later commented that she felt it 'jarred' to read this write-up of her account, with what she felt was an over-emphasis on smacking.

In addition, reasoning could be important as they grow older, as discussed in relation to Zoe's tantrum at 2 years old over not being able to play with a friend who was not at home. Here Penny felt she had successfully changed her tactics from one of seeking to assert direct control over the tantrum, to one of allowing the child to 'see reason':

> So I said, 'Well you can't play with her because she's gone out.' 'I want to play with Janie, I want to play with Janie.' So I carried her back screaming. I mean they are just so unreasonable, you just can't reason with them. And left her screaming and carrying on, and then I just went to her and cuddled her, and I said, 'Never mind Zoe' . . . And then in the end she said, 'I can't play with Janie because she's gone out.' It was like a sudden turning point, she realised that for herself, that she was being unreasonable, and why she couldn't play with Janie.

When asked to describe her children, Penny's main response centred on their good behaviour, particularly in terms of immediate obedience and ability to occupy themselves. Penny expressed the belief that children have to learn to fit in with the adults in the household – 'You've got to live with them, so you've got to get them to live by your rules.'

Penny commented later that she sounded 'Victorian and authoritarian', although agreeing that this was a real basis of difference between herself and her sister in their childrearing ideas, her sister being more inclined to fit her own life around the children rather than the other way around. Penny stressed that her concern with discipline arose from the belief that this is the basis on which to build the fun and enjoyment of childhood.

While discipline makes life workable for the mother, it may also be for the child's own good – 'in some ways, as a caring mother, you've got to be cruel to be kind'. Imposing discipline could be an effort, and an obligation.

> I find the disciplining them the hardest thing . . . It isn't until David's there, that I realise what an effort it is to summon up the energy to be angry about something, because you know they need to be told, when really you can't be bothered.

Discipline might also benefit the children in other ways, by enabling Penny to cope with messy activities:

> I hope I don't suppress their creativity or anything like that . . . Because they are so well-disciplined . . . I can get all the paints out, they can take their shoes and socks off, splodge through the paint, and do foot and hand pictures. They can have water play and all this, and I can have baking and everything going on . . . if I've got discipline, I know I can do all these messy yucky things, and the results won't be too drastic.

Nevertheless, Penny worried that the emphasis on discipline might not always benefit the children and in particular, might reduce the scope for individuality:

> I sometimes think I'm a bit too strict and don't let their own personalities develop, in a way . . . [My sister] and I are really mother clones basically. We are very like our mother and the two of us are very much like each other. But David's family, I would say, are very individual.

Taking responsibility

Penny suggested that this burden of discipline and responsibility falls largely on the mother's shoulders. Part of her definition of how a mother shows her children she cares for them centred on taking her responsibilities seriously, whether for their diet, their safety, or helping them to develop independence. Furthermore, she did not define any limit to the responsibility a mother should take for her children:

> I don't think she puts any limits on herself, what she would do . . . I wouldn't put any limits on myself as to what I would do.

The sense of responsibility had hit Penny hard when she first brought Zoe home:

> . . . when you start a family you really are on your own – well this is how I felt anyway . . . It's really awful to realise the responsibility, and how it all comes back to *you*.

Nevertheless, in some areas she felt David had influenced their family lifestyle, particularly coming from a different background. There were jokes about different language at times – 'knickers' should be referred to as 'pants' – and David emphasised certain behaviours at table. While she described him as largely sharing her own views on childrearing, when he was at home she wanted her judgement to be recognised:

> . . . we find that we tend to agree on everything, most things anyway. I mean occasionally I'll check back with David, 'What do you think?' sort of thing, but it is usually me.

Beyond the boundary of home and household

Over the years, Penny had developed confidence in her own child-rearing abilities inside the home, but she also wanted to have more confidence in making her own judgements about acceptable behaviour with the children outside the home. While taking pleasure in compliments from strangers about her well-behaved children, she also felt she had worried too much about others' opinions:

> When they were little I told them off at times because I felt the pressure of people watching and thinking, what a naughty child, and I'd got myself really worked up and got really angry with them, and when I've calmed down I've thought, well, it wasn't that bad really. I was reacting to *them* more than the child, so I try and control that now. I think to myself now, are you doing this because *you* think it, or because you think these people expect you to do it?

In dealing with a child's introduction to playgroup, Penny took it for granted that she would make her own assessment about how to handle the situation, rather than being conscious of the leader's advice.

> I think playschool is more accessible, isn't it? Because they're really just parents themselves who are helping out, aren't they?

When it came to schools, however, Penny felt it was less appropriate for her to mediate on the child's behalf. While she had herself been a teacher, she described a considerable divide between parents and teachers.

> . . . a lot of parents around here are frightened of going into school, they are frightened of having contact with the teachers. I'm not like that, if there's something bothering me I'll just go in and tell them.

Nevertheless, she had kept quiet about some things that had happened at school which she did not like. She believed schools must break children's ties with home, and did not want to identify herself with 'pushy parents' – of whom she felt there were many in the area. Ultimately, the responsibility came back to her again:

> . . . underneath it all I feel that ultimately they are my responsibility and they'll only get from school and playschool what I have given them the ability to get from these things.

Looking ahead

While Penny generally described herself as happy in her mother-hood, much of its meaningfulness came from an orientation to the future – 'I think preparing them for life [is important], that's what you're working towards isn't it? All the time.' While her children were well-behaved, she considered whether they might rebel later, not having got it 'out of their system'. However, her confidence might be greater than this suggested – 'because I like them as people I feel quite happy that they'll turn out all right'.

For herself, she wanted to return to teaching in the near future, and had a desire to 'prove herself' at work. In the longer term, she anticipated good times ahead with David – 'just having time together really as a reward because it isn't easy bringing up kids'.

Update on Penny

By 1990, Penny and David had moved to a detached house literally just round the corner, bought from one of her close friends. Also through her friendship networks, she had become involved in supply teaching, which she felt was difficult for Samantha but having started she did not want to stop. She had since obtained a part-time teaching post, with hours individually tailored around Samantha's playgroup hours – a result of a great shortage of teachers in the area. She wanted to become a deputy headmistress before she reached 40.

Her employment led her to revise some of her earlier ideas about routines. These had had to become more flexible, with sudden job changes, the house move and then building work in the house as well. She had also asked David for more help, and he had started taking responsibility for family shopping. Tuesday shopping days had, after all, become a routine of the past. David had also occasionally been involved in childcare responsibilities, for instance, when one of the children was ill. Penny felt that he was becoming more involved as the children grew older and as his hours of work became rather less demanding.

By 1994, Penny described their lifestyle as having changed completely, and she was back in full-time teaching. She had enjoyed reading her earlier account once again, although it made her aware of how her views had changed over time, sometimes coming back to earlier ideas (see the quote in the Introduction to Part II).

Sandra Hopkins

Date of first interview – 1987. Source of contact – playgroup. Aged 34, two younger sisters. Village primary schools and then girls' grammar school. Left school at 16 with O-levels. Worked in supermarket and went to college on day release. Later became branch clerk, training others. Married and gave up paid work with first child. Returned six months later to full-time book-keeping work. Currently working with her husband running the family shop.

Husband – Jack Hopkins, aged 36, runs his own shop, earnings unclear.

Children – Andrew aged 7, local village school; Gemma aged 3, local playgroup.

Housing – when first married, lived in company flat, then bought own house in an expanding town some twenty miles away – moved back to the area over two years ago, to detached house with shop, with some financial assistance from her father. The shop is at the front of the detached house where they now live, in small rural village in commuter area.

While there were other women in the sample whose husbands worked largely from home, Sandra's household was more obviously unusual than most, in that the family business was an integral part of the house. The demarcation of boundaries between work and home, public and private, was thus difficult to achieve – 'You've got no privacy living with the shop.' Sandra wanted to meet me before committing herself to the research, but quickly agreed. I felt this reflected a sort of cautious openness about their position in the village generally. Their family life was fairly visible for all to see, but some areas were kept private. The shop at the front of the house always felt very much present, even in the evenings, and Jack would often be working out there when I arrived.

Sandra had not found early motherhood at all easy, and with Jack's agreement, early on she returned to full-time employment,

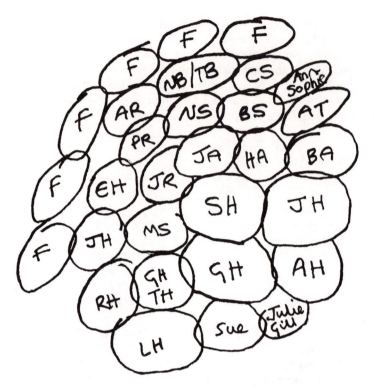

Figure 5.2 *Sandra Hopkins' spatial map of people important to her*

later combining her childcare with work in the shop. Throughout this time, her own mother had played a central childcare role and their households overlapped in significant ways. In her map of significant others, her immediate household was portrayed as closely enmeshed within other circles (Figure 5.2).

Sandra had not moved far from her origins, in either social or geographical terms, her father having been a scientist working with alloys. Jack's father was an electrician but died some years ago.

'You can't tell anyone what it's going to be like, can you?'

When Sandra and Jack had their first child they had bought a house and Jack was employed as a butcher. Sandra at that point gave up her job although money was tight. The pregnancy was not planned as such (although Sandra was a little ambiguous about this), and the birth itself was good.

Yet caring for the baby was something of a shock, and on one occasion Sandra feared she would harm Andrew – 'this awful feeling of, "You've got to stop crying somehow"'. She described him as hyperactive, and blamed some of his problems on the colouring in the medicines she was given for him. She felt she only slapped him when he deserved it, while someone else might have 'thumped him', but she had left him in his cot to cry and shut the door on him. (On reading an earlier version of this account, Sandra commented – 'It makes me sound like a battering mum'.) Thus she experienced motherhood in these months as very fraught, and she felt very miserable at home. Eventually, with the advice of her doctor, she asked her mother for help, and Andrew started spending weekends with his grandmother. Sandra expressed guilt about some of these early difficulties, and blamed herself for not handling them well – 'But it wasn't really one thing, and one thing led to another.' When Andrew was 6 months old, with childcare help from her mother, Sandra took a full-time job again. Andrew then split his time between his grandmother and his parents, spending several nights each week away from home.

This pattern of shared care continued with Gemma, who spent six months as a baby living with her grandmother when the household moved to the shop:

> . . . we did have her back for the odd nights and odd days, and we always went over there. I mean we never lost contact with her . . . I missed all her crawling . . . But she was very good about it all, and Mum got her into a nice routine.

Family business

Six months after Gemma was born, Sandra and Jack bought their present business, and a host of relatives came round to help clean up, since the place was very run-down. Business picked up well, and Sandra felt they had considerably improved their standard of living. But the shop dominated their lives, with the whole pace of family activities determined by patterns in trade. After getting up at 6, Sandra's day 'depends entirely what is going on out there'. She tried to spend lunch time with Gemma, and the child played in the house while her parents worked, or accompanied Sandra when she went out. It was in relation to her housework that Sandra most resented the time spent on the business:

> You don't get up and make the beds in the morning, you make them before you get back into them at night . . . it would be nice to go back to that, so that everything is all neat and tidy and clean and spick and span, but it never will be, so what's the point in wanting it really?

Although Jack was almost constantly present in the house, family time distinct from work time was very difficult to find. They had not been able to take a holiday together – 'the most we get is a long weekend', although Sandra had taken the children away for a week without Jack. Sandra described the pace of work as almost impossible to cope with at times, especially for Jack – 'at the rate he works at times, you couldn't do it for too many years, you would really do yourself in.'

Jack's family role had altered considerably with the acquisition of the shop:

> . . . he went out for the day on a business thing and I spent the day with the children . . . That was lovely, but oh, were they pleased to see Dad again when he came home . . . they're so used to having him here, that when he's not here they really did miss him.

Sandra expressed mixed feelings about these changes. In some respects he had a greater understanding of the strains of parenting – 'He didn't realise, I don't think, how hard it was having two little ones around you all day long' – but on the other hand – 'he used to have a lot more patience than he has now, but then he's with them all the time you see'.

Sandra nevertheless described herself as still taking primary responsibility for the children, with Jack's main commitment being to the shop. While they often disagreed over the children, generally she had already decided what to do on any particular matter, and felt that discipline is really down to mothers, because they are with children more than fathers.

Practical caring and adaptable children

Sandra in many ways gave the impression of being a very practical woman, and this seemed to hold true also for her concerns in childcare.

> *Jane:* Do you have any kind of image of what your ideal family would be if you could only be like that?
> *Sandra:* No, not really. As long as you are warm and you are well fed, and you are happy and you are healthy.

She described childcare as hard work, that has to be fitted around other obligations, with children being quite capable of fitting into a variety of situations:

> . . . really neither of my children has had a stable family life, with one thing and another, but I think really it's been good for them, and made them more adaptable and outgoing.

While other families had routines with their young children, Sandra described their own lifestyle as one of 'broken routines'. The adaptability of children applied to children generally, so that families can live quite different lifestyles and children will fit in – 'children are adaptable, they get used to it.'

'I'm not cut out to be a mother.'

Sandra had found it stultifying being at home with a baby – 'I think your brain gets a bit stale when you are at home with the baby . . . I really did feel stagnant, awful.' Her worst fault as a mother was described as lack of patience – 'I haven't got a lot of patience and I should have, but I haven't, I wish I had really.' Nevertheless, Sandra found children more enjoyable as they got older, so that they become more independent with regard to the practicalities – 'Once they can do for themselves, and they can sit and play a game properly, I've got far more patience then.'

In describing a mother she particularly admired, Sandra referred to someone who was full of patience and ideas with children. Yet for Sandra this was balanced out against the need to get other things done too – implying perhaps that ideal motherhood is incompatible with the realities of life. She described the mother's role more in terms of being there for children when they are upset:

> Just to be there when they need her really. Sit and listen, sit and talk to them, if they are upset. I'll always say goodnight to them, I don't like them to go to bed upset . . .

Learning the realities of life?

Sandra also stressed the importance of children themselves learning about the realities of life, in the shape of work and money.

> *Sandra*: If Andrew does certain jobs he gets 10 pence per job, and if he doesn't do them he doesn't get his pocket money.
> *Jane*: What sort of things?
> *Sandra*: Makes his bed in the mornings, keeps his bedroom tidy, dusts it for me, brings down all the washing, puts it in the machine for me. Just things like that, that just save you a few minutes . . . It's just one way of teaching him . . .

Poor attitudes to work were a source of concern about young people generally, and such standards were something Sandra expected gradually to teach her children:

> . . . you can't push them too far. At the moment, it's trying to get into them the importance of money, and why you can't just lose it and not

bother to look for it, and things like that. Andrew is not so bad now because, like the other day, he made a potion, which infuriates me. A whole thingy of talcum powder, brand new, £1.50. So I made him work it off at 5p a job until he'd earned back £1.50, and I said to him, 'Now perhaps you will understand money just doesn't grow on trees, Andrew, you have to work to earn it to buy things. And when I tipped the whole lot down the toilet it's just like throwing three 50-pence pieces away and flushing them away.' It's sunk in now.

Money was identified as the crucial aspect of working, and the basis of a good job (though not the only one) – 'I mean a dustman earns good money doesn't he? That's basically what it boils down to nowadays.'

'Good as gold' – care and control

Discipline was a central issue in Sandra's account, evidenced by the immediacy of her description of the children in these terms – 'I've got a good one and a bad one.' When asked about differences from other mothers, Sandra quickly described herself as stricter than others. She was also explicit that children should fit in with adults. In this respect she was critical of her sister's childrearing:

Their whole life revolves around her, instead of hers revolving around them. They've adapted their life to suit her totally. Rather than her fitting in with them, they fitted in around her . . . You should bring the child up to grow up to your ways . . . They've got to learn, bit by bit, to fit in with you.

Besides the management of the daily routine of bedtime, food had been another area of concern in the past with Gemma, but Sandra felt she had solved this successfully:

. . . she didn't want it, she wasn't going to eat it. I put it in the fridge and served it up for tea. The penny had dropped by then, so she reluctantly ate enough to take the edge off the appetite. 'Not good enough, Gemma.' So I served it up for breakfast, she had the lot, that was it, it cured her. She was just playing up and she's not done it since, so it works, she's quite good with her food. I wouldn't normally go to that extreme, but she was going to that extreme, and she'd pushed me enough. I mean, every meal was just sort of, 'I don't like that', for a while.

Nevertheless, Sandra implied that some rebellion might be inevitable, and might have to be accommodated. In discussing choice of clothes, she remembered how she rebelled sometimes as a child:

. . . you only rebel against it, we always did and they'll do the same, so you might just as well, as long as they're not going to go berserk . . . Andrew has one pair of jeans at the moment . . . looks like a tramp, he loves them, he lives in them, but he only wears them round the garden, he doesn't go out in them, so that way he gets his way, I get my way . . . that way we both win really . . .

Issues such as getting children to clear away their toys might evoke some complex judgements. One factor was how to judge the authenticity of a child's excuses, which might determine whether or not the issue was one of control. It might often be easier just to do it yourself, although this was not right:

. . . Gemma's awful. I must say, nine times out of ten I end up doing it because it's just not worth the hassle of arguing with her . . . but I shouldn't do it really, I should make her . . .

On special occasions, Sandra implied childhood could be given some leeway, evoking happy memories. Christmas time in particular was a special time when parents might 'go soft', and provide treats – 'It's just a time for children, and you get no greater pleasure than seeing the faces on Christmas day.'

Overall, the control of children was not easily achieved, and might be modified by various considerations, not least the nature of childhood. This could sometimes be very difficult to understand, since children might be quite mysterious. At the same time, Sandra clearly implied that control of children is associated with caring for them:

. . . [it is] mum who is for ever pulling them up, because mums do, that's what mums are there for, isn't it? All the smacking, all the sorting out of the arguments. But then it's always mum they come to when they are upset, isn't it?

Private boundaries

The analysis of how Sandra's childrearing account varied between public and private settings was complicated by the degree of overlap between her own household and that of her mother, and by the loss of privacy with 'living over the shop'. In relation to divisions of both time and physical space, there was less of a boundary between family life and the rest of the world. Sandra liked to keep the door shut between the shop and the rest of the house, but this was not always easy:

Sandra: I used to worry and keep my voice down and that. Now I think oh, to hell with it, it's my home . . . we do try and keep that door closed as much as possible.
Jane: What, the door into the shop?
Sandra: Yes, but there's times when you can't always keep it shut.
Jane: It's almost like having the front door of your home open to everybody?

Sandra: Oh it is, yes. Especially if the door gets flung open by one of the kids and there's a queue of customers and you can guarantee they will peer. They will hang over that counter as far as they can. It does infuriate me, and you can guarantee it's the day when you've got piles of washing all over the kitchen. Yes, it isn't the ideal situation really, you have a lack of privacy . . . I love closing time, I watch that clock from quarter past five onwards.

Moving beyond the home and household

The control of children was a central issue for Sandra in social contexts outside as well as inside the home. While some 'push' might be necessary, and some rebellion inevitable, it must be contained in acceptable channels or it might become quite out of hand – 'as long as they are not going to go berserk'. Several times Sandra expressed her concern that children must not become 'too outrageous' – the implication being that it was people generally who would be outraged, although it was parents who interpreted what counts as outrageous.

She described shops as places where you could be exposed by badly behaved children, so that it was preferable not to take them:

. . . mothers don't like to be shown up in the middle of a shop . . . before you have children you see mothers yelling and giving them a whack, and you always think, I wouldn't do that when I have kids, and you do . . . All the people that look at you, but the same people are the ones that disapprove of the children running riot, and they have to behave themselves . . .

Some of Sandra's key aims for her children concerned their social acceptability generally, and what could perhaps be described as honest citizenry:

You try to maintain a decent standard of living and just try to bring the children up to be well-behaved and polite, and don't let them go round smashing up cars and windows, and things like that. Just teach them the rights and the wrongs then, and just hope that they are honest enough to be able to come to you if they are in any trouble before they get themselves into more trouble.

Nevertheless, while valuing acceptability to the wider community, how this actually worked out in particular social situations involved some differences of emphasis, so that it did not always entail a straightforward deference to others.

Sandra described both children as sociable – 'my two are very outgoing and independent'. However, there were some children she did not want to invite to play at her house – 'A couple of them are little monsters and once was enough.' She was also ready to assert herself with children who came visiting, and she described how she had smacked a visiting child one day – 'Some of them really need a good hiding and would be much better for it.' In reading this through later, Sandra commented – 'It makes me sound as though I'm always whacking kids! He was really vicious, but he was a little angel after that.'

Generally Sandra's children had been happy to go to playgroup, but before Christmas Gemma had been clingy:

> I've had one morning at playschool when she was very clingy, very cuddly. That was Christmas time, there was so much going on . . . she got very upset, but she hadn't seen very much of me, you see . . . we just sat and had a little cuddle and started playing with playdough and that. And she just announced I could go, so I went. That was it, forgotten, but my two aren't clingy anyway.

Sandra also suggested that it is good for children to be used to being without mother, and the sooner they learn this the better.

In relation to schooling, it was the parents' job to create a basis for discipline in the classroom – 'I think if they are disciplined at home they're fairly well behaved at school . . .'. Sandra described contact with the school as very good, partly because of its small size, yet there was a difference from the relationship with Sophie, the playgroup leader:

> . . . it's slightly different there, I mean Sophie . . . and I are friends anyway. [The headmistress] is a lovely teacher, and she is very approachable but – and it doesn't just apply to me, it applies to all the mothers – she gives that aura over, you should be saying, 'Please Miss', and putting your hand up, and then she'll talk to you . . .

Nevertheless, while school was clearly a different sort of place from home – being concerned with educational work, within a larger group and with a teacher in authority – there was also the implication of quite an open boundary between the two for Sandra.

Looking ahead

> [I hope they won't grow up to be] layabouts, punk rockers. As long as they grow up to be reasonably well-mannered, average people, I'll be happy.

Sandra expressed her hopes for her children's future largely in terms similar to her own life, projecting a continuity with regard to both work and family life. For herself, future years might provide more opportunities for work, study, travel and for her marriage. But for herself also she implied a future in terms of continuity of family life over generations:

Jane: One mother said to me, she said your life is over when the children leave home. You don't agree with that?

Sandra: No, nonsense, it starts again, doesn't it? I don't believe it at all. You've got the grandchildren to look forward to, haven't you?

Update on Sandra

This continuity was apparent in Sandra's life in 1990, when life seemed to be carrying on in much the same way as before. They had made some house improvements and the children had moved on at school. Sandra talked about going back to college for a business course. Jack had some part-time help in the shop but they had still only managed a weekend away together the previous summer.

By 1994, however, Jack had given up the struggle with the shop and closed down – 'we decided we just couldn't be bothered to keep fighting the supermarkets all the time' (Sandra). Sandra appeared quite content with this decision. Jack had found work doing a variety of self-employed jobs, Sandra herself was 'being very lazy at the moment', and not in paid employment. They had also been able to take their first 'decent holiday' in ten years, and were hoping to move house to a different area altogether. The children were well, with Andrew happily settled in to State secondary schooling.

Comparisons

Both Penny and Sandra had a central belief in the idea that children have to be taught to fit in with social life as it exists, and that adults have a vital part in imposing this on children through discipline. Crucial within this view was the belief that this is what is beneficial to children and that discipline thus constitutes a crucial aspect of caring for children, that might actually be quite hard work for mothers. Both women were confident about their maternal authority inside the home, even if there were occasional differences with their husbands' views. Penny was also becoming increasingly confident about taking authority for defining her children's needs and standards of behaviour outside of the home as well as within it.

Yet there were also important differences between these mothers, concerning the relevance of routines, which were important to Penny but not to Sandra. For Sandra, while children could be mysterious at times, in most areas children were seen as adaptable. For Penny, children needed routines, and to this degree adult life had to be shaped to fit the needs of children, although it was adults who defined children's needs. Over time, however, routines also gave way for Penny in the light of other practical demands in adult lives, including her own paid work.

There were also contrasts between the women as regards their own roles at the time their eldest children were aged 7. While Penny had found mothering a lonely and overwhelming responsibility at first, at the time of the initial interviews, she expressed confidence in her maternal role and satisfaction with her lifestyle outside paid employment. Sandra, on the other hand, found early motherhood extremely hard to cope with (for various reasons, including a baby who hardly slept). Early on in her 'motherhood career' she sought out other significant identities besides that of mother, with a return to employment followed by immersion in the family business.

Having considered two women similar in their orientation to the idea that children should learn to fit into social life under the direction of adults, in the next chapter I will present two women with a rather different approach.

6

Fitting in around the Children

The two mothers to be introduced in this chapter regarded childhood as a special time for freedom from restriction. During very early childhood particularly, adults should be ready to meet children's needs as children themselves express them. The job of mothers is to provide the sort of space in which children's own feelings can be accommodated and the demands of adult life can be modified and minimised around children's special needs. There were also, however, considerable differences between these two women in the practical outcomes of their childrearing styles.

Emily Warren

Date of first interview – 1988. Source of contact – mutual acquaintance involved in Education Otherwise. Aged 28, one younger brother. Village primary school and then secondary modern school. Left at 16 with some O-levels, became university secretary. Left home to live in rented flat in town when 17, and later moved in with Tom Warren. Started nursing training but left when pregnant and then married. Part-time evening work, as care assistant and later barmaid, earnings unclear.

   Husband – Tom Warren, aged 29, quantity surveyor, earnings about £14,000 (increased to £18,000 during the early phase of interviewing) plus company car.

   Children – Edward aged 7, not in school; Robert aged 5, not in school; Jack aged 21 months.

   Housing – shared house with Tom's sister when first married, later moved into council house in urban area. Moved out of the region altogether for short while, then moved back into a shared ownership house, and then bought older-style end-terrace house in small rural village. It is the house where Emily lived as a child.

Emily was very concerned with her family life, and was highly reflective and self-scrutinising about her mothering. In drawing her spatial map (Figure 6.1), at first she drew her children and husband as separate but adjacent circles to herself. Deciding that this was

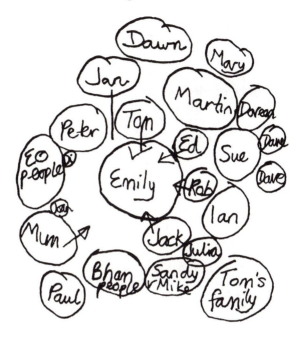

Figure 6.1 *Emily Warren's spatial map of people important to her*

not right, she added arrows to indicate their incorporation in the circle that represented herself. In many ways, Emily's family shared characteristics of the stereotypical 'conventional family'. Yet while many women presented themselves to the outside world as creating an 'ordinary family', Emily seemed to present her household as 'alternative'. She placed particular importance on her children's individuality which should take priority over social conformity. Her children did not attend a school and had not attended a playgroup.

While the household had been geographically mobile, they were living at the time of the interviews in the house where Emily was herself brought up, which she described as coincidental – 'Don't read anything into that.' Emily had also been socially mobile, her mother having been a wages clerk and her father a factory worker. Tom's father was a plumber, while his mother trained as a teacher, divorced Tom's father and married a teacher.

'Before he was even a year old, I felt I was very different to the other mothers in my attitude.'

Emily described her adolescence as rather difficult, and she left home at 17, while working as a secretary. Later, while living with Tom, she decided to train as a nurse, but became pregnant, married and withdrew from the course. She felt they coped with the change of plan quite easily, and they were allocated a council house after the baby was born. She made friends with neighbouring mothers, but felt under pressure for being different from the other women – 'I used to get really upset and come home and cry.' This difference focused in particular on the issue of breastfeeding, since Emily was the only one still breastfeeding at 3 months, and she decided to seek out some support for her own ideas. As a result, she responded to an advert in the newspaper for La Leche League, 'a breastfeeding support group':

> I went along to their meetings and found it really supportive. I thought they were very weird because they were feeding these big babies and toddlers, and I thought that's not for me, but I still found it very supportive to find people who were still feeding . . . I learned a lot from those people.

In contrasting herself with other neighbouring mothers, Emily became aware of how many issues she felt differently about:

> I felt quite different because I liked the children to do what they wanted to do. And I liked them to be playing with water and paints even – this was before Edward was one, so he was really quite tiny . . . lots of experiences like that, which other people didn't like, because they were messy, and they like everything pretty . . . And also they would smack their children, tiny babies . . . other people thought they could be trained by smacking them . . . I wanted to convert them all to my way, which is not – I thought that mine was the right way.
>
> Partly I suppose it comes down to how my mother treated me. She was very gentle and kind, and would let us do things like cooking and make a mess . . . I don't know why, whether it was, I'm sure a big part of it again was my influence from La Leche League, seeing how lovely and gentle they were with their children, but I already had it.

The move to initiate contact with La Leche League was the first in quite a long line of such moves, to find like-minded groups of other parents. Emily had thus been involved over the years with the National Childbirth Trust, a birth centre, Pre-school Playgroups Association (PPA), and Education Otherwise. She had also developed a long reading list of books on relevant topics. While she had first sought out these contacts on her own impetus, they then had a further impact in changing her ideas – 'I think La Leche

League and PPA were the two, I feel, important beginnings, and this sort of set me off on this path.'

Emily was very explicit about having an overall philosophy of childrearing – 'I think that my way is the right way. I can't help thinking that, but I'm sure there are other ways'. This philosophy underlay how she dealt with diverse issues, so that the various aspects of childrearing constituted a seamless web. Before Robert's birth, Emily felt she had this philosophy coherently worked out, with the help of her new contacts:

> So by the time Robert came along my attitude was to relax much more. I fed him much more on demand – although I'd already done that, I was much much more relaxed and fed him all the time. I think Edward had always been in a carrycot by the side of our bed, whereas Robert immediately slept with us always. So I changed, in that I'd got more child-centred. Like I would have maybe smacked Edward, whereas I wouldn't smack Robert. My attitude had moved, shifted in that direction, in general my attitude had shifted.

'Needy children': setting out to meet children's special needs

Emily regarded babyhood as a special period of immediate needs, which she should respond to unstintingly. In this respect, she felt some regrets at her handling of Edward when he was a baby, whom she now described as 'needy' rather than 'difficult':

> I think he was difficult. Well, I thought at the time he was difficult, they were both very needy babies. Well, Edward didn't have his needs met so fully as the other two have done.

Defining him as difficult and fussy was associated with a response to his crying which she since regretted:

> . . . when he was very tiny . . . I feel that he was really needing us, and we left him to cry . . . I did try it because that's what everybody said you did, and I wish to goodness I didn't do that now . . . I didn't leave him to scream for hours or ages. I'd leave him for a minute and if he didn't settle then I'd probably pick him up and carry him around.

In caring for Jack, Emily felt confident that 'his time' had been as perfect as she could make it:

> I think he has had everything as right as I can feel it is . . . I feel his every need has been met. He's been fed whenever he needed feeding, I'd never try and make him wait . . . He's had lot and lots of bodily contact, so I think he's had a lovely time of it, it's been really nice for him.

For Emily, prioritising and responding immediately to babies' needs is important to create security. Again, it was clear how all these issues inter-linked:

Jane: Is it the babyhood that you see as being the crucial time?
Emily: All of it is important . . . Like way back to when you're pregnant. I think it's important to have as calm and stress-free a pregnancy as you can . . . I think it's very stressful for a baby to have a difficult birth. And I see breastfeeding as very important. And I see sleeping together as very important too. I feel that's important to the child, that they have some very secure — but again, I mean that's not to say that parents who go out to work — I mean that's not at all what I would want to do . . .

I think security is everything . . . I think they become very confident and secure people, because they've had a lot of input at an early age . . . their self-esteem will be very high, I hope, and I hope they will be loving and caring because they've seen that as a role model really, and had it given to them, that they'll have it to give back.

For children's needs to be met, however, their wants have first to be perceived. Contact and listening to children are thus central aspects of affection.

It was thus difficult for Emily to find that she could not always meet her children's total needs. The period after Robert's birth was very difficult, feeling socially isolated after moving to a new area, with a baby who was extremely sick all the time — 'I mean I did cope, but only just. It was very, very hard.' It was some years before a physical basis was diagnosed for this sickness. Her third child, Jack, had colic, and Emily could not stop him from crying:

It was quite a shock to me that he would be awake in the night, so that was quite difficult, and he did have colic, and that was distressing to see a baby crying and not really be able to do a lot with it.

Boundaries and limits: how far is it possible and desirable to go, in meeting children's needs?

Experience had not always matched up with theory then:

All the theory that I've read about [colic] is that if you carry them and feed them whatever, they shouldn't get colic, but he still got colic.

Similarly Robert's babyhood was undermined by the sickness problem — 'it was awful, Robert's time'. Other factors could thus prevent the perfect time that Emily wanted for her children, including unavoidable daily tasks around the house, and her own inability to live up to her theories — 'Loads of times I would scream.' Furthermore, she was not quite sure how far she ought to recognise adult needs:

> I'm not as strict about tidying up as [Tom] is. I'm very soft, I think, I so
> much see it from their point of view that I overdo it, I know I do. I
> should think of myself more, and of us as a couple more, but I see
> everything from their point of view.

Adult interests may be balanced out against the children's learning
process:

> The mess in the house, that's a difficult one . . . We let their bedroom
> get in the most awful mess . . . it made a problem for washing . . . they
> didn't have any clean clothes . . . It was awful, but that's part of
> learning, they've got to learn to sort that out for themselves, I think,
> but it's very difficult to live with, the mess.

Emily suggested that it was she rather than Tom who had taken
the initiative in childrearing – 'I think I got the ideas first always,
and he caught up with me . . . we've got a similar outlook.' Like
other mothers, Emily mediated sometimes between her husband
and children:

> He really does do an equal share when he's here, but I'm here more
> than him . . . I'm much more in tune with the children . . . I'm much
> more gentle than him, but mostly it's because I spend more time with
> them . . . I think he's too hard on them. I'm always saying lay off,
> particularly with Edward.

Emily was also concerned about how to shift the balance between
household members as children grow older:

> When they are little their demands and needs are immediate, but the
> difficult part for me has been the changeover between their needs
> being all-important, and as they've moved on their needs aren't quite
> so all-important . . . It was a little bit bumpy saying, 'No, Edward, you
> can sort that out, or, I'm not going to do that.'

As they grow older, also, Emily expected to teach them to recognise
other people's needs:

> I think people are important . . . considering other people is impor-
> tant, considering other people's needs . . . I teach them to care for the
> younger ones . . . to be aware of little children and aware of their
> needs.

A further issue was who takes responsibility for identifying needs
– such as children's dietary needs – and who is responsible for
setting up the environments in which they will express their wants.
Emily felt she may have overprotected her children against stressful
feelings, but that she was less protective than other mothers in
terms of safety issues, such as the use of knives. Near the end of the
research period Emily started seeing a counsellor, who suggested to
her that one of the children's needs might be to have clear

boundaries, but Emily was not sure whose needs are actually met by such boundaries:

> There is a lot of talk of boundaries, which I haven't really thought about before . . . I do say some things are not acceptable and I say no. I don't know whether that's important or not, or whether that's important for me and the family running.

Emily inter-linked all these issues around taking responsibility for herself and the family, with the idea that the children can learn to take responsibility also for themselves – 'It's all part of being in charge of yourself.'

Boundaries with the world at large

While Emily made links between different issues within the household, she also suggested that there are no boundaries between childrearing concerns and wider world issues outside the family, such as world poverty and peace, and environmental issues. The analytic division between issues within the household and outside the household had a rather different application in Emily's account from those of the other women, since her children are not in schools, which perhaps sheds some light on processes these other mothers took for granted. Emily developed her own ideas partly as a process of contrasting herself with others – to adapt Cooley's description of the looking glass self, a sort of 'looking glass family' effect (Bell and Ribbens 1994). The pressure she felt to conform had come primarily informally from people she met, rather than from any formal authorities.

In protecting herself from this pressure, at times Emily evoked a clear sense of authority and territory within her own household, and in doing so drew a very clear boundary around her family. At other times, she wanted to be more active and outgoing, almost to the point of evangelising her vision of childhood. In doing so, she sometimes opened up her family very visibly to public scrutiny if she could do so on her own terms, for instance, in the form of newspaper and magazine articles. One impulse towards doing this came from her desire to define all social settings as places where children's needs may be recognised, and perhaps met. Thus while at times she used the privacy of the family defensively, at other times she sought to break down the boundaries between life within and without their household. Emily herself expressed a strong need for approval from others, which sat very uncomfortably beside her adherence to a different perspective, making her very vulnerable.

Taking a middle line: high visibility and balancing acts

At times, then, Emily sought more privacy, while at other times she tried to find congenial social contacts. Yet some activities brought her childrearing into public scrutiny:

> I remember Robert screaming because he wanted to feed on the bus, and often I would feed on the bus, but I was sitting right at the front . . . he was about two or three, it wasn't when he was a baby. I don't normally feed openly, I would do it on a bus, but I would go and sit right at the back and be very discreet about it.

Emily regarded shopping as an activity that could provide an interesting outing for children, but could also be full of crises and public judgements:

> Lots of people glare and I feel very frowned upon. I always feel we look so scruffy . . . I often get a lot of people say what lovely children they are . . . and that's really lovely . . . I suppose everybody when they are going shopping gets children having screaming fits . . . I used to distract the children but now I let them go with how they are feeling and let them scream. It's awful when you are walking along.

In such situations Emily felt she had to mediate between her child's feelings and people around:

> Robert was cross with me and he hit me and somebody said, 'Don't hit Mummy, you must never hit Mummy.' And I don't agree with that at all, but I think I just sort of smiled at Robert and rubbed his head and just didn't say anything . . . I think often I'm partly apologetic for how they are behaving . . . and yet still acknowledging to the children that I understand . . . I think I've got to take the middle line somewhere between them and the world, whilst still acknowledging how they are feeling.

Again, Emily described a difficult balancing act:

> Really I want them to feel good about themselves. But I think it's important how other people view you because you've got to somehow fit in with life, and much as I don't like most of it, you do have to. You are part of society and you've got to fit in in some way.

The preferred solution was for children to want to fit in of their own accord, and she was proud of them when they behaved well in a restaurant:

> They'd got there just because they want to be there, because they can see that other people sit down and talk at a meal, and not because they are being made to, and I felt really proud about it . . . our way is working in our own way.

Self-responsibility

For Emily, taking responsibility for yourself included self-reliance in health and education. She had felt socially pressured to send her children to playgroup, but had never found a group that really adopted the approach she wanted. She also felt she could provide the same experiences and activities at home, and moreover the children themselves did not want to go. Thus, when the expected time came for moving her children outside of the immediate family circle, Emily found it very difficult to find an organisation for the children that reflected her own values. When she did find a toddler group that did more than 'just tip out a box of toys in the middle of the floor', she felt the activities were too adult-directed – 'they were all adult ideas . . . And they're quite structured, I'm very anti-structure . . .'. However, she described the decision to educate at home as having crept up on them, particularly because of her feelings about the schools in the area where they were living when Edward reached school age.

Emily's concerns about the formal educational system centred on a number of issues, including processes of learning, the organised structure of social relationships within schools, and issues of conformity and individual freedom.[1] She perceived a marked contrast between their family life and the demands that school would make:

> He couldn't have coped with the discipline of school because we've led such an undisciplined life really with few constraints or things put upon him that he has to do things, he could do what he chose to do . . .

As for peer group contact, Emily felt she could provide this on her own terms.

By not sending the children to school, then, Emily had avoided their encounter with school structures and values, and also kept her home life free from constraints other mothers learn to take for granted, in terms of the timetabling of family life, and the effects on family roles and concepts of education – 'We just do absolutely everything you could think of, but not in any particular pattern.' Thus Emily had avoided compromising her family life by relationships with an outside authority. Nevertheless, she expressed concerns about their lifestyle, such as the intensity of the relationships within the house, her powerful position as role model, and uncertainty about her adequacy for this responsibility.

At the same time, she wondered whether or not she should try to change outside organisations in line with her beliefs, particularly the playgroup:

I feel quite guilty because I think that just maybe if I went along I could actually improve them but that's being very bigoted, but I think that my way is the right way . . . I feel in a way I'm opting out instead of getting in the system and improving it for other people, I'm opting out, but I haven't got the energy or the personality . . . at the moment I've got to think of my own family and that's what I'm doing, I'm putting us first . . . . I feel it's all I can manage at the moment.

Looking to the future

Emily did not orientate her childrearing towards the future, preferring to 'take one step at a time', although she hoped they would have interesting jobs as adults. In the immediate future she had ideas of living in a village of like-minded people, with Tom reducing his commitment to paid work. In looking further ahead, she hoped to undertake further training herself, and perhaps try harder to change the system more widely. A life ahead without children provoked mixed feelings:

Jane: I had one woman say to me that your life is over when the children leave home.
Emily: No, I don't think that. I'm quite frightened about that . . . I can't imagine what it would be like . . . It's quite exciting as well, I suppose, there's lots of new prospects open to you when they leave home . . . I haven't got a plan laid out.

Update on Emily

By 1990, Emily had given birth at home to a baby girl. She and Tom had had a large extension built to the house, doubling its size, and they had also employed an au pair. This was Tom's idea, and Emily seemed quite resigned to the fact that he liked his work and would not give it up. Emily's own life had changed somewhat – she had become involved in running a holiday playscheme for children, and also acted as an agent selling children's books. More significantly, she had developed a close friendship with a woman living in a co-operative house about twenty minutes away by car. There were various children's activities running in this house, which Emily attended on an irregular basis, with the possibility also of setting up a Free School. She had also changed the household's diet to vegetarianism, and become interested in homeopathy and in Green politics. She still felt that once you question one thing in life, it opens up new issues – 'Once you've started you can't go back.' She was also considering training as an ante-natal teacher.

By 1994 the children were continuing their lives without school attendance. Jack had expressed a desire to go to school and went for three days, and then 'wouldn't go any more'. After a considerable gap, Emily herself had resumed her sessions with a counsellor, which she said had become quite traumatic and had recently ended. It had led to much heart-searching about her parenting:

> It's such a weird thing to do, not to send your children to school . . . It has made me realise there is quite a lot in it for me, allowed me to avoid facing certain things I needed to face . . . But my other reasons are still there . . . I don't think we're any more screwed up than anybody else!

Emily had also applied for midwifery training, having completed some years as an ante-natal teacher. Tom was still very involved with his work, being now a company director. 'He's okay and we're okay which is nice.'

Shirley Wootton

Date of first interview – 1987. Source of contact – playgroup. Aged 35, no siblings. Village primary school and secondary modern school. Left school at 16 with CSEs, worked in London as supervisor of computer operators, married and gave up work with first child. Undertook part-time evening office jobs when child aged 1 year. At time of first interview, working 20 hours a week, take-home pay £300 monthly.

Husband – Stephen Wootton, aged 38, works manager in small engineering company, earnings unclear, about £14–15,000, plus perks.

Children – Mary Rose, aged 7, local primary school; Paul, aged 5, just started at local primary school.

Housing – semi-detached house in a large plot in small village, built by Shirley's grandfather.

Shirley had clearly enjoyed motherhood, and drew herself in her spatial map unproblematically (see Figure 6.2), at the centre of a cluster of significant others, including her parents (who live in the same road) and her dog, as well as her husband and children. Shirley was unsure how satisfactory her employment circumstances were, either to herself or her husband. She was brought up in the village, and Stephen had come from an adjacent hamlet. While her current household was higher in social class terms than her family of origin (both her parents had been factory workers), her grandfather had a small business. Stephen's father was a carpenter in a local factory.

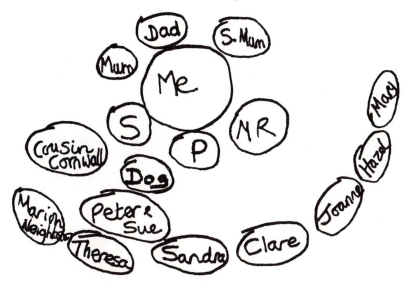

Figure 6.2   *Shirley Wootton's spatial map of people important to her*

Happy memories

Shirley's first child took some time to conceive, but the birth itself was quick and easy. Once the baby had arrived, Shirley looked to the hospital staff and later the health visitor for advice in caring for her:

> I didn't feel as though she were mine. I felt as though I needed someone to tell me what to do.
>
> I went into it thinking, oh yes, I'll know what to do, but once you've got this little tiny bundle then I felt so green, and not knowing what to do with it. [*Laughs*] But you soon get into the swing.

In several ways, Shirley seemed to have certain expectations of motherhood as a significant step. As well as having looked forward to the birth, and to breastfeeding (which required much persistence), Shirley had bought a large coach-built pram to take the baby out for walks, and a rocking chair to help settle her. Later she had been very keen to prepare her own meals when weaning her babies. She appeared to enjoy talking about the early babycare in some detail and to look back at the pre-school period with fond memories, and a sense of a job well done. She had given up her full-time job in London when she had her baby, which she had not been sorry to do after 11 years. When Mary Rose was 9 months old, Shirley took a local part-time job in the evenings, and later helped to run the village playschool:

> I would never have had children if I hadn't intended to stay at home. That's me personally because I think you miss so much . . . I helped at the playgroup and that. I did my bit for them, and everybody else's children! . . . I quite enjoyed it. Playing and having to do the chores in between. I enjoyed it.

Feeling that she 'did her bit' for the children when they were pre-schoolers, Shirley believed it was easier for her to adjust when they started school, and she did not want to return to the babyhood period:

> I don't think I could go back to babyhood after so big a gap, I prefer to get them both together and — not to get it out of the way, it sounds as if I haven't enjoyed it, and I have, but I don't know if I would want to go back to it now.

Changing times

Shortly before the research, Shirley had changed her work to 20 hours weekly during the daytime. While she had easy childcare available from both grandmothers, she felt conflicting priorities:

> I still want to have time with the children. I suppose really I want the best of both worlds, which is hard to get. I suppose I get the guilty feelings, it's not really guilty feelings, I just like to be with them when they are at home . . .
> I do enjoy the work, you see. It's difficult, isn't it, you get torn between the two . . .

Shirley was uncertain about Stephen's attitude to her work:

> . . . he feels that I should be at home with the children during the school holidays which I find hard to understand, because he wants me to go to work because we need the money, but he still expects me to be at home with the children . . . .

With the chores to be fitted in as well, there was little time left for Shirley herself without the children also around:

> I don't really have any time without them here . . . as soon as they are home I'm here as well and then it's — get the dinner ready, walk the dog . . .

'Being there'

Shirley believed it best not to leave a baby to cry:

> I don't like to hear babies cry. . . . I found that if you do that you end up having to spend twice as long because they're really then in a state and you can't calm them down . . . If they cry it's generally for a reason . . .

When Mary Rose went through a particularly troublesome time at night when she was older, Shirley either took her into her bed, or she spent time in the bedroom with her:

> I can remember having a sleeping bag or a mattress on the floor just so that if she woke up in the night I could go in, just so that she'd got someone there.

Shirley particularly emphasised the importance of physical contact, and in her description of 'cuddle times' she symbolised her availability to the children in 'having time' for quiet activities.

> *Jane*: How would you say you express any affection for the children?
> *Shirley*: . . . mainly cuddles I think, we'll have cuddle time.

When the children were younger she felt it was important to compensate for her absence at work in the evenings:

> I always made a point, and still do, of having our cuddle time in the morning. We have the cuddle times at night *and* in the mornings now! . . . so I always felt that I have got time for them.

Besides such special times with children, there was also the suggestion that mothers should 'be there' for children if there is a problem. This was part of the dilemma about Shirley being at work during the holidays:

> . . . the silly thing is, I mean when I'm at home . . . I rarely see them anyway. But it's just the point that I'm here should anything happen.

'Being there' for children could involve more than just the mother's physical presence:

> *Shirley*: . . . love and understanding, being there when they've hurt their knee, and when they've hurt themselves is when they need you most . . .
> *Jane*: . . . you mentioned understanding?
> *Shirley*: Well, trying to reason things out with them. If they've got a problem, sit and talk it out with them, trying to understand how *they* feel and what *they're* thinking.

However, bickering between the children could sometimes destroy the 'cuddle times' when Shirley would like to know that they are all 'happy together':

> Sometimes they start fighting and arguing and that upsets me, when it's supposed to be our quiet cuddle time, and they're playing snakes and ladders, and they're arguing about who's going to have the blue . . . . Sometimes I get really irate, get really upset, and tell them that

that's not how I planned it at all. I wanted two children so that they could grow up and be happy together . . . if it doesn't work, I walk out.

'You are only young once': unrestricted childhood

While Shirley was cross when the children did not respond to what she saw as her own legitimate requests, she was perhaps unsure whether to be cross or amused by Paul's 'funny little tantrums':

> . . . he's a little horror when he's at home, he's quite temperamental sometimes, funny little thing really . . . the trouble is he can run faster than me now, I can't catch him!

In several ways, Shirley felt childhood should not be restricted, and she expressed images of children running freely. This was most apparent in a discussion in relation to Stephen:

> We have conflicting ideas . . . sometimes, like when we are out walking he'll say, 'Don't run, you might fall over,' and I think, well, why can't kids run? I'm all for letting them enjoy their childhood while they're young . . . it goes so quickly. But he'll stop them . . . I don't want them to look back on their childhood and think they've been restricted.

One childhood freedom that Shirley emphasised was making a mess – 'I think it's all an important part of learning and growing up. . . . That's children, to me.'

> I don't care what mess they get into. If they want to make mud pies, they can have as many pots as they like out there to make mud pies, their clothes will wash easily. Their latest thing is to make potions . . . Mary Rose and the little girl next door made each of us, their mothers, some perfume for Easter . . . and gosh, it nearly knocked me out. I don't know what ever they put in it. And I had to wear it to work yesterday! . . . So we've got trays of this and that, they're making gardens there, potions in the kitchen, we've got mud pies outside the back door, but I don't really mind.

Other areas for freedom from restriction included watching television and choosing clothes, as discussed in response to a vignette[2] about a child's choice of clothes:

> I'm a bit of a softy. I think I would let her have them because you are only young once . . . I mean Mary Rose loves new shoes and high heels, and she had a pair of very tiny heels which I didn't really think were quite practical, but I let her have them, and she loved walking up and down in them, she was the bees-knees in these shoes.

Similarly, Shirley distinguished between mothers who do and do not keep the 'sweet bowl down' within reach of the children.

'A united front'

Shirley described herself repeatedly as 'soft' with the children in comparison with Stephen. In response to a direct question about how she makes a good and bad job of being a mother, she said that perhaps she was not strict enough:

> I don't know whether it's because they don't see him as much, or maybe I'm just softer and they know they can get away with it. Or whether it's because I'm doing other things at the time, and perhaps I don't follow it through and don't notice that they're not doing it. I don't know, but they definitely do [take more notice of him].

Shirley's preferred method of control was through reasoning, though she also smacked them:

> I try and tell them. I don't hit them to start with, I try and tell them straight that I don't agree, and then if they still continue then I threaten a smack, and then if they don't, I do do it. I do hit them, and I don't think it does them any harm once in a while. Or else to send them up to their bedrooms and give them time to calm down, and then perhaps we can talk about it . . .

In reading through this section later, Shirley commented that it sounded as though she 'wallops' her children, but 'the occasional smack does get a response'.

In terms of everyday issues, Shirley would often make her own decisions because Stephen was not around – 'I mean, mothers are with the children, even in our circumstances, I'm with the children more than my husband is.' However, when they were both present, differences of approach could be quite a difficulty and source of discussion:

> . . . he feels that, whatever he says, I'll over-rule it if I don't like it . . . Some of it's true, I do feel sorry for them and then I let them go and – which is not right. If he's made like one rule, I shouldn't over-rule it, I know I shouldn't, but then some of the things I think are so trivial, is life really worth it for all the hassle you get afterwards? But I do agree that I shouldn't do it, but it doesn't always stop me, I'm afraid.

While stressing the importance of children being respectful towards parental authority, Shirley did not want them to be afraid of either parent:

> . . . when [Paul's] wet the bed before, he's dreaded telling Daddy that he'd wet the bed, and I don't like it to be like that. I think that's awful, if you can't – if you've got a fear of your parents – frightened of what they are going to say, I mean, not to smack them. I don't like the idea of them being frightened of us . . .

Beyond the boundary of home and household

Inside the home, Shirley was concerned to meet her children's
needs, as she understood them, with as little restriction as possible,
especially when they were younger. While she expected more from
them as they became older, and reproved any cheekiness, she was
also prepared to 'back down', and respond to their requests if they
seemed reasonable. Moving outside the home and family, however,
she showed more concern with her children's acceptability to other
people, and she was proud to have reports from others that her
children behaved well when out without her.

In this context, manners were particularly emphasised:

> Well, I think good manners don't really cost very much, just to say,
> 'Yes please, no thank you', and just to be polite. It seems to make
> everybody feel so much happier when you've got polite children. It'll
> make them a better person when they grow up, I don't know, perhaps
> to make them more tolerant, that's important to me . . . I think they
> will be more well-liked if they are polite, it's important to me that
> they are liked and have friends, get on with people.

A vignette concerning a child who would not eat a meal grandparents had prepared seemed to make Shirley feel quite uncomfortable – 'How embarrassing! . . . They've never been rude and said
it's absolutely horrid. I'd die, I think.'

Apart from informal play with other children, where Mary Rose
was quite confident, Shirley described her children as reluctant to
join activities outside the home – 'both are very shy'.

> Paul's now got the hurdle of – he's been invited out to tea with one of
> the friends from school, and he's saying he doesn't want to go . . .

This shyness was felt to be undesirable, with perhaps some self-
blame:

> I was quite a shy person when I was younger, and so whether it's sort of
> come from that I don't know. I mean, you try not to put your own fears
> and things into your children, but I don't know.
>   . . . looking back, I wish perhaps my mother had pushed me into
> doing things, because then I wouldn't have been so shy, and it seems
> like a real hurdle at the time. I don't want to bring my children up
> feeling the same, but there again, I don't want to upset them. Tricky!

Both health and education are matters where Shirley respected
the advice of professionals, and she seemed to give education some
centrality.[3] Yet, while she was pleased to undertake educational
activities at home with her children (often as part of 'cuddle times'),
there were also clear limits to the goal of using education to
progress in life.

I'm not saying that most people don't want qualifications these days, but if it's going to upset the children in the process, then I don't think it's worth it.

Mary Rose had been difficult to leave and had been sick when she first started school:

It's very difficult when they have that . . . I always used to make her go to school, unless she was actually being sick . . . she used to hang on to a coat peg and hang on to my skirt and it was heart-breaking. Terrible being dragged away. I mean they've just got to stay, haven't they, and there's nothing you can do?

This assumption of the authority and compulsion of the formal educational system underlay Shirley's continuing contact with the school, where she was inclined to 'tread a gentle line'. Her apparent preference in her relationship with the school was to be helpful to the school, to help the children at home, and to see the teachers over matters worrying her without making undue demands on their time. At the same time, she would not expect to lay down the law, and wanted her children to be smart and well thought of, within an institution that she regarded as concerned with central aspects of her children's characteristics.

Looking back and looking ahead

In general, Shirley felt she did not normally look ahead in her family life – 'I'm more the sort of person to live now, and take whatever comes.' However, social acceptability was a theme from the present that she also projected into the future, in relation to their teenage years:

I would hope that they would be polite and well-liked . . . Just to be generally likeable, and active, and God willing, just to be presentable and not too punky . . .

The crucial issue for Shirley's own anticipated happiness was how far Stephen has time for her, apart from his consuming interest in cricket. While she might feel freer to pursue her work when the children are older, Shirley had mixed feelings about the time when they leave home. However, pictures of the future are perhaps difficult to conceive, unlike pictures of the past. When I reviewed with Shirley how she had felt about the research, one of the reasons she felt she had enjoyed it was precisely that it had made her think about the past, reminiscing and bringing things back to mind that she had not thought about for a long time.

Update on Shirley

When Mary Rose had come to change schools, her abdominal migraines had started up again for a while, but in other ways Shirley felt the children had become more confident about going out to places, especially Paul. Stephen's cricketing interests were still an issue, although she felt he had become rather more aware of childcare issues during the school holidays.

Shirley herself was about to be made redundant but did not anticipate difficulties obtaining another job. Her attitudes towards work had changed: she was no longer experiencing guilt and was feeling the children were adaptable enough to be happy at a childminder's. She still did not want full-time work, however, because she wanted the children to be able to invite friends home for tea after school.

By 1994 Shirley had changed jobs, still working less than full-time and going into school to help with cookery once a week. Paul was leaving primary school at the end of the year, and she would then consider full-time employment. Little else had obviously changed in her life, while both children had sat exams for selective secondary schools and not been selected. 'I felt like it was me that had failed.' Shirley had appealed on Paul's behalf against the school allocated (which was not the one Mary Rose was attending), and she regretted not having appealed against her daughter's rejection from the selective secondary school she had wanted.

Comparisons

There are some quite striking parallels between the childrearing accounts of these two women. Shirley and Emily had both enjoyed their experiences as mothers, and both described themselves as 'soft'. They were also alike in using this self-description in the context of comparisons between their own and their husbands' childrearing ideas, although Shirley expressed greater concern about having different ideas from her husband. They both laid considerable emphasis on children's special neediness, stressing the importance of freedom from restrictions, and messy activities. There were also, however, differences of emphasis between them, since Shirley believed that children should be respectful to parents and was prepared to enforce this with a smack.

There are also some significant differences between these accounts. Emily was totally committed to mothering as her central occupation, while Shirley was seeking to balance out her maternal role against her own paid employment, which she valued both financially and personally. While Shirley wanted her children to have greater social confidence than herself, she did not doubt that social acceptability and good behaviour should be enforced with children. In this sense, she defined the home as a different sort of social setting from other contexts, drawing a clear division between public and private, such that children can experience a freedom in the family that they cannot expect to find elsewhere. Emily shared Shirley's concern with other people's opinions, but did not expect to teach her children to be deferential to others outside the home, and sometimes sought to convert others to the ideas of childrearing which she had developed inside the home. There were, however, occasions when she was happy to draw firm boundaries, and, like Shirley, to regard the home as a special and different social setting from others, because here at least she could feel confident about providing her children with room for the freedom she believed they are entitled to as children.

Notes

1. Fuller details of Emily's educational ideas can be found in Ribbens 1993b.

2. The final interviews with the case-study mothers included the use of vignettes as a form of stimulus material that would allow comparisons between interviewees. Verbal pictures were drawn using little story lines involving children, and asking mothers how they would proceed next. These pictures were drawn from my own experiences with children and were deliberately set up to explore dealings with children in a variety of different social settings. These vignettes were also used in the interviews with fathers and grandmothers. For a slightly different usage of vignettes, oriented more towards the elicitation of public ideologies, see Finch (1987). For further details, see Ribbens (1990a).

3. Fuller details of Shirley's educational views can be found in Ribbens 1993b.

Overview of the Portraits

All four women discussed so far presented subtle and varied discussions of their childrearing, such that there is a danger of underestimating the complexity of each woman's perspective. However, for the present analysis, they have been categorised according to some of the broad themes in their accounts. In this concluding section I will refer also to a further two women – Pauline and Christine – whose accounts seemed altogether more ambivalent and to contain more mixed imagery.

Furthermore, I have discussed the four women so far in pairs, enabling me to show certain points of comparison. However, these women could have been paired in different combinations to demonstrate rather different contrasts. In concluding the portraits of the case-study women, then, I shall draw out some rather different issues and points of comparison.

'Fitting in' and 'adapting' – adults and children living together

These childrearing accounts varied considerably in how far they suggested children should learn to 'fit in' with adults, or adults should learn to 'adapt' to children in their shared domestic lives (and this is the basis for the paired comparisons used in chapters 5 and 6). While explicit references to such differences might be only brief, or might be embedded in the use of particular sorts of imagery, such differences of approach carried implications across a wide range of different substantive issues.

Thus Penny (chapter 5) was clear that children should learn to live with the rules that adults define, and should be obedient. However, discipline was also an obligation for the parent, particularly the mother, since discipline was for the good of the child as much as for the convenience of adults. While Shirley (chapter 6) also valued respect for adults, she was concerned to restrict her children as little as possible and she hated to leave a child to cry. For her, the nature of childhood and of growth meant children should run freely.

Nevertheless, Penny and Shirley both appeared to hold views that could predominantly be seen to express one sort of imagery or another fairly consistently. Christine and Pauline, however, at times took the view that children should fit in with adult ideas, but at other times seemed uneasy about this approach and preferred a different attitude.

On the whole Pauline believed that she should enforce certain things on her children, but she also showed ambivalence about this. In response to the vignette about the child who won't clear away her toys, she said:

> . . . I think that is downright defiance . . . I don't really feel that you can give in . . . [the child] wouldn't win. *But perhaps in a happy household she would* (emphasis added).

Pauline had a particularly vivid memory of a disagreement with her husband over how to handle night-time waking when her first daughter was a baby.

> I remember one night when [Susie] was very tiny, she was crying and crying, and wouldn't go back to sleep, and in my own feelings I would just sit and hold her. And Mike just got up out of bed, got the carrycot, dumped it in the living room, and said, she can cry all she wants in there because she can get on with it, and she went to sleep . . . I felt awful about it . . .

Christine stressed 'the family' as a unit, but she also stressed the importance of individuality, whether her own or the children's:

> The children need their space as much as you do, but that's much harder as parents to learn, I think. I think you've got to learn and appreciate the child as being a whole individual before you can then give them perhaps the space they need.

Within the home Christine described decision-making as occurring co-operatively. However, a central dilemma appeared to lie at the heart of Christine's emphasis on the individual spirit:

> The one phrase that I think should be given to every mum who has a child is — it is your job to shape the will without breaking the spirit, because so many of us damage a child's spirit, almost deliberately, because they feel that is the only way to make them conform or shape them up. But the most important thing is to make the children want to do, or want to be whatever. Children have to be socially acceptable to move forward in society, as they grow up. We all don't lose our individuality, but we all have to conform to an extent, and this degree of conformity which my son finds just so hard, is something that has to be achieved by shaping the will. Very spirited children especially are often children that would derive a lot of self-satisfaction out of life, that will be very satisfied as people, and so it's very important that you don't detract from any of that . . .

While individual spirits also had to fit into family activities, it was in public places that control issues came to the fore. While Christine was clear in some ways that children must learn to conform, there was also some deeply felt ambivalence about fitting in – for herself as well as her children – 'As you have probably gathered, we are totally unusual weird people.'

These further two case studies, then, both provided rather shifting ideas and some ambivalences about how adults and children should relate to each other. Both women were prepared to smack children and enforce obedience, but they also both suggested at other times that children should have freedom to experiment and express individuality. While Pauline gave priority to the care of the house, such that respect for the home was a major source of conflict with the children, in other issues she did not seek to impose her own ideas particularly and preferred not to let her children cry. In some discussions, she showed quite conflicting views about how far to seek to control her children. Christine's ambivalence, on the other hand, was expressed most strongly in relation to settings outside the home, in her general uncertainty about how far she wanted her children to 'conform' in a society about which she had mixed feelings.

Happy and difficult times

Pauline and Christine were alike in discounting the rosy images of motherhood which they felt are portrayed in the media. Yet their feelings about motherhood contrasted sharply. Christine had hesitated to become pregnant, but later was shocked to discover her pleasure in her children.

> I didn't expect that I would enjoy having children that much. I thought it would be nice, but I didn't expect that it would be such a wonderful pleasurable experience that it's been. It's been a total shock and a wonderful revelation, and I've really enjoyed being at home with the children.
>
> . . . if you didn't have them you would lose everything.

This was not to say that motherhood had been an easy experience – far from it. Early motherhood was especially difficult, since Christine had a difficult labour, and immediately afterwards Richard had a back operation that left him paralysed and hospitalised for four months – 'It was hard in a way I can't even begin to put into words.'

Pauline became a mother more quickly than she later thought wise, and she also suffered quite severe post-natal depression, for

Figure 6.3   *Pauline's spatial map of people important to her*

which she sought help from a psychologist. Yet her family life, to outward appearances, might be thought to be a success story. She and her husband had both been upwardly mobile, coming from working class London families. They had just moved to a brand-new detached house, comfortably furnished and well decorated. She had two pretty daughters, and her own employment was minimal. However, for Pauline, the reality of family life and motherhood had not lived up to her expectations – 'There's something in me can't come to terms with how things are.' She found drawing her spatial map for the research (Figure 6.3) an uncomfortable experience, because it seemed to express her sense of isolation.

For Pauline, early motherhood had been fraught with depression and a sense of failure, and these feelings were an integral part of her childrearing account. Her mother, to whom she felt very close, died suddenly a year before Susie was born. Pauline had high expectations of motherhood, and especially wanted a daughter because she looked for 'a role reversal' – having lost her own mother, she would now gain a daughter.

> I was expecting to come out [of hospital] and have this happy time, and in fact I felt a failure.
>   . . . the overall thing was that I felt that things weren't right, that I wasn't doing the sort of things a mother should be doing.

The sense of failure recurred with a difficult second pregnancy that stopped her from doing her normal activities. While both children slept quite well at night, they were more demanding than she had expected and did not accord with her images of babies – 'Neither of them have been the sort of, put-baby-into pram, push-pram-into-garden, and leave them for two hours.' 'Very inquisitive, not a you-sit-there-and-stay-there-while-I-get-on-with-things sort of child. She was always there.'

While Pauline did not rate herself very highly as a mother there was also a sense of being let down by idealised images. Other research has also found that first-time mothers who experience post-natal depression tend to have more idealised images of what a mother should be like, and to feel incapable of living up to these images (Breen 1989, Mauthner 1994):

> I suppose it all becomes very sort of cute. Nice little baby clothes and nice little prams, but when you get down to the nitty-gritty and you are having to get up and wake up every few hours, you're tired, you're not looking radiant with your baby and visiting all your relatives.

However, Pauline also expressed a recurrent notion of being responsible for her strong sense of failure – 'I don't know why, most other people just seem to have children and to just get on and cope.' She described herself as failing through a lack of patience, and this was associated with not spending time with the children:

> I can't see that there is anything I'm particularly outstanding in as a mother . . . I don't really spend a lot of time with them, which again is probably because I'm not very patient . . .

Yet Pauline defined her greatest strength as a mother as her willingness to spend time taking them around where they want to go. The schedule of their activities was a considerable complication – including four dancing classes as well as Brownies each week. In the end, she consoled herself with the thought, 'they've obviously reached this age without anything major happening to them.'

Like Pauline, Sandra (chapter 6) found early motherhood very difficult, for different reasons. Both women on occasions felt close to harming their children, and blamed themselves for lack of patience. Both were rather more hesitant about being included in the research, and I was unable to complete all the interviews I sought with their significant others. However, Pauline expressed greater continuing dissatisfaction with her life now, and, unlike Sandra, she expressed no clear optimism for the future, say in ten years' time. She might look for more part-time work, but without much enthusiasm:

> *Pauline*: I would be just like thousands of other mothers with children at secondary school . . . I can't see now that I'm liable to suddenly

change and become anything else, you know, to suddenly start my
own successful business . . . I feel very much that I've done what I
suppose I was put here for, I've got married, I've had two children
and that's it, I'm now in the decline. It isn't a good way of putting it,
but I don't think I'm going to have much excitement to come, I think
it's all past.

Jane: I've had one mother say that she thinks your life is over when
your children leave home, would you think in those terms, or – ?

Pauline: In some ways I think your life is over as soon as you've had
them, you become somebody else, you become a mother and that is
your role. It is frightening once they grow up and they leave home,
you're not really going to have anything . . . The way people last in
my family, I probably won't be around much after that anyway.

On the other hand, while Penny and Shirley differed considerably
in their childrearing approaches (chapters 5 and 6), they were alike
in deriving satisfaction from motherhood. While there were some
tensions for both women in their lives as mothers, through their
differing approaches each woman had felt able to express and enjoy
her mothering and each woman's childrearing perspective was
plausible and coherent in its own terms.

Among these case-study women, then, there was much variability, both in some of the basic childrearing attitudes, and in their
satisfaction with their own roles as mothers. These two dimensions,
of attitude to childrearing issues, and satisfaction with their own
roles, appeared to be quite separate in this small group of women.
This conclusion has some parallels in the findings of Oakley's
(1980) study of childbirth. This research, involving larger numbers
allowing the measurement of correlations, found that women's
satisfaction with new motherhood constituted a quite separate
dimension from their feelings for their new-born babies.

Maternal employment

While Pauline and Sandra both found early motherhood very
difficult, they had responded to these difficulties in different ways.
Sandra had moved away from the role of full-time housewife and
mother when her children were very small (although she had given
up any paid work again by 1994), not only by taking a full-time job
but also by sharing her childcare with her own mother for
substantial periods. In this her husband was supportive, and she no
longer expressed such doubts about her mothering. At the same
time, she did not present her family style as any different from any
other, except in terms of the demands of running the shop. Pauline,
on the other hand, had kept more closely to a commitment to
motherhood as her sole occupation, and was still not in paid

employment at the time of our last contact (1994). She was concerned about childcare responsibilities during the school holidays or if the children were ill:

> I do get a little fed up . . . I'm here all day on my own . . . I would like to find something useful but I wouldn't like to compromise my situation here.

While both Penny and Shirley had enjoyed motherhood, and neither expressed regret at having given up work to care for children, they both had ambitions they still hoped to fulfil in their work lives, although they worried about how to do this while also caring for their families. Emily (chapter 6) and Christine, however, expressed less interest in paid employment in the present or near future. These women shared an approach to childrearing which involved much conscious reflection and ideological soul-searching. While there were thus some strong parallels between their interviews – including their shared tendency to discuss issues in great detail and with considerable enjoyment – there were also some striking contrasts in their childrearing views. Again, both of these women had derived much satisfaction from motherhood.

Sharing parental authority?

All the women described themselves as taking primary responsibility and authority with their children. They also all discussed ways in which they mediated between their husbands and their children. However, they varied in the extent of any differences of view with their husbands, and also in how they dealt with such differences. While four of the women all appeared assertive about their own childrearing ideas and maternal authority inside the home, Pauline and Shirley both expressed some anxiety about their husbands' attitudes to childrearing issues. Shirley had decided at times to follow her own ideas rather than those of her husband. She herself did not like to leave babies to cry, and there were hints that Pauline might well have felt the same, but for her husband's tendency to cut across this. Pauline's principal concern was to mediate the tensions between herself, her husband and her children.

The house could be a serious source of conflict between Pauline and her husband. When first married, Pauline and Mike made considerable efforts to buy their own home and do it up and furnish it well. While Pauline believed that children should not use the new three-piece suite 'as a trampoline', she was concerned that Mike wanted to apply stricter rules – 'It's their home, and you can't have them scared about sitting on a chair or spilling something.' She had also been concerned about her husband's views about the telephone when Susie was younger.

> . . . we had this big thing about the telephone . . . Mike used to say, watch she doesn't play with the phone, so I used to spend all day making sure she doesn't do it, because I don't think they can live by one rule through the day . . .

As Pauline talked to me about her life with the children, I thus felt a strong sense of her husband's presence as an important part of the context of her childrearing, even when he was physically absent.

> I suppose we are all different . . . there's things that are acceptable, I think, for children to do, that my husband doesn't think are acceptable.
> . . . we pull against each other most of the time, and often it's the children that are the issue.

Social acceptability and maternal assertion

While Penny and Shirley took different approaches to childrearing, they had both received reports from others about the good behaviour of their children when outside the home. All the women discussed their children's social acceptability to others, but they varied in how far they deferred to the ideas of others when dealing with their children in contexts outside the home.

It would appear, then, that Penny took a good deal of authority within the home as well as outside it, and looked to her children to follow her expectations fully. Shirley, however, described herself as 'a softy' inside her home, while deferring to the opinions of others outside. Sandra sought to take control of her children both inside and outside the home, although her children's social acceptability generally was also important, while Pauline was less sure of her authority either within the home or outside it.

However, all four of these women were quite clear that there were limits to their authority with their children once the children left home to enter the school system. Christine and Emily, on the other hand (both part of the theoretical sample – see Appendix), had resisted this loss of authority, and had sought to assert their views of their children's educational needs beyond the confines of the home (even though public spaces raised difficulties with Christine's children that did not occur at home). Christine had done so by the use of additional resources – whether money or professional expertise – to obtain the sort of educational environment she saw as appropriate for each child (discussed further in Ribbens

1993b). Like Christine, Emily had strong beliefs about how to bring up her children, and had sought to maintain control over what happened to them outside as well as inside the family. But for Emily this had been achieved by withdrawing from the educational system, which had enabled her to control their childhood experiences and avoid compromising her own childrearing. While at times she used the privacy of the family to maintain her authority over such issues, at other times she was assertive towards wider social contexts, hoping that society more generally might recognise and respond to the needs of children as individuals.

Throughout all these different strands, there were both common assumptions and themes, and variability in the meanings used to make sense of childrearing. Some of the common assumptions concerned the nature of individuality and of family life and responsibilities (see chapter 3), and the awareness of, and sensitivity to, children's wider social relationships (see chapter 4). These cultural themes are embedded in the accounts, but are manifested in certain symbolic activities. The variability in childrearing meanings, on the other hand, were often expressed in very concrete form, in the daily issues of living with young children. In Part III I will develop these issues further, to see how they are played out in the accounts of all the women interviewed.

Part III

Developing the Pictures

7

Conceptions of Children

Introduction

In considering the everyday detailed issues of childrearing, I discussed earlier (chapter 2) how I came to reorientate my analysis around the contrasting images and understandings of children and childhood which underlay some of the different meanings in the women's accounts. I turn now to a more direct discussion of these images, discussing them as *'typifications'* (Schutz 1954) *of children* which are widely available in our culture, which women may draw upon in various ways to make sense of specific childrearing issues. I shall then consider at a fairly abstract level what each typification implies in the way of appropriate parental responses. While there is not space to explore these meanings in relation to the range of nitty-gritty issues of daily life, I shall go on in chapter 9 to consider how they may lead to different ideas in relation to some of the *central preoccupations* which unite many of the concrete issues discussed in the women's accounts. These preoccupations could perhaps be seen as middle range themes, in the sense that they move beyond daily issues such as sleep, food, and cleanliness, and yet they are less abstract than the underlying cultural assumptions discussed in chapter 3. In this chapter, I am moving some distance from the details of the women's lives as discussed in the earlier case studies (see Part II), but will nevertheless seek to move between abstract typifications and more grounded issues.

Typifying children

Since industrialisation, childhood in Western cultures has become increasingly defined as a special phase of life (Hendrick 1990). The cultural specificity of this understanding of childhood has not been widely recognised, although some writers have contested its inappropriate application to the lives of children living in non-industrialised societies (e.g. Scheper-Hughes 1987). The study of childhood as a social construction has become an important emergent paradigm within recent sociology (see chapter 1). Childhood is defined in Western societies as a time of dependency, and indeed Hockey and James (1993) suggest that childhood is the model by which we understand all forms of dependency in contemporary Western cultures. During the twentieth century this dependency of children has been extended, both in terms of the *number of years* over which children are considered dependent, and in terms of the *range of needs* that they are considered to have (see chapter 1). 'Caring' for children implies the recognition of their special dependency needs. The meeting of these needs (however defined) is construed as showing a caring response, signalling that the child's needs have been recognised and the adult has responded to them. I suggest that such dependency needs are central to the definition of being 'a child' and not 'an adult' – hence the possibility that fully-grown people may be described as behaving 'like children'.

The notion of child as a particular category, then, defines children as individuals who are not-adults, who have their needs recognised and met by others who are adults. Because they are not-adults they are not responsible for meeting the needs of others. George Kelly (1955) discusses how we may understand and identify a construct by defining how it is different from something else – a process of construing through the perception of difference. Thus Jenks (1982) suggests that adulthood is only recognisable through being contrasted with childhood. Children are regarded as 'strange', and Jenks suggests a parallel with the ways in which early anthropologists made distinctions between savages and civilised/ rational beings. 'Children are all foreigners. We treat them as such' (R.W. Emerson 1803–1882). In the present study, the view of children as different-from-adults was very widely taken for granted, and might only be referred to in passing in the childrearing accounts – 'children will be children' (Kay). In this sense children are construed as 'Other' than adult; from the adult perspective, children are defined as 'Not-me'.

Nevertheless, there may be great variability in the definitions used to specify the content or *nature of children's needs*, and such variability is closely associated with variations in the underlying images of what it means to be a child. One of the ways in which Schutz (1954) suggests that social life is possible is through the use of typifications, which are available in the socio-cultural world to be drawn upon to make sense of other individuals' behaviour:

> . . . only in particular situations, and then only fragmentarily, can I experience the Other's motives, goals etc. – briefly, the subjective meanings they bestow upon their actions, their uniqueness. I can, however, experience them in their typicality. In order to do so I construct typical patterns of the actors' motives and ends, even of their attitudes and personalities, of which their actual conduct is just an instance or example . . . Here, I submit, in the common-sense thinking of everyday life, is the origin of the so-called constructive or ideal types . . . (1979: 33).

In chapter 3 I argued that the family is a major site for the construction of individuality, and I considered how some women stressed the importance of paying close attention to the child's unique understanding and perspective. However, children may also be described at times as mysterious and beyond understanding – '"they sort of live in a funny little world"' (mother quoted in Newson and Newson 1978: 278). Sandra suggested that such aspects of children's behaviour are the ones she is most likely to want to discuss with her mother:

> It's the mysterious things you tend to tell, like Gemma took the scissors to her hair the other week and ended up with a fringe a quarter of an inch long which stood like a little tap, and she lopped four inches off the sides! . . . Gemma is just Gemma, she just does these things.

Backett (1982) suggests that her middle class parents regarded a primary parenting task as being to 'understand' children's uniqueness. However, while – to paraphrase Schutz (1979) – parents may at times seek fragmentarily to experience the child's uniqueness, they also draw upon wider typifications of what it means to be 'a child', such typifications being the basis on which family life can be constructed.

I suggest that *three broad typifications* can be discerned in the childrearing accounts given in my own study. The identification of these typifications developed through a process of close analysis of the details of the accounts, and can, I believe, be regarded as 'grounded theory' (Glaser and Strauss 1968). I have certainly experienced their identification as surprising 'discoveries', but the typifications I am outlining are presented as working hypotheses. They may well need modification in other contexts, or may contain ramifications that I have missed, but I suggest that these typifications do draw upon quite deeply rooted and pervasive notions of children and parenting. Once I had developed their initial analysis,

I also became aware of possible links with wider images and with religious and philosophical issues discussed by writers and thinkers over many years. Some of these further ramifications and wider cultural links will be discussed in chapter 9, but here I shall concentrate on their elucidation in the women's own accounts.

I have labelled the typifications identified as:

1   children as natural innocents,
2   children as little devils, and
3   children as small people.

The last typification, in contrast with both of the others, minimises the view of children as not-adults. Thus the first two typifications are alike in sharing a perception of *children as different-from-adults*, although this difference is construed in quite opposite ways.

Children as natural innocents
This typification defines children as different from adults in that they have a natural innocence, which adults have lost. Thus not only are children typified as innocent, but this is something that is 'given', in the sense that it is something that children are born with and that they will retain if allowed to develop without distortion from society:

> Children are different, they're lovable little beings . . . you just think they're the most wonderful thing that's come on earth. (Amy)

This view of children can extend to a construction of childhood as a very special – almost magical – phase of life (Peter Pan):

> It is important to respect and protect the child's childhood, it will never come back again, when it's gone it's gone and they can never catch up. (Ellen)

> I think children have the reality – we strive all our lives to recapture what we have as a child, I think. (Christine)

Such childhood innocence may be lost as children become more aware of social life and more 'knowing':

> . . . she's getting a bit more knowing now, and she may know she's been naughty and she'll give you a sort of defiant look. (Sally)

> . . . one little girl in particular is just so adult . . . this little girl turned round and looked at me with such a knowing look . . . I felt absolutely squashed into the floor. (Christine)

The magical specialness of childhood is perceived in various ways, notably the idea of childhood as a special carefree time for play, fun, 'mess' and creativity. Although some educational theories regard play as part of the serious business of learning adult skills, this was not very apparent as a perspective in these parents' accounts. Indeed it is the view of play-as-fun, and therefore not-work, that underlies criticisms that children 'play too much' in the early years of school life. Ellen's account was unusually explicit in its positive valuing of play – 'precious playtime'. She viewed play as a vital part of childhood, describing her children's messy play with pleasure – 'I really strongly believe that very young children should play, they shouldn't try and read and write so early'.

Some accounts clearly made consistent use of this typification, notably those of Emily and Shirley (see chapter 6), and also Amy and Ellen. However, other accounts also made use of such imagery even if only fleetingly. Kay and Angela both used this typification in the context of something which had been lost through the disruption of 'family life' resulting from divorce. Angela thus discussed the possibility that the 'break-up of the family' had reduced the time available for her son to enjoy 'being a child', a view of childhood which his father promoted.

> I say, 'He shouldn't be doing that, he ought to be reading', and [his father] will say, 'Let him be a child, don't expect too much of him at this age', and maybe I am a little bit over the top. He says, 'Don't be so serious with him all the time' . . . It's always a lot of fun and laughter when they are at Dad's and they make a special point of going to the park . . . They are having fun all the time, whereas there isn't always the time for us to have fun all of the time . . .

Kay also suggested that her son's childhood might have been left unprotected because his father was not part of the household, so that the child showed signs of becoming an adult before time. Kay defined childhood at times as innocent and also silly, while adults are rational and sensible. Descriptions of children's activities as 'silly' carry some ambiguity. If children are silly they are not part of the adult world of rationality and responsibility, yet this silliness is not necessarily seen in quite such a destructive light as the potential for anarchy, and parents may allow themselves to join in children's silly games – 'We play quite a lot of silly games . . . I suppose that's quite fun' (Margaret).

However, it is also important to note, within this typification, that images of innocence do not just view the child as 'all sweetness and light' but may *encompass a variety of emotions* in the child, including 'anger':

> I sometimes find with [my daughter] that I'm about to correct some aggression, and then I think, no, you're going to need that. (Amy)

Such emotions are regarded as needing expression as well, but such expression is regarded as expelling the anger which will then be 'spent', without unleashing unlimited forces as the next typification suggests. There is thus a sense of *natural self-regulation* underlying this typification.

Children as little devils

This typification also sees childhood as a particular phase in life, because children are viewed as very different from adults. However the nature of this difference is regarded as potentially destructive – '"She's on the fiendish side"' (mother quoted in Newson and Newson 1965: 184). The imagery used here refers to the possibilities of children disrupting social life with their asocial tendencies, with hints of the possible setting free of latent uncontrollable forces unless the child is shaped to fit into social order. However, there may also be some ambivalence in how this is evaluated: '"He's such a little devil that I think you can laugh about him and enjoy him completely all the time . . . Even when he's being a devil, 'cause he's got such a way about him you know"' (mother, quoted by Newson and Newson 1978: 283).

Children are thus seen as potentially anarchic – 'I'm not saying my children are angels . . . but her children do run riot' (Rosemary). If children are left unrestrained, anything might happen. Lindsay described children as potentially infinitely disruptive:

> [If] you just give in to them all the time . . . as soon as you start doing that they just push you, and push you, and push you, until they're doing the most awful outrageous things, and you're not able to control them at all . . .

Mary also suggested that an absence of restriction on children might unleash almost limitless and unknowable lawlessness:

> I think we're probably too strict, but it's the trend nowadays, isn't it, not to be too strict. Free-thinking, and let them do what they like. Let children rule. You wonder what's going to happen, don't you?

Janet's mother, on the other hand, quoted her own mother's saying by way of contrast – 'If you drive one devil out another will only come to take its place.'

In Stephen's account, this typification of children led to a careful consideration at times of children's real 'needs', since 'attention-seeking' children might 'play on' their needs to obtain unjustified concessions from their parents, leading to almost unlimited possibilities:

... once that starts I think that's the thin edge of the wedge −
probably there until they're about nineteen or twenty!

Accounts which repeatedly used this typification were those of
Sandra (chapter 5), Stephen, Lindsay and Mary. Again, however,
other accounts drew on such imagery at times. Kay referred several
times to her son's resistance to restriction, and in this context
described his behaviour as 'diabolical'. At another point in the
interview, she discussed her response to a complaint from his
teacher, with hints again that his undesirable behaviour could be
potentially limitless unless stopped by adults − 'I said to her, "if it's
not stopped now who knows where it will go" . . . The funny thing
was I was going through exactly the same at home.'

Children as small people

This typification did not appear in the accounts as frequently as
either of the two outlined above, and no-one drew exclusively on
this sort of imagery. What this typification does is to minimise the
notion of childhood as a special phase that occurs after babyhood
(babyhood as a phase is discussed in chapter 3). From babyhood
dependency, the child becomes an *individual*, a *person* like any other
− albeit rather smaller in size − '"she's an individual . . . she can
argue, she's got a mind of her own already"' (mother of 7-year-old,
quoted by Newson and Newson 1978: 280, original emphasis). Such
a perspective clearly links with the earlier discussion of mothers'
construction of individuality, with age status being minimised (see
chapter 3, particularly the discussion of Janet and Margaret). There
is consequently much less tendency to identify children and adults
as separate categories, and less notion of an implicit hierarchy
based on age. While dependency needs are minimised, independence
is valued.

In Margaret's account, individuality − being your 'own person' −
was something that could potentially be hindered and stopped and
it therefore required some nurturing from the more powerful adult.
In Janet's account, there was more of a sense of her son being his
own person here and now, having an individuality which he
expressed vigorously and which she did not have the power as an
adult to stop, even if she wanted to.

This typification also appeared occasionally in other accounts,
particularly in the belief that children should be respected. Children
might thus be defined as having rights as well as needs. Tom's
account used imagery of children as small people, although there
was also, as in Margaret's account, the suggestion that adults are in

fact more powerful and may thus choose whether or not to recognise the child's perspective.

> I wouldn't say they have equal voting rights to us, there's not quite a democracy, we do tend to have the casting vote if it comes to a tie, but we certainly do listen to them and you just don't see that with other people. The great majority, the children are under the thumb . . .

Children may thus also be construed as different-from-adults, not because their needs are different, but because they occupy a less powerful position.

Appropriate responses

In his discussion of concepts and theory formation in the social sciences, Schutz (1979) describes how it may be possible for sociologists to move beyond the description of typifications, to the construction of a model. He suggests that it is possible to proceed through a consideration of 'typical behaviour or course-of-action patterns', upon which can be built a model using 'homunculi':

> . . . [the social scientist] co-ordinates to these typical course-of-action patterns, models of an ideal actor or actors, whom he [sic] imagines as being gifted with consciousness. Yet it is consciousness restricted so as to contain nothing but the elements relevant to the performing of the course-of-action patterns observed. He thus ascribes to this fictitious consciousness a set of typical notions, purposes, goals, which are assumed to be invariant in the specious consciousness of the imaginary actor-model (1979: 35).

This description accords quite closely with how I actually proceeded in the analysis of the childrearing accounts. Thus, having outlined the typifications of children and childhood, it is possible to proceed further by considering what they imply for mothers' responses to such typifications. In this procedure, following Schutz, I am considering what these responses may be, if we assume the women's consciousness to be *free from any other considerations*.

Following on from the earlier typifications of children, the ensuing discussion shows that in these implied maternal[1] responses, while the first two types are very contrasting, they also share the view of fundamental difference between adulthood and childhood. The important features of how to deal with this difference centre on *three inter-linked questions*:

1   Who are the best people to know and understand children's needs – children themselves, or adults?
2   Should adults fit their own needs and lifestyles around children, or should children be taught to fit in with adult guidelines?

(Backett 1982 reports that the parents in her study saw this issue as a fundamental source of difference between parents.)

3 Is social life fundamentally beneficial to the individual by regulating anarchy, or does it serve to distort natural goodness?

In the third typification of maternal response to be discussed, the issues are not the same since children are not regarded as fundamentally different from adults anyway.

Children as natural innocents – 'let him be a child'

The typification of children as natural innocents implies that the appropriate response is to interfere with nature as little as possible, since the social environment is only likely to serve to distort. It may therefore also be necessary to ensure the child has freedom and security from the harsh realities of the wider world and the potential distortions of social life. The appropriate maternal response is to protect childhood, and for adults to adapt themselves to children's needs as they themselves express them – 'growing from within' (Ellen). Children are regarded as the ones who are best able to know their own needs, and family life should fit around them.

In some accounts, then, childhood was described as an idyllic period, which should be respected and should be interfered with as little as possible. In discussing her children's broken sleep patterns, Amy said, 'That was the one thing that got in the way of this wonderful idyllic childhood they were all going to have.' Furthermore, she also believed this disruption was not due to the broken sleep as such, but to her unnecessary worry about it. She blamed this worry on child clinic professionals who did not inform her that broken sleep was quite normal: 'They never said, that's just the child's sleep pattern, which is all it was necessary to say to save all those hours of terrible worry over it.'

Here the needs of children are construed as being defined and known from within them – the appropriate maternal response is to create an environment in which these needs can be freely expressed, and met as fully as possible.

Ellen's ideas on play have been developed in conjunction with notions of play discussed by the teachers at her children's Steiner school. In her account, not only was play considered to be very important, but it should occur without the imposition of adult ideas. There were therefore clear limits to the type of toys that should be provided. One of the key features of avoiding adult impositions was to avoid conformity and provide scope for creativity/individuality:

> Look at children playing with Fisher Price toys, they have their ready-made dolls' house and they put the furniture in the dolls' house and they put the dolls in bed and then the game is finished . . . Lego is much better, there they can make their own dolls' house and it takes them ages to put it together. Even better would be just bricks or sand, because they then have to imagine, they can't actually make an exact image of what they want, they've got to imagine with materials what this is going to be like.

Ellen was thus concerned to allow room for individuality and for the development of the inherent nature of the child, not 'putting the lid on' what may 'come from within':

> It's something that should come from within the child, not the adult putting it upon the child . . . There is something about putting your own ideas and expectations onto the child, it's like a lid onto a pot, isn't it? It's like cutting a plant, you prune it so that it grows the way that you want it to grow to suit your own needs, but not to make a nice strong natural plant, the growth has got to come from the roots of the plant, so a parent can water a plant and give it the right environment but the growing still comes from within.

There are clear parallels here with what is sometimes described as the 'horticultural' model of education, but Ellen did not regard her ideas as being derived from the Steiner school her children attended. Rather she described herself as having actively sought out a school that would reflect her own strongly held beliefs.[2] Indeed, Bernstein (1975) suggests that such approaches to education may have been introduced by mothers who had first developed such views of children and their needs in childrearing within the home.

Amy held the view that a secure and happy childhood is the basis for qualities needed later in life. She believed that her life and routines should be accommodated to the individual natures of her children. She did not consider that there are general rules or guidelines on how to bring up children, as everything depends on the individual child:

> That's what it's all about, you have to accept that child, that it doesn't sleep or whatever . . . I can remember with [my oldest child] sitting at the bottom of the stairs and crying because I had to go upstairs to get a nappy and I just didn't have the physical strength to go up those stairs to get the nappy. Of course with the next one I organised everything to be near at hand and took every opportunity to sleep. I still continued a normal life with the first one, going out visiting, shopping and being super-efficient . . . you learn that sleep comes first![3]

Recognition of the nature of the child should lead the mother to foster the development of the child by allowing his/her own characteristics to manifest themselves – 'You have to accept the kind of child you've got' (Amy).[4]

The view of childhood itself as a special time of natural innocence, with particular needs for freedom from social restrictions, thus implies certain types of maternal responses, for which I suggest the term '*adaptive*'. This response is thus concerned to allow room for individuality and creativity and for the development of the inherent nature of the child. The mother believes that her job is to provide the child with the right kind of environment to develop this potential, and that if this is done then the child will naturally develop into a desirable kind of person. The nature of children is perceived as inherently self-regulatory and self-limiting.

In addition, there may similarly be an acceptance of the woman's own 'instinctive' reactions and emotions as a mother, as a basis for maternal behaviour. However, as the mother is the mature adult, it is she who must learn to provide the right environment for the child, and must mould herself to fit around the child's needs. Children should not be imposed upon, or this inherent capacity to grow straight and strong will be distorted, and their creative individuality will be submerged under adult/social impositions. The job of the mother is to adapt herself/the family environment to meet children's expressed needs. Shirley (among others) described this approach as 'soft' (chapter 5).

Children as little devils – 'children need limits'

Where children are typified as potentially anarchic and destructive, the appropriate response is one of regulation and direction, not only for the sake of adults but also in order *to meet children's own needs*. *Adults* are seen to understand children's needs best, so that adults should direct children and take responsibility for defining and meeting their needs before children become overwhelmed by their own anarchic potential. Children should therefore learn to *fit in* with adult guidelines in family life. What might happen if children are left unrestrained was often left unstated, and only hinted at darkly:

I think children need to know the limits. Otherwise they'd just push until – I think *they* are happier if they know the boundaries. (Hilary)

For such adult direction to be achieved, there also has to be established a sense of respect for adult authority and definitions:

I think you see things in other people's families as well and you think, 'Oh, I wouldn't do it that way.' If I can give an instance, it's over this calling adults by their Christian names, to me it grates because to me

> it's disrespectful . . . I think there are certain phases in a child's
> development where they have to respect authority . . . . (Kay)

While other mothers might not show this particular concern, there were common beliefs about the importance of children being respectful to parents and other adults, with 'rudeness' and 'cheekiness' in particular being frequently cited as undesirable behaviour. This was a strong theme in many of the accounts although there was also quite a common tendency to believe that it was *other* parents who did not show sufficient concern in this regard. Parents who stressed respect for adults also often described themselves as 'old-fashioned'.

In this maternal response there is a high level of concern with maintaining control over children, in order to define appropriate rules of behaviour beyond which they may not stray and become 'diabolical':

> He knows how far he can go, what he can and cannot get away with, and that he doesn't go overboard because he knows if he goes over-board then he suffers the punishment. If he's really diabolical, like over thank you letters . . . he's really been rebelling . . . I just banned the television . . . . (Kay).

Similarly, there were recurrent themes in Veronica's account of children needing direction. She stressed that children should respect adults, and used an elaborate system of controls to achieve the direction of her children which she believed they needed.

In seeking to regulate children's anarchic impulses, Lindsay expressed a clear belief in the resulting benefits to the children themselves. In directing her children and controlling their anarchy, a mother can help them bring order into their own lives. Additionally, the mother may feel she must *control her own feelings* and emotions to produce good mothering. Thus Lindsay believed that at times she herself should not act on her own emotional feelings as a mother, but should consciously seek to develop other ways of behaving with her children:

> I find all the time that I have to make an effort . . . to encourage them to do things for themselves, because it is an instinctive thing to protect them and do things for them . . .

Mary similarly believed that she should bring her own emotions into order in order to do her job properly as a mother.

Notions of 'losing one's temper' and *'temper tantrums'* have particular significance from this point of view, implying loss of control and the letting go of undesirable forces. This may apply to both children and adults, and where they are not accepted in children they may also be unacceptable in adults. While Emily referred to her children's 'anger', her husband Tom was upset by what he described as their 'temper' – a shift of language which carries quite different connotations, of legitimate self-expression or loss of control.

Kate discussed ideas of maternal 'detachment' as suggested by the parenting group and book she has used (Dreikurs 1972) – 'The main thing is to say, right, be detached . . . and you must never lose your cool – so they say.' While she was very positive about some of the changes in her children's behaviour which she felt had resulted from this approach, she also had reservations about it, since an absence of 'temper' might also mean an absence of 'warmth' and 'enthusiasm':

> If you read it thoroughly I think they just take things a bit too far. You become so detached from your children if you're not careful, you lose that sort of warmth and spontaneity. And everybody loses their temper sometimes, and we all do stupid things and wish you hadn't afterwards.

The typification of children as anarchic and anti-social is thus intrinsically bound up with ideas about appropriate maternal responses, which I shall call '*directive*'.[5] Not only are children viewed as needing direction, or guidance, but so also are the mother's own impulses. Perhaps the implicit goal here is that of self-government, which is defined as necessary for good mothering and expected of mothers as adults. However, it should also be noted that this description of appropriate maternal responses does not incorporate definitions about the *content* of the appropriate regulations for children's behaviour, only that there should be *direction of some sort*. Penny suggested that while she and her husband might have some differences in their ideas about how to bring up their children, these differences centred on the content of the rules considered appropriate. Since she and David did however agree more fundamentally that children need direction, the content of the rules could be negotiated between them.

Children as small people – 'he's not doing any harm'
Within this typification, there is much less explicit ideology which lays down predetermined guidelines as to how mothers and children should interact. This is because mother and child are construed as different individuals of equal standing, without special reciprocal obligations centred on the dependency needs of childhood. Indeed, the very notion of 'child' is less relevant. There are thus less clear-cut implications for relationships within the family unit, since age

status is not construed as the basis for hierarchy, either of power or of dependency – 'We feel the family is standing in a circle, equal spaces between each other' (Ellen). There is thus less scope for a guiding framework of beliefs about how older individuals in the household should respond to younger ones. Instead, there may be a focus on responding to the individual natures (or 'person'-alities), of those involved, with scope for negotiations about how best to meet the needs/wishes of the different 'family' members. (Indeed, the notion of 'family' may also be less relevant when the notion of 'child' is minimal.) I have therefore labelled this response as *negotiative* since there are no overall rules about who should accommodate to whom within the household. The desired relationship may often be described as one of friendship between older and younger individuals. Where these negotiations break down, however, there may be recourse to power relationships.

I have discussed above how both of the previous typifications may imply responses from mothers that lay obligations on them, either to adapt themselves around children's expressed needs, or to govern their own impulses in order to regulate children in line with beliefs about their real needs. Negotiative parenting is to be distinguished from these as it carries *fewer implications of adult obligations* towards children. Children's expressed desires and demands are generally regarded as legitimate (but not necessarily given priority, as with the typification of children as natural innocents), but so also are the mother's own needs and preferences. However, neither is there a conception of a pre-existing social order that children must learn to fit into before they overthrow it to the detriment of all (as with the typification of children as little devils). Instead, the emphasis is on the needs and demands of household members *as individuals*. There is a requirement to treat the younger person's point of view with respect – 'You certainly shouldn't talk down [to children], you must respect children' (Ellen).

> Jane: How would you say you express affection for her?
> Margaret: . . . . I suppose respecting her really, respecting her opinions and her ideas . . . . I think affection and respect kind of go together.

If there are obligations towards each other within the household, these are seen as being parallel between all family members, rather than a reciprocity of obligations for adults to meet children's needs and for children to defer to adults in return:

> [My parents] always asked my advice about things even when I wasn't very old, and I would hope that I would be able to do that for [my daughter] because I think that's something that isn't terribly usual between children and parents. (Margaret)

Within this approach, there is *less conscious ideology* than in other approaches, few references to what a mother 'should' do, and less expression of 'guilt' by women. This is exemplified in Janet's account, which included discussion of her own feelings and those of her child. Janet took these feelings as an appropriate basis for decisions about childrearing. Several times, decisions were explained on the basis of what was needed to make Russell happy, and Janet described him several times as a 'happy child'.

> . . . some of the things Russell does my mum will say, 'You shouldn't let him do that', but I think, why not, he's not doing any harm.

Sally's account was also noticeable for its absence of explicit ideology and strong imagery of 'children', without explicit rationales except in terms of what 'worked' for her. For example, after being unable to get her first child to sleep well at night, she decided not to fight what she could not seem to alter, and carried this through with her second child when he cried in the evening:

> I just used to lay with him on the settee, and I just used to feed him, change him, wind him, all evening . . . I'd learned not to fight it by then. I just gave in. And I was much better like that.

This strategy was not explained in terms of an ideology but of what *made her feel better*. Sally's account overall was noticeable for the absence of any reference to feelings of guilt as a mother.

This raises a wider issue concerning the extent to which *the majority* of all mothers in Western societies tend to hold images not only of children, but also of mothers. I discussed earlier (see Overview of the portraits) the unattainable rosy images of motherhood that seem to be associated with postnatal depression. Indeed, Mauthner (1994) has suggested that women only start to move away from such depression when they are able to 'let go' of some of these images. My present analysis suggests that this may be part of a much wider pattern for most women to hold some imagery of how they are supposed to be, and – even more importantly – to feel, as mothers.[6] Hence the widespread tendency to expressions of guilt when women 'fail' to live up to these images. The women discussed here, who do not hold such strong imagery of mothering, may well be in a minority (although we do not have the evidence to know very clearly). This may also relate to the distinction made in the Introduction to this book, between a view of children that suggests they need 'bringing up', in contrast with a view of children as 'growing up'.

I have suggested that the typification of children as small people is used less in the accounts given in the present study than other typifications described above, and no account drew exclusively on this sort of imagery. Its use is undoubtedly limited by wider institutional frameworks in contemporary Western societies which construe people below certain chronological ages as different from people who are older – the educational system, exclusion from paid employment, or other legal contexts. In this sense, the childhood phase of life is heavily underpinned by a framework of legislation and social policy, which is almost impossible to avoid within family life. We can therefore perhaps only speculate (with some insights from historical and other comparative evidence) about the full implications for 'family life' that arise from the view of children as different-from-adults, rather than small people. If children were not seen as dependent, how would this affect contemporary Western understandings of family life? If we typify children as small people, we emphasise the significance of individuality regardless of age status, and can be correspondingly construed as freeing mothers from the obligations to meet those needs, providing more scope for their own individuality. If we typify children as *different*-from-adults, then mothers who pursue their own individual preferences may be described as 'selfish', since they are construed as failing to meet their obligations, undermining the framework of *reciprocal obligations based on age status* that are believed to underlie the family unit.

Overview of the model of typifications

What I have been seeking to do, based upon the analysis of the accounts women gave of their lives with their children, is to describe differing cultural understandings of what it means to be 'a child'. Such understandings are a central aspect of childrearing and of socialisation. In their accounts, the women drew upon these understandings, or typifications, to help make sense of the substantive issues of daily life. Each typification carries different implications of how we are to understand the needs of children, and consequently of how mothers may best meet children's needs. However, women did not use these typifications in any automatic or simplistic way, but rather they drew upon them, combined them and extended them, in ways they found useful to make sense of their particular 'child/ren' within the context of their particular 'families'.

Starting from different theoretical concerns and using different methodologies, other researchers have described various 'types' of parenting (reviewed by Maccoby and Martin 1983). The central difference between these typologies or dimensions of difference, and

Typification of children	Appropriate maternal response
Natural innocents	Adaptive
Little devils	Directive
Small people	Negotiative

Figure 7.1   *The model of typifications*

the model of typifications described here, is that the typifications are concerned with the *potential meanings* that *women themselves actively draw upon* to make sense of their childrearing, while other typologies seek to classify behaviours, beliefs, and/or mothers themselves. Thus the typifications suggest that differences of approach to childrearing are fundamentally related to differences in cultural understandings of what it *means to be 'a child'*. Such differences in understanding are expressed in varying imagery, and imply quite different views of children's needs and family obligations.

Indeed, it seems likely that researchers themselves inevitably draw upon these underlying typifications and images of children in making sense of their 'data' about maternal behaviour. The degree of parallel between expert typologies (see chapter 1) and the present model of typifications suggests that the underlying imagery of children may be pervasive, and be found in contexts well beyond the limits of my particular sample of parents. However, I suggest that the 'expert' descriptions of childrearing styles by psychological researchers carry strong evaluative overtones of 'good parenting'. Indeed, this often appears to be their explicit intention.

It may well be that my own model of typifications also carries within it the seeds of implicit evaluations. It may be that *any description of differences* will attract evaluations, and this may depend upon whether other people use them as judgemental labels in practice. A rather different question is whether people may identify themselves and their own understandings within the present descriptions of the typifications.[7]

My purpose has been to describe some common-sense ideal-types (which Schutz calls typifications) which are available in our culture for women to draw upon to make sense of their own experiences with their children. These various typifications are *themselves drawn upon* and elaborated in *expert psychological typologies*, so that there may be a complex *inter*-play between expert theories and common-sense understandings. I have thus been seeking to map some of the variability in how mothers described their childrearing, using terms by which the women might recognise themselves without feeling evaluated. Each typification is intelligible within its own terms, and is therefore potentially useful to women in making sense of their experiences with their children in various contexts.

Most fundamentally, then, I am not seeking to describe actual childrearing behaviours or values, or to classify the women themselves under the model, but to understand meanings, as these are employed within particular contexts. While some women's accounts drew very heavily on one particular typification, most drew upon different typifications at different times, and in relation to different issues and settings. It is for this reason that I have not sought to discuss some of the central preoccupations of childrearing under the model so far described. In the next chapter, I shall turn to these preoccupations to show how women might draw upon and combine the typifications in various ways in discussing these daily preoccupations of childrearing. I shall return in chapter 9 to the relevance of particular contexts for the use of different typifications, and the consequently political nature of their usage. The central preoccupations discussed next, then, concern life within the family home.

Notes

1. Much of this discussion about implied responses to typifications of children may be relevant to fathers' responses as well as mothers', but I shall refer to mothers to be in line with my central focus of study.

2. For a fuller discussion of Ellen's educational views, see Ribbens (1993b).

3. Contrast this approach to dealing with a sleep problem with that discussed by Penny Barton in chapter 5.

4. There is an interesting side issue here in relation to handicapped children – parents are often told they have to accept the child with the handicap, and yet there is the possibility that this is a much wider issue in relation to all children. Handicap is simply seen more clearly as an obstacle to parental shaping of a child, rather than accepting the child 'as she is'.

5. I had intended to call this typification 'regulative', but this term has been used by others e.g. Walkerdine and Lucey (1989) and – rather judgementally I feel – by Raphael-Leff (1983).

6. Maternal emotions are discussed in greater detail in Ribbens (1990a), chapter 4.

7. Part II includes some information about the reactions of the case-study women to their readings of my accounts of their interviews.

8

Childrearing Philosophies in Action

Maternal balancing acts – mothers as mediators

Jane Lazarre, in her autobiography about motherhood, eloquently points out the invisibility of maternal achievement when she describes her feelings at watching her husband's graduation ceremony:

> I am nowhere near finished with my degree. I couldn't leave [our son] as often as you did, just couldn't manage to do it when he was so little. What do I have to show for these years, James? I have a baby. No one cares about that. So I go back to my sandy beach where the water is rising, where no ritual or long black costume marks the changes I have known, where no audience acknowledges my struggle with their tears and clapping hands, where, with every low tide, another storm threatens. (1987: 98)

Hilary Graham (1982) suggests that a capacity for *invisible 'coping'* is the primary task of new motherhood in our society. I suggest that part of this coping is about establishing independent maternal authority (Ribbens 1993a), and linked to this, there is also for many women the expectation that the arrival of a baby will create a new 'family' or enhance an existing one. By the time family life has reached the plateau of the middle years of childhood, a woman is expected to be coping happily with the various internal and external processes that constitute her invisible production of family life (chapter 3).

Motherhood is a key 'Act' in a woman's life (in Goffman's dramaturgical sense), and may perhaps be most likened to either a juggling act, or a balancing act – riding a bike with no hands. However, the metaphor of 'look no hands' does not hold up in one important sense – there is no-one to look, no audience and no accolade – unless of course one falls off the bike, when the audience suddenly materialises. While various writers discuss women's roles in terms of a balancing act between motherhood and *employment* (e.g. Gerson 1985, Gieve 1990, Sharpe 1984), the mothers in the present study also described themselves as performing other balancing acts in bringing up their children, both within and without the household. In carrying out these balancing acts, women positioned themselves as mediators between their children and others. In this chapter, I will consider some of the mediations and balances the women described within their households, and how these were played out in issues of childrearing. I shall consider women's mediations outside the household in chapter 9.

The different aspects of the maternal balancing act within the household can be understood by reference to three inter-linked concerns:

1 Children are regarded as individuals, but individuality itself may be seen as composed of various parts, each with its own needs, such that these different needs require balancing out within the life of the individual.
2 Certain individuals are seen to be components of a social unit defined as the family, such that the needs of the individual child require balancing out against the needs of other individuals within the family.
3 The family itself is seen as an entity in its own right, such that it may have needs of its own, requiring a balancing between the scope for individuality and the life of the family as a unity.

Within the accounts given, there was considerable variation in how these different elements were perceived, evaluated and given priority. The other variability concerned how the mother placed her own sense of individuality within all this (chapter 3). Consequently, in seeking to develop the ideal balance, any conflicts and issues might be internalised, as the woman took it into herself to create the balance. Hence beliefs that, if mothers have lives on their own, 'the family' is under threat as a social unit.

> 'It's something to do with mothers being the centre, the centre-pin of families, I think. I think they really are. Everything revolves – I mean if I go over to, um, Jeff's parents' house, if his mum's not there the house is empty. There can be five other people in it but if she's not there it's empty you know. And it's the same with my mum and dad . . . you're the one that, even totally unconsciously, you're the one – you hold everything together'. (Mother-student, quoted by Edwards 1993b: 52)

In chapter 3 I discussed the taken-for-granted cultural assumption of the significance of individuality. However, the notion of individuality *itself* may be constituted of various parts, each with its own needs. Thus one of the balancing acts concerns the various components which are seen to make up the child's individuality. These may include the physical body (itself requiring a 'balanced diet'), the emotional being, the intellectual capacity, and (perhaps less often) the spiritual soul. This is therefore a balancing act that occurs *within* the space defined as the single individual.

However, the child is of course only one of the individuals within the household. Children's individual characteristics and rights have to be balanced out with the other members of the household. This was a responsibility the mothers took on themselves, and in fulfilling this responsibility they acted as mediators between the different individuals within the home.

A mother's position as mediator between her child and the physical and social world can be seen as potentially occurring even prior to birth. The physical processes by which the baby receives sustenance across the placenta within the womb represent a biological mediation whereby the woman's body intervenes between the foetus and the external world. Breen (1989) discusses how the boundary between inside and outside the womb may itself be regarded as rather more permeable towards the later stages of pregnancy.

After the birth, psychologists and sociologists alike have pointed to the processes by which the mother mediates between the baby and his/her experience and knowledge of the physical environment. While some writers have thrown a great deal of light on the ways in which people are intrinsically social, they have not considered how these processes occur in various social environments which are mediated by mothers for the majority of children in our society (see chapter 1). Mead and his interpreters thus tend 'to elide the "generalised other" with *actual* others (principally the mother)' (Ingleby 1986: 307).

Bertaux and Delacroix (1992) suggest that it is because women act generally as mediators between children and their fathers that there may be problems for fathers in relating to their children after divorce. The women in the present study perceived themselves as mediating their children's relationships within 'the family', between children and father, or between quarrelling siblings. In this sense, they sought to balance out the needs and rights of different household members, as individuals with specific needs structured according to their gender, age and personal characteristics (chapter 3). However, while part of this particular balancing act concerned a balancing or evening out of each family member's individual needs and rights, in that very process a mother was also defining and placing them as members of the family unit. As Bell (1990) has pointed out, women deal with the economy of emotion, and as such they are the book-keepers who seek to balance the family's emotional budget. But by the very process of defining the relevant items for inclusion in the budget, they define the boundaries of the family unit.

But further, there may be a balance to be kept between allowing scope for individuality and maintaining the cohesion of the family unit – how far the individual may 'opt out' of the family unit, undermining family togetherness. Any activity undertaken by individuals outside the family may reduce family cohesion. Some of these activities may be seen as imposed and unavoidable, though the imposition may not always be total in fact – such as children's participation in the educational system, and fathers' participation in the economic system, both of which have been questioned by Emily (chapter 6). Other individual activities outside the family may be seen as more optional and arouse greater debate – such as maternal employment, men's sporting pursuits, or teenagers' peer group activities. Perceptions and priorities of individual needs are therefore balanced out against the need to 'be a family', doing things together, and using individual activities to maintain the family unit rather than to undermine it.

While mothers may hope to have reached a plateau of established family life in the middle years of childhood, the processes of 'family' production are also relevant whenever the illusion of effortless and natural family life is threatened or the boundaries have to be redrawn and new balances struck – say, at the birth of subsequent children, or when some crisis strikes, such as father's unemployment or child's drug abuse, which throws out the existing balances that have been negotiated. Such crises may represent serious imbalances, requiring overt and stressful renegotiations. However, the everyday experience of bringing up children in family units requires a *constant and subtle negotiation* to achieve some balance, and the responsibility for this balancing act is largely the mother's, as primary mediator within the family.

In this position as mediator, mothers draw upon various taken-for-granted cultural assumptions and resources, including notions of 'individuality' and 'family' (chapter 3), and variable typifications of 'children', each of which construes 'the child' as a particular sort of being (chapter 7). In the remainder of this chapter, I will explore some of the ways in which mothers drew upon these notions in relation to three areas – scarce household resources (especially time), control, and independence. Each of these areas constituted a central preoccupation in these accounts of childrearing. As such, they act as middle range themes, being less abstract than the typifications of children described in chapter 7, but also more wide-ranging than specific concrete issues of everyday childrearing. Nevertheless, through the discussion that follows, I hope to show how the typifications of children were drawn upon in varying ways in dealing with everyday concrete issues, such as babies who will not sleep, children who have to be dressed, or children who ask for toys and sweets.

Following the overall aim of the book, I am not, of course, suggesting right or wrong ways of handling these issues. Instead, by paying close attention to the language the women used, I seek to point out the various meanings such situations might hold for different women. It is only by considering these underlying meanings that we can understand why certain methods of dealing with childrearing issues are considered suitable by some and not by others. These underlying meanings raise profound questions about the nature of individuality and social life, such that differences of childrearing can be regarded as representing different philosophies in action (a point I will elaborate in chapter 9).

Central maternal preoccupations

Balancing scarce household resources
Certain resources within households are regarded as finite, and issues arise as to how they are distributed. Household space, for example, may be organised to provide room (literally) for children and adults *as individuals*, or to provide more *shared space for 'the family'* as a unity. Ted expressed his disapproval of a household where he felt the children were too much separated from the parents:

> *Ted*: . . . the kids have their own room where they can watch telly, they have *their* own room. Cor, I'd never have that.
> *Jane*: Why's that?
> *Ted*: It's half the fun sitting here watching him enjoy himself. Getting all excited over the A-team or something . . . If he was shut in a room, errh, you'd miss half the fun.

Not all of such scarce household resources will be within the control of mothers. The provision of *material resources* for the family is of course a central definition of paternal responsibilities. Nevertheless, in this regard, the mother may well again act as mediator between her children and their father, as well as between siblings.

Some of the potential tensions may be seen in the contrasting meanings attached to notions of *'spoiling'* and *'treats'*, even among these women living in broadly similar economic circumstances. Indeed, Jamieson and Toynbee (1990) suggest that there is no straightforward relationship between notions of 'spoiling' and economic circumstances.

Thus in one sense, 'spoiling children' could mean expending an unreasonable amount of resources upon them:

> . . . [this girl up the road], she was always one of these kids . . . if she couldn't get her own way she'd sulk . . . Mum always reckoned it was because she was so spoiled, she had everything she wanted. And she's even like it now. (Janet)

As a result, the child may be irretrievably spoiled or damaged, in the way that any piece of work may be damaged, with echoes of the old saying, 'Spare the rod and spoil the child'. This usage of the notion of 'spoiling' carries overtones of directive parenting.

In another sense, 'spoiling' could mean indulging children in a desirable way, showing that individual needs are recognised, and the parent seeks to meet these in an unstinting fashion. This usage carries overtones of adaptive parenting. It was Janet's own mother (referred to above) who remarked about Janet's childhood:

> . . . with three children under 4, they didn't have the individual attention, it was always three together . . . you never spoiled one without the — when, er, when they ever had anything, three of them had it . . . three small ones together like that, they didn't get what they should have had. (Grandmother)

Emily's mother explicitly questioned the notion of 'spoiling'. Thus she checked herself in describing children nowadays as 'spoiled' — 'not spoiled, that's a funny word isn't it?' — and described how her mother-in-law believed that 'you cannot spoil children too much'. Jacky did not use the term 'spoiling', but discussed her mixed feelings about buying things children ask for:

> . . . if . . . you're shopping and they say, 'Can I have a packet of crisps, or a bar of chocolate or things?', I'll say yes. Whether it's to keep them quiet or shut them up, or whether that in a way is subconsciously showing them that you love them, giving them what they want . . . you like to give your children what they like, within reason . . . And if you're refusing, are you refusing, do they see it as — ? No, they can't think that. But often people buy things and shower people with things by way of love, or as a substitute for love and affection perhaps. I don't know, it's a very difficult area that.

Mary, on the other hand, unambiguously regarded some treats as 'buying children off', representing a failure to show love through the meeting of their real needs as she would define these. She said of parents who buy lavish Christmas presents:

> . . . they see that as loving them. I don't see that as love. I see reading to them, and talking to them about leaves and things, as love. They're trying to buy love . . .

Some of these disputes, then, are about differing definitions of children's needs, and who takes the responsibility for defining them, and it is such differences which are at the basis of the various typifications discussed in chapter 7. For many, the tensions may be dealt with by allowing ritual spoiling at certain times, most notably Christmas and birthdays.

The households in the present study were relatively affluent and stable financially – this was indeed often described by the parents as a major difference from their own childhoods (Newson and Lilley 1989). However, *time* was a commodity which was experienced as being in short supply and this was the medium through which many family balances were expressed. How mothers spend their own time may be *circumscribed* in some respects, such as by school timetables, or husbands' work hours. Indeed, Karen Davies (1990) discusses the gender implications of contemporary Western notions of time, particularly the ways in which women's domestically based lives are dominated by a male-oriented, publicly based understanding of linear time, to the detriment of other understandings of time. However, within these overall constraints operating through other family members, in many ways women's own time is a resource over which mothers themselves may have *direct control* when not in paid employment (Oakley 1985):

> It was great being able to potter around in my own time, which I'd never done before, it was quite an eye-opener. I really enjoyed that. (Clare)

The freedom for new mothers to allocate their own time may even be experienced as disturbing in the terms of Fromm's discussion of a 'fear of freedom' (1942), and may lead to a desire to establish 'timetables' and 'routines'.

Time in family life can have at least two rather different meanings. First, time is something that passes by and denotes change (see e.g. Backett's 1982 discussion of phases, and Morgan's 1975 application of the term 'project' to family life). James and Prout (1990) suggest that the notion of time passing is central to the meaning of childhood as such (to the extent that researchers have neglected to give significance to the lives of children as they are in the present). Children's presumed incapacity to take a long-term perspective may be a crucial element in the way they are defined as different-from-adults.

Secondly, however, time can be perceived as a finite quantity, although it may be possible to use financial resources to increase the amount of time available to the household – 'I had a lot of time with her, because of the help with the au pair' (Ellen). In this sense time is a resource, like money, such that decisions have to be made about how to spend it. It is in this sense that researchers have studied household and individual 'time budgets'. In reviewing this work, Tivers (1985) describes it as influenced in the twentieth century by time-and-motion studies (in other words, rooted in public sphere concerns of work), and as largely quantitative in orientation. I am here concerned more with women's descriptions of the *qualitative meanings of time* as a 'family' resource, for which mothers generally do the accounting.

Thus, just as spending money on someone can denote caring, so also spending time with someone is central to many parents' notions of *caring* for children. If you love someone it is expected that you will want to spend time with them. *Spending time together* is seen as the essence of building a relationship, and a crucial part of developing awareness of children's needs as individuals. This is especially relevant with new-born babies, when mothers are expected, and may feel obliged, to have unlimited time available (Boulton 1983, Breen 1989). On the other hand, just as money can be demanded and given under duress, so can time. Thus the allocation of time can also be seen as the basis for control and a *site for power struggles* within the family.

Not 'having enough time' for children was thus the commonest ground on which women expressed *guilt* about failing in their mothering. Similarly, lack of 'patience' was often described as a serious failing in a parent, and patience is partly to do with enduring delays, living in the child's time-scale rather than the adult's. Such tensions were again indicative of how women might feel torn between a linear understanding of time, rooted in publicly based, male-oriented lives, and domesticallly based understandings of time oriented around caring. Angela was employed full-time, and felt unable to balance her time budget:

> There is never enough time for him, as much as I try to there is always something to do . . . . You physically can't fit in more than you do . . . . We always get in the bath together every evening . . . I don't know why, and we have a chat in the bath . . . and the conversation will start to flow.

Diane, similarly, stressed special times for talk:

> I think if you can present them with a time and a comforting place and environment, whereby they can open up to you and you to them, I don't think you need worry about anything else, because anything that's there will come out . . .

'Caring for children' was defined in terms of *'being there'* by many members of the case-study families in response to my direct question:

Jane: What are the ways a mother can show her children she cares for them?

Penny Barton: That's a hard one, Jane. Well, just to be there when they want you for something . . . spending time with them, I suppose, and doing things with them . . .

David Barton: . . . spending time with them really, doing things with them, things that I don't do!

Pauline Davis: I suppose always being there.

Shirley Wootton: Having time for them . . . being there when they've hurt their knee, and when they've hurt themselves is when they need you most . . .

Grandmother: I suppose being there, at any age, just being there ready if they need you there . . .

Sandra Hopkins: . . . just generally be there for them . . .

Jack Hopkins: . . . spend a bit of time with them . . .

Part of the belief about time, then, seemed to centre not just on 'spending time' on children, but on 'being there', so that mothers are available when their children need them. There might thus be negotiation not only about the amount of time, but when and how it is spent with children. Lynn Richards (1990) found that her Australian respondents stressed 'having time and giving it' in their descriptions of 'good mothers'. Similarly, Hallden (1991) found that her Swedish parents stressed the importance of 'being there' for children, and that this involved an understanding of time as indivisible, whereas involvement in employment conflicts with this view of time.[1]

A mother's time may thus be expected to be organised around children's needs, as expressed in the idea that maternal employment should 'fit around' children. On the other hand, there were marked variations between parents about *how far this obligation extends*, for maternal time to be 'fitted around' children's needs. Did this obligation include night-times, particularly as regards sleep patterns? Evenings might also arouse different expectations about time. Jacky remarked that, 'You don't mind what they do during the day within reason, as long as you've got the evening to yourself', while Mary referred to 'uncaring parents' who 'shove [children] off to bed at 6 o'clock . . .'.

A major issue expressed through notions of time, then, concerns the different typifications about who can best know and define children's needs – children themselves, or adults? While parents/ mothers should have time available to allow for the identification and meeting of particular children's needs, the definition of children's needs as regards the organisation of time at a more general level may itself be open to different interpretations. Much of this difference is encapsulated in ideas about *'routine'*. This concept could be used, on the one hand, to suggest that children are expected to learn to live by the rhythms of the households of which they are members – 'Don't put a pattern of your formal routine in the house onto the child' (Amy). On the other hand, it could be used to refer to a need in children themselves for predictability as a source of security: routine could be regarded as valuable in itself for children.

> I think routine creates stability in the child. Oh yes. They know the pattern, the routine's there, the stability, the security, all come into it. (Grandmother)

Whether routines were beneficial to mothers themselves was a separate issue again. Some of the contemporary mothers appeared to value routine for enhancing their own ability 'to cope'. Kate valued routine partly because it provided a framework that enabled her to balance the family time budget, providing time for each family member as an 'individual'. A 'crisis' was defined as something that disrupted this balancing act by creating extraordinary needs to be met:

> I mean I think [routine] is good for them in a lot of ways, because they know that somehow they have a certain amount of time that they'll get, and it's very hard to give them more unless it's a crisis . . . You only need one of them to be ill one day and the whole thing goes out the window.

Control of time through the establishment of routines could be a very important consideration in relation to breastfeeding. Breastfeeding is generally seen as making it more difficult to establish routines, requiring instead that mothers respond to the demands of the baby – although not always: 'They were fed on *my* demand. I decided when I was getting too heavy for comfort and they were not demanding sort of babies' (Ellen).

A very central part of the description of new babies concerned how *demanding* they are of the mother's time – 'easy babies that you can put down' (Jo). 'Good babies' were referred to as 'easy' and 'contented', whereas babies that demand time were described as 'hard work':

> I knew it would be hard work . . . some people are lucky, if you get a baby that's very placid and doesn't cry and goes to sleep when it's meant to . . . . (Hilary)

'Demanding' babies might seriously threaten women's ability to balance out their family time budgets, which was a central aspect of 'coping'. With older children sleep generally becomes less of a central issue, and it was children's inclination to 'amuse themselves' that was valued as relieving the mother:

> Actually he's the best − not the best, I haven't got a favourite, but I mean he will amuse himself and just fit in. He's always had to really, and he's been no trouble at all. (Susan)

Children might be demanding not only in terms of the *amount* of a mother's time they took, but also in terms of *when* they wanted her time. '*Attention*' was a term which incorporated some of the tensions about *control of time* in relations with children. Children were construed as both 'needing attention' − and therefore having some right to attention − but also as potential 'attention-seekers'. The latter concept might be invoked if children were thought to demand unreasonable amounts of time, or time at inappropriate occasions, the latter constituting part of children's potential to embarrass (chapter 4).

Gaining the mother's attention might be seen as rewarding to a child, and therefore a site of potential power struggles. Kate defined her first child particularly as an 'attention-seeker', which she took as a sign of her own failure to control time allocation:

> I suppose he was an attention-seeker, and not having had the experience to know what to do with an attention-seeker, I sort of let him get away with it in a sense . . .

Part of the child control strategy advocated by the parent group she attended was to avoid being 'at the beck and call' of children.

Nevertheless, 'attention-seeking' was not always evaluated negatively, sometimes being viewed as showing signs of a child's active determination in dealing with the world. An *un*demanding baby could give cause for concern for being *too placid or boring*:

> She was easy, even easier. Actually she had a fit when she was 48 hours old, and she had always been a very, very placid baby until about six months, so we were quite anxious that it might be related to some minor brain damage . . . there was very little response . . . . (Ellen)

Similarly, Kate said of her daughter who has Down's syndrome:

> Very placid as a baby. Well, I say that, but she wasn't later on. I was very glad she wasn't later, because she's very determined, she wants to do things.

Order, care and control

While some could thus see time as a control issue, almost all the women implied that control over a child was, *in itself*, something they should be able to achieve as mothers. There is evidence that fathers' involvement in the control of children has lessened in post-war Britain (Newson and Newson 1974). When the women compared themselves with other mothers (as I specifically asked them to do), the sources of contrast and comparison often centred on this specific issue of levels and types of control over children – 'The lack of discipline is one thing. I don't allow screaming' (Kay). Control over children was also important in women's self-descriptions as mothers.

> I think everybody brings their children up differently. I'm not saying mine are angels, I do smack them, but I don't very often have to smack them because if I tell them not to do something they know I mean it. (Rosemary)

There was certainly no evidence from this study that contemporary British parents are unconcerned about issues of discipline with their children (and see also David et al. 1994). On the other hand some parents were concerned to give their children 'choices', and more 'independence' than they had experienced as children. Alwin (1990) describes a shift in the attitudes of American parents over a 50-year period, valuing conformity less and autonomy more highly.

The term often used in the research literature to discuss the issue of control over children is 'discipline', but the concept of 'discipline' itself presupposes certain evaluations, such that 'discipline' is often assumed to be a 'good thing' (although being 'a disciplinarian' is not necessarily positively evaluated in the same way). Weber suggests that discipline is bound up with the value of consistent rationality, rooted in the wider social order: 'The content of discipline is nothing but the consistently rationalized, methodically trained and exact execution of the received order, in which all personal criticism is unconditionally suspended and the actor is unswervingly and exclusively set for carrying out the command. In addition this conduct under order is uniform' (1968: 253).

Newson and Newson imply that discipline – defined as 'the prevention of "naughtiness" and the promotion of "goodness"' (1965: 184) – is central to motherhood. Thus they refer to the 'mother's disciplinary function' (1978: 331), a 'function' being defined by the dictionary as 'the natural action or intended purpose of a person or thing in a specific role' (*Collins Concise Dictionary*). Some parents in the present study suggested that discipline is intrinsically valuable in itself, saying that they 'believe in discipline'.

However, *whether or not* a woman described herself as 'believing in discipline', I am suggesting that they all had to develop an approach – perhaps intuitively rather than intellectually – to the issue of maternal authority/power (whether this was great or small) within the context of their family balancing acts. This was the case even if a woman's approach to maternal control asserted the *un*desirability of 'discipline', prioritising children's own expression of their needs as 'natural innocents'.

Since children are defined by their dependency needs (chapter 7), women are very powerful in relation to their children:

> the future of childcare is an uncomfortable subject, not because it is to do with liberating mothers, but because it is also to do with empowering children ... A lot of childrearing consists of calming children down, controlling and managing them, getting them to submit and to accept the unacceptable. These processes are not at all neutral. Inevitably they are carried out by mothers who have enormous power over their children, even though they are otherwise not very powerful (New and David 1985: 21–2).

However, not all women seek to use this power to the same degree nor in the same ways, and 'discipline' is only *one* of the concepts available for women in developing an understanding of, and an approach towards, their maternal power. There is thus no neat relationship between the three typifications of children (chapter 7) and the extent of control mothers talked about, although the typifications might relate to the use of different *concepts* for describing maternal power. The same piece of maternal behaviour can be described using different terms rooted in varying frameworks of meaning – 'physical punishment' and 'corporal punishment' (Newson and Newson 1989), 'a good hiding' (Veronica, Stephen), 'marking a child' (mother quoted in Newson and Newson 1965), 'physically hurting a child' (Amy), 'a slap' (Amy), 'a smack' (Susan, Rosemary, the Newsons), 'spank' (Kay), 'lashing out' (Jo), 'hitting them' (Susan, Shirley), 'swiping them' (Susan), 'a quick clip' (Christine).

The first sense in which women discussed maternal power was in terms of a straightforward power struggle to achieve control over the child:

> I used to count to five, I'd say, 'I'll count to five, Anna, and if you don't do anything then you'll get a slap', and I thought, no, five's too long, so I said I'd count to three, and I never get to three, I mean I very rarely have to smack them . . . . (Marie)

Sometimes, this power struggle was something that was seen to have been already won in the past:

... they're fairly good now and I find I don't – I've sort of gone
through all that and I find I don't have to discipline them quite so much.
(Lindsay)

The majority of the women expressed in some way the implicit
expectation that they should have the power to control their
children's behaviour. While such power may not always be easy to
obtain, there was a widespread assumption in these childrearing
accounts that competent mothers *ought* to achieve some degree of
power over their children – as indeed, is implied by Newson and
Newson's (1978) reference to the mother's disciplinary function
(discussed above). The ability to control children's behaviour – for
whatever purpose and in the service of whoever's interests – was
regarded as desirable in its own right. This is to use the concept of
power within a traditional Weberian sense, as 'the probability that
one actor . . . will be in a position to carry out his own will despite
resistance, regardless of the basis on which this probability rests'
(1968: 53).

Women referred to a variety of methods of achieving power,
including deprivations such as no television-watching, and restriction of their movements, for example sending children to their
rooms. Veronica had an elaborate system of rewards and
punishments – 'I'm a great one for bribery.' Many women referred
to their tendency to 'shout' at children, and almost all had at some
point smacked a child – although this might not be accompanied
by a 'belief' in smacking. Susan felt that smacking could occur for
the 'wrong' reasons:

I mean, I believe in smacking, but yes, I think sometimes I do do it on
the wrong occasions, but you can't help yourself if you've had a bad
day, and it makes you feel better . . . And I wish I didn't shout really
but you can't help it.

A further issue concerned whose interests were being met in the
assertion of maternal power. A woman's power might be used to
promote her own interests, but if children are typified as little
devils, this implies the *necessity* for the suppression of children's
potential for anarchy, to subdue the 'will' in favour of *social order*
– 'They must understand what the word "No" means' (Clare). On
the other hand, while Hilary described her 'wilful' daughter as
'awful', she also described her as having a 'lot of character' and a
determination to 'go and do things', which Hilary felt might help
her in adult life:

. . . she won't do something she doesn't want to do. . . But [my son]
has always been completely the opposite . . . you didn't have to
chastise him at all. I remember once I put him by the front door when

eating dinner and he was very very upset about it and I never had to do it again, but [my daughter] wouldn't care two hoots if I put her by the front door, she would just stomp back in again and say, 'I'm not eating it, it's yuck.'

Several women raised the question of whose interests are being served when mothers assert power over a child. Jacky suggested that her husband regarded her as 'too soft' with their children, but she also questioned who 'the law' was meant to benefit:

He's going to say I'm too soft and I don't lay the law down enough . . . I question, when I say 'No', whether it is to make things easier for *me*, whether it is definitely for a very good reason that I say 'No' to a thing.

A grandmother made a similar point:

. . . a lot of parents try and keep children down, and it's not for the child's sake, it's for their own sake. I found that out. It's me.

Ellen also distinguished explicitly between the different *purposes* for which maternal power might be used:

Why do you give the child discipline? . . . Do you give the child discipline . . . because if they don't behave they are a jolly big nuisance with parents . . . are they a social embarrassment? . . . Or are you thinking of disciplining the child for their own development, that's what I'm interested in. Yes, of course it's very important for social reasons, and for myself, but the most important thing is to help the child . . .[2]

Traditionally, sociological concepts of power are rooted within a framework that assumes the pursuit of self-interest even against the will of others (see chapter 9). However, while maternal power might be valued as a good thing in itself, towards the maintenance of social order, its exercise in the *mother's* interests was regarded generally as a dereliction of maternal duty. However, its exercise might be justified as serving *children's* individual interests as well as the interests of wider social order. Women who valued 'discipline' and 'firmness', then, might take care to explain that this was not in order to pursue their own preferences, but because this is needed for the child's sake. While they did not refer to the Bible quote – 'He that spareth the rod hateth his son' (Proverbs 13: 24) – there was the expectation that children's own needs will not be met without some exercise of maternal/parental power, and that the exercise of power is thus an *expression of caring*.

I think children . . . do need to have discipline. I'm not saying they need to be beaten and tied to a chair, but they do need it. I think they actually need it for their growth and development . . . There's this great school of thought at the moment, isn't there, for children to be very liberated and find their own level, and, oh well, he's just expressing himself, when he's doing the most awful thing, and I agree up to a point . . . but not letting them have so much freedom that they actually don't know which way they're going because it would be very confusing for them . . . (Lindsay)

Lindsay thus saw discipline as aiding the child's own growth and movement towards independence. Clare, by contrast, regarded discipline as necessary for social order, but also construed it as suppressing children as individuals because it restricts their choice and self-determination. She thus regarded it as inimical to children's developing independence:

I think they still need the discipline, they need to know the rules, you know, where the lines are drawn. In practice I found it much easier to be participative in a working environment, much harder in a home environment, and much easier to be autocratic at home. To say, 'You will or you won't do this.' At the same time thinking, well this is wrong. And the dividing lines between allowing them the choice and the freedom but also knowing where to draw the line and say, 'This — well, you don't overstep the mark', is quite a finely divided one.

In considering discipline as necessary for social order, different emphases could be discerned. A mother might exercise her power to the benefit of all family members,[3] or the social order might be seen as bound up with independent rational principles. Christine's husband and mother both gave childrearing accounts which explicitly used notions of rational justice in parenting. Such consistency and uniformity parallel Weber's description of discipline, and relate to ideas women expressed about the importance of 'being consistent' and 'following things through'.

Within this framework, then, it is the *mother's duty to exercise power* over the child, to uphold the social order to the benefit of all, including children's own needs. Penny explicitly described the amount of effort she felt was involved in undertaking her *responsibility to exert discipline*. (I shall return to the concept of power in relation to childrearing in chapter 9.)

A rather different balancing act occurs with the notion that children need '*boundaries*'. Much of Ellen's account referred to the specialness of childhood, with typifications of children as natural innocents who require freedom from adult restrictions to be able to grow without distortion. Nevertheless, she suggested that the application of this typification should be limited at some point, as explicated by the notion of parental 'boundaries' which will help keep children 'upright' while they 'find their own boundaries':

I don't like the word, 'discipline', because it gives me the taste of an adult dictating to a child, and that I don't approve of. I don't approve of the idea, the attitude that you should always treat a child as your equal, that you should always discuss and explain and share everything with your child, I don't approve of that either. But there is a way in-between, and that's this nice word of 'setting boundaries', or letting the child feel where the boundaries are. They've got to kick their head against something, they've got to have some push and give to keep them upright, and it's the boundaries that give the child stability. A child that has no boundaries, if a child has no routine, they can become very insecure . . . . The most important thing is to help the child find their boundaries for their own development.

This concept of 'boundaries' was explicitly suggested to Emily by a counsellor, but she was doubtful about its value for the children:

I think I don't actually set very strong boundaries, but I don't think it's right to have very strong guidelines or rules or whatever laid down . . . I do say some things are not acceptable, and I say no, I don't know whether that's important or not, or whether that's important for *me* and the family running . . .

While Clare described her own belief in the need for consistent discipline on matters of 'principle', she also suggested that at times this was hard to live up to in the realities of daily living. Some accounts suggested, however, not only that power over children may be difficult to exert in daily life, but it may not be necessary and may even involve *pointless effort* – 'it's easier to let things go.' This view seemed to be underpinned by the typification of children as small people, since there is no predetermined guideline that children are different from adults with special needs which adults must meet, or obligations which adults must enforce. Other everyday realities and priorities may therefore loom larger within this approach. Whether or not the woman exerts power over the child seems to be more of an individual choice, rather than a duty she has to fulfil.

Janet, Shirley, Sally and Margaret are all women who described themselves as settling any conflicts of interests or demands by doing what comes most easily – 'sometimes, at the time, it is easier to get out of things by giving in sometimes'. Within this approach, the preferred solution is generally to do whatever will make everyone happy. Janet implied that she cannot stop her son from 'being himself' (chapter 3), but in addition she implied that any undesirable behaviour might be self-limiting or self-regulating:

I didn't see the point in keep stopping him and smacking him and telling him not to do it. Because even now, you tell him not to do something, and he goes and does it. So it's easier to let him get it out of his system himself.

I have described how different women used different concepts and language to describe the ways in which they sought to exert some power over children. What they had in common is the assumption that mothers are obligated to exert some control, even if they vary as to the amount, method, meaning and purposes of such control. However, the typification of children as natural innocents implies that adult control is *potentially harmful to children*, distorting their natural growth and denying their self-expressed needs. This may account for Emily's doubts about her counsellor's suggestion that children need boundaries. From this perspective, the mother's duty is to exert power, not over children, but to *keep harmful social influences at bay*, seeking to create a safe space within which children can grow with as little harmful restriction as possible. The accounts of Shirley and her mother both seemed to delimit such a space for freedom from adult restraint, in terms of the physical/psychological space of the family home (chapter 6). Amy and Emily were quite explicit about their underlying ideology in using such a typification to minimise restraints in all directions – 'I'm not prepared to break a child's spirit. You don't want to face it like a cornered rat' (Amy).

> Possibly I'm not a very good disciplinarian in that I don't like to physically hurt children, and therefore I don't like to slap, and I don't like to mentally – which I think is even worse – mentally punish children, or emotionally punish children . . . therefore probably they're very free souls . . . My mother was observing [my daughter], and she said, 'Really, for you to get that child to sit down and be quiet you'd need to break its soul', and that sums it all up. (Amy)

Amy thus uses a language of 'spirits', 'souls', 'freedom' and 'hurting', that contrasts strongly with notions that 'children need discipline'. What it means to be a child, and what will count as caring, here involve very different understandings.

Independence, individuality, protection and freedom

While issues of maternal power and control are very much bound up with the need to balance the family's needs as a whole as well as children's individual needs, the notion of 'independence' conceptualises children as individuals apart from 'the family'. If children are defined by their dependency needs, which in our society are generally met within a family unit, then their independence makes it possible for them to be *individuals without reliance on the family*. In the women's accounts, a concern with children's 'independence' was likely to be integrally linked to a positive evaluation of 'individuality' (although see chapter 3 for discussion of the complex and ambiguous links between notions of individuality and of family), and to be based on a typification of children as small people. Where individuality apart from the family was valued, then, women were likely to be seeking a different sort of maternal balancing act stressing independence. In this sense, the typification of children as small people was implicit in many women's accounts, even if only as an orientation to the future rather than an image considered centrally relevant to 7-year-olds. Thus the central issue for mothers of adolescents of 'letting them go' is anticipated throughout the child's earlier years.

As with the themes already discussed, however, the concept of 'independence' could carry a number of different meanings. Firstly, the *content* to which it refers could vary. Is independence a matter of physical self-care and/or independence of ideas? Secondly, there were issues about what sort of *skills* are needed for independence – these could include physical skills, decision-making skills, a capacity for rationality, and (most problematic of all) a future orientation. Dilemmas about how far to 'push' children become relevant here, and the paradox becomes apparent that training for independence can be seen as another form of dependency need. Thirdly, independence may be *evaluated* within different frameworks of meaning. Is independence about increasing *freedom to* make choices, unrestrained by childhood limitations, protections and incapacities, or is it about increasing responsibility, with the need to be self-reliant in a hard world, such that it entails a loss of *freedom from* the irresponsibility and protectiveness of childhood?

Several women discussed the value they placed on encouraging children to be independent in *self-care activities*, such as dressing. Once children are able to cope with such activities without help, they reduce their dependency and increase the resources of time available to the mother. However, in the shorter run, encouraging such independence was seen as time-consuming – 'It's always time' (Jo) – and something which women might have to make an effort towards.

Besides independence in self-care activities, Kate also suggested that it was important for her children to be self-determining in other areas, such as religion. Her son had asked to go to Sunday school in company with his friend – 'I don't believe in a lot of it, but I don't want to make their minds up for them.' One of the ways in which Margaret defined caring was in terms of independence, which for her included intellectual as well as physical independence, 'being her own person'. In discussing the expression of affection, she suggested the importance of treating children as rational small people, rather than asserting adult power/authority in its own right:

> I suppose respecting her really, respecting her opinions and her ideas, and trying never to say, 'You've got to do it because I say so, or I tell you', which I know I do, but I actually consciously don't think it's a very good idea. She's old enough now for lots of things, to actually give reasons.

However, independence might be seen to require certain capacities and skills. 'Being your own person' in Margaret's account seemed to centre quite strongly on being rational and intellectually self-determining. Margaret valued individual confidence in 'standing on her own two feet' by arguing for ideas:

> I think it's easier actually with political things to respect people who hold strong opinions on things, even if they are different from yours, than people who have no particular opinion at all . . . And you can actually end up respecting people over quite a wide range of different sincerely held beliefs if they can argue for them well, but I don't know, that's what I'm aiming to do for her.

In this approach, then, training for independence was based upon an intellectual process of developing rationality (a view of self-determination which has much in common with that of John Locke, discussed in chapter 9).

Clare explicitly valued 'decision-making' as a skill that she wanted to encourage, and which might not be entirely dependent upon rational cognition and intellect. Nevertheless, training children in such individual skills within daily family life could be problematic, and she had revised some of these ideas in the light of her experience of balancing out activities within the household:

> One of the things that everybody says you ought to do is to give children choices and encourage them to make decisions, which is all very well and good, but in fact if you give them choices about too many things you never get a decision, or they find it hard to make the choice. Perhaps in the long run it is good for them, but I know in a practical sense, when you're trying to do something in an hurry, it can actually be very frustrating. You do it automatically because that's what you've become accustomed to doing, and then you wish you'd bitten your tongue off and said, 'Well, you're going to have orange squash', and not given them a choice.

If children are to make choices for themselves, however, they may need the capacity to identify their own needs and best interests. Self-determination in terms of choice of clothes was an area where Lindsay expected to direct children in their own best interests:

I met [my friend] at the school gates, and it was freezing cold, it was snowing, and she said, 'Eleanor wouldn't wear her boots and she's come out with little socks and no gloves, no scarf and no hat' . . . She said, 'Well she's always been like that.' But somehow that seems a very incongruous thing to say really, because it's almost like this child from a baby popped out of the womb and said, 'Right, I'm not going to wear my boots, I'm going to be a real horror' . . . It's only because she's got away with it in the first place . . . In the end, you let them do all kinds of things that may be detrimental, because you cannot assert yourself and get them to do what you feel is right for them . . .

While Margaret, by contrast, defined self-choice about clothes as unlikely to be harmful to her daughter's needs, other areas could be more problematic, if her daughter did not perceive her own needs in line with Margaret's views. This particularly applied when looking into the future, raising the question of whether children are able to define their own best interests when they have less experience than their parents. Margaret referred to potential difficulties ahead, since she would prefer her daughter to choose freely, but she also wanted this free choice to lead her to the same sort of standards as her own. Education was a key value for Margaret, but in the short run her daughter's *self-determined choice* might not include carrying out her homework conscientiously:

It might be that you will nag that much more to work for the exams . . . it might mean that I'll end up sitting over her and saying, 'Do your homework, you are not going out until then', or whatever. I don't know, I think things like that have changed a bit [since my own childhood].

A paradox therefore appears at the heart of these ideas about independence, whatever form independence is considered to take. Valuing independence tends to involve an intrinsic future orientation, yet children are construed as lacking in experience, without the capacity to take a future orientation. These factors in themselves are understood to limit children's ability to know their own best interests, and be self-determining. Consequently, they may need training and 'pushing' towards independence, such that the development of independence may constitute another form of dependency need, requiring training and effort from mothers. There may be concerns about who takes control over definitions of children's *long-term* and *short-term* needs for freedom and opportunities, and education was a recurrent issue in this context.

Such dilemmas were also apparent in Marie's account, with education again a central theme, valued for opening up doors onto new worlds. She was very explicit about her desire to push her children educationally, and ensure that they did not leave school at the first opportunity:

> I hope I will be more pushy than [my mother] was because, having met loads of friends of ours, especially ones who have gone to university, I think it opens up a whole different world.

Such '*pushiness*' had been the source of discussion between Marie and a friend:

> . . . she said, 'Oh well it's whatever they want to do themselves', and I said, 'I know that, but at the same time I think you have to push children a bit . . . I want them to go to university and I want them to travel', and she said to me, 'You're just making your children do things you have never done yourself', and I said, 'That may well be true but at the same time I think if you don't give them the idea, they might go on placidly and not push them the least wee bit they might end up not doing anything at all.'

Thus Marie understood education as an opportunity that opens up doors for travel and interesting jobs, but the dilemma was that if children have no perception of what lies behind these doors they may miss out. Some pushing could be necessary to make them aware of the doors and what lies behind them, since her children (unlike the children of her much-travelled graduate friend) would not have experienced these other worlds directly for themselves. Similarly, Janet suggested you may miss out on what there is to see in life if you do not get pushed to keep up at school:

> It's like when you're going for a walk, if you lag behind, you miss out on everything that's going on up the front, you should always try and keep up . . . .

On the other hand, Hilary suggested that children may in the end 'do well' if they are 'free' from other people's expectations, but are given opportunities to define their own needs/preferences in terms of 'interests' outside school. In Hilary's account, then, there was less sense of conflict between short- and long-term goals of self-determination at home and at school, and work opportunities:

> I think sometimes people who are very good at school, who find it easy, that's the high point of their life and then they perhaps don't do so well when they leave school . . . and then they disappoint themselves by not fulfilling other people's expectations. There are perhaps other people who aren't so good at school, don't have these expectations to fulfil so they're more free to do what they want to do and they come out and do well . . .

Independence and self-determination are thus ultimately about children becoming adults who deal with the world beyond the home without the protection of the family, and this could carry different evaluations for different women. Thus a further difference of emphasis within the notion of 'independence' could be seen in Lindsay's account. While Lindsay valued independence, she discussed it in terms, not of *self-determination*, but of *self-reliance* in dealing with various contexts outside the home:

> I suppose in a way I push them to be independent, more than perhaps I would be myself . . . For instance [my daughter], who is only 7, we bought some plimsolls from Mothercare but they were one size too small . . . I didn't want to park and everything, I gave her the receipt and the shoes and I said, 'There you are, just pop in and say we bought the wrong size and ask to have a size larger.' Now if my mum had asked me to do that when I was 7 – well, she wouldn't have asked me to do it I'm quite sure – I would probably have been absolutely terrified . . . But [my daughter] didn't bat an eyelid . . . I felt really delighted actually . . .

There are parallels here with dilemmas about how far to push children to be independent in other contexts outside the home, through independent social visiting without mothers, and attendance at playgroups (see chapter 4).

Lindsay also contrasted 'doing things for themselves' with the concept of '*protection*', a notion through which she implied that a woman is unnecessarily prolonging her children's dependency:

> I still have to make an effort to encourage them to do things for themselves because it is a very instinctive thing to protect them and do things for them.

Lindsay thus suggested that a good mother is supposed to encourage children to *leave their dependency needs behind them*, and Kate similarly implied she had done well not to be too 'protective' with her daughter who has Down's syndrome:

> I wasn't very protective, I'm not that sort. If [her brother] dragged her around from room to room it didn't really matter, she didn't seem to get hurt. She bounced well! And I think it did her the world of good, because everything he did, he tried to do with her really.

In such discussions of self-care activities which reduce children's dependency needs, independence was not necessarily seen as something children would develop and seek for themselves. 'Doing things for themselves' is not always the same as 'finding things out for themselves', then. On the other hand, the research interview itself led Rosemary to experience her regrets at her children 'growing up too quickly', so that they would be 'off her hands' before she wanted it.

'Pushing children to be independent' might therefore be seen as difficult not only for mothers, but also for children. 'Pushing children' could be described as 'hard' as distinct from 'soft', since such 'pushing' was perceived as curtailing a desirable and enjoyable period of childhood dependency, when children can rely on the family to meet their needs. In Angela's account, the term 'hard' was used (in contrast with 'soft') to describe an attitude which seeks to minimise childhood as a special time for protection and nurturance:

> [My childminder] is probably more protective of him than me. My mother says I've changed a lot and I'm harder than I used to be. I mean we still have lots of cuddles and kisses but if he falls over – 'Come on, don't be silly, rub your knee, you're okay', whereas Julia will say, 'Oh, are you all right, now are you sure?', and I say, 'Oh, he's fine, Julia, don't worry'.

Adult independence might then be seen as a mixed blessing, carrying overtones not just of self-determined choices, but also of self-reliant responsibilities. Jo valued independence defined as 'responsibility' in terms of economic realities, and expected her daughter to look after the chickens on the family smallholding. If she neglected to do it, she was fined, with the explanation that if she did not do it properly, it created more work than if she did not do it at all.[4] Ted, on the other hand, wanted his son's childhood to be a special time for *ir*responsibility (by contrast with his own rural childhood):

> Jane: Does (Russell) have any particular jobs he has to do or anything?
> Ted: (laughs) No.
> Jane: Silly idea, is it?
> Ted: Yes, of course it is. He enjoys hisself . . . he don't have no set job. Good luck to him and all.

Childhood dependency may thus also be construed as a time for freedom, not in terms of freedom to make choices, but in terms of *freedom from adult responsibility* and from the realities of a harsh world. 'Freedom' may be construed through typifications of children as natural innocents, whose childhood should be protected and nurtured, *or* through typifications of children as small people, who have the right to be self-determining and to be free from *adult restrictions*, free to make their own independent choices.

Aspects of independence may thus be conceptualised through varying notions of individuality, protection, responsibility and freedom, which may be combined and construed in quite different ways. Around these different concepts, issues of parental control and caring are again given quite different meanings within different accounts. Such variability hinges upon whether childhood dependency is positively valued as signifying freedom from adult responsibility, or negatively valued as signifying potential restrictions from powerful adults and loss of individuality. Furthermore, different balances are invoked between ideas about individuality and ideas of family obligations, values and continuities.

Conclusions

Overall then, I have argued that these central preoccupations of motherhood – of time, control, and independence – signify how the mother seeks to develop her particular balancing Act within her family. In this sense, they are all issues wherein the woman uses her available resources of power and authority to mediate all the different factors which she defines as relevant to her maternal balance. Among these factors are notions of 'individuality' and 'the family' as a unit, both of which require much effort towards their production. The particular balance the woman seeks will also be expressed in language that draws upon different typifications of what it means to be 'a child', each typification implying different responses from the primary carer.

It is possible to discern parallels between particular typifications and particular childrearing preoccupations. Thus the adaptive response may have particular links with the issue of time, since 'having time' may be a significant way in which caring and maternal adaptation are expressed. The directive response may have particular links with the concept of control, since rational control of children is an important method of caring for them by directing their undesirable anarchistic impulses towards social order. The negotiative response may have particular links with the concept of independence, since caring for children is understood in terms of encouraging them to be individual people in their own right. However, while such links are apparent, in daily life women have to deal with *all of these central preoccupations* in their lives. Typifications may thus be interwoven in a variety of ways within all these themes, so that this neat linkage actually becomes a great deal more complex when we examine how they are discussed in the accounts. Thus while time may be a focus of maternal adaptation, it may also be a site of struggles for control. While control may be construed as rational discipline, discipline itself may hold a number of different meanings. Furthermore, maternal *absence* of control over the *child* may relate to maternal *power* to create a space for the specialness of childhood, an area of freedom for the child as a natural innocent. While the encouragement of independence may be a focus for the development of individuality, freedom to develop independence may also be construed as pushing children to grow up too fast, missing out on the special period of childhood freedom from adult responsibilities.

In all of these areas, 'loving children' can hold quite different meanings according to how their needs are defined and prioritised. However, what we can conclude is that these central preoccupations of motherhood – time, control, and independence – may in daily life be expressed through all sorts of apparently 'trivial' issues of childrearing, while underlying the trivia of childrearing are major philosophical and political debates about the nature of individuality and the social order, and of power and freedom. I will elaborate these points later in the concluding chapter, although first I will pay rather more attention to the relevance of the contexts within which mothers deal with these issues in their daily lives with their children.

Notes

1. These varied understandings of time in Western culture, and their gender dimensions, require more attention than is possible here. See e.g. Karen Davies' (1990) discussion of male linear time and female cyclical time. The notion of 'being there', however, seems to involve other qualities again, perhaps invoking more a sense of psychological time (akin to ideas of psychological 'space'). It is also likely that the meanings of time in children's own lives may raise different implications again.

2. Writing more from the position of an outside observer, Stolz (1967) suggests that conversely, children's needs may be overlooked since 'some parents may need help in identifying, understanding and responding to children's behaviour that is painful to the children themselves, but not disturbing or annoying to the family' (1967: 290). Blaxter and Paterson (1982) similarly suggest that mothers were more likely to attend to children's symptoms of ill health if they caused the mothers themselves inconvenience.

3. This viewpoint would seem to have much in common with a Parsonian non-zero sum concept of power, where power is seen to further the interests of all, rather than being a finite quantity such that to increase one person's power is necessarily to reduce another's.

4. See Sandra Hopkins – chapter 5 – for another example of children's independence being signified through an understanding of economic realities, within a household that relied on a family business.

9

Sociology and Childrearing Reconsidered

Numerous important questions remain to be explored about the domestic lives of men, women and children, and their relationships with each other – the experience of parenting children of other ages, in different household structures, or within different ethnic and class/economic groups. In all these areas, however, the present study points to the need to *fundamentally conceptualise issues from within private settings*, rather than concerns that originate from more public spheres (Edwards and Ribbens 1991, and chapter 2).

There is also great scope for exploring how children themselves learn about such social boundaries as public and private. In chapter 2 I pointed out the absence of an *ethnography of family life*, equivalent to the well-established ethnography of education. While issues of privacy within the family/home make direct observation here difficult, there would be much to be gained from *observational studies of women and young children in semi-public settings*, such as friendship networks and toddler groups, to consider how women and children construe different social settings and negotiate social boundaries when they are participating in different groups. We need to consider how mothers and children together accomplish the fundamental taken-for-granted skills which are required for ordinary social interactions, including understandings of the different skills required in different settings. (See chapter 1 for some empirical studies that have made a start in this direction.) The study also points to fascinating issues in the meeting ground of traditional psychology and sociology – of the *inter-relationships* between individual experiences within family dynamics over time, and the movement of those individuals in other social settings, more commonly known as social structure. I will explore some of these issues a little further later in this last chapter.

This book has concentrated on women's own voices as they talked to me about their lives with their children. At the start of the project I had anticipated that I would be describing, and possibly explaining, variations in what women had to say about the nitty-gritty daily issues of childrearing. As it turned out, I found I could not begin to explore women's varied understandings of such issues without developing a more sustained analysis of the *cultural themes* the women drew upon to help make sense of their lives with their children.

These themes are rooted fundamentally in understandings about what 'family', 'individuality' and 'childhood' mean in Western contemporary societies (chapter 3). The notion of 'child' is fundamental to our understandings of what 'family' is, while the notion of becoming and being an 'individual' stands in a complex and ambiguous relationship with the notion of being a 'family' member. Yet these are all unequivocally culturally specific notions, which the women both drew upon and *actively (re)created* in their lives with their children. 'Childhood', 'family' and 'individuality' could be seen to be produced by the women themselves, rather than simply given, 'natural objects'. Nevertheless, the women varied considerably in exactly how they understood these notions and balanced them out in their childrearing accounts.

Part of the process of creating 'a family' for these women involved mediating relationships within the household and actively working to secure a cohesive unit. In addition, however, the women also at times drew boundaries to demarcate their 'family' as a clearcut and distinct social unit. Nevertheless, these boundaries were by no means fixed or given, and women might use a sense of boundary in flexible ways towards their own purposes (discussed further below). Much of the women's lives with their children did not occur within nuclear 'family' units at all, but in complex networks of interactions with other women and children. Contacts with female relatives, particularly maternal grandmothers, were also significant. The women showed much concern about their children's interactions with others, encouraging their social acceptability and social confidence, as the mothers actively mediated between their children and others in social settings outside the family unit (chapter 4).

In the interviews, each woman thus drew her own particular portrait of her life with her children, making sense of her experiences within a particular set of circumstances and background. Each woman's childrearing account developed some central themes and concepts that were important for that particular mother. Thus within its own terms each account could be seen to make sense of that woman's situation and perspective. In the case-study portraits (Part II), I have sought to demonstrate how each woman's account shows particular and central themes, and also how it makes sense as a whole. In order to understand what a woman was saying about any particular childrearing issue, then, we needed to 'place' her remarks within this overall picture of her situation and understandings.

Yet, while each woman developed her own unique family portrait about her life with her children, she did so by drawing upon existing cultural understandings of what it means to be a child. In analysing these understandings (chapter 7), I used Schutz's notion of typifications, to develop descriptions of these common-sense ideal types of 'the child'. Children may thus be understood to be natural innocents, little devils or small people, and each of these typifications carries quite different implications for appropriate maternal responses. In this connection, I depicted such maternal responses as adaptive, directive or negotiative. Each response carries a different answer to three central questions: 1 Who is best able to know a child's needs? 2 Should adults fit themselves and their lives around children's needs, or should children learn to fit into pre-existing adult patterns? 3 Is social life fundamentally beneficial or harmful to the individual? The answers to these questions carry quite different implications that could be seen to be worked out in the women's childrearing accounts in relation to everyday practical issues of childrearing. These different implications are conveyed and portrayed by the use of quite different concepts and languages, and these variabilities could be seen in relation to some major maternal preoccupations, namely, issues of time, control and independence (chapter 8).

Throughout these central chapters of the book, I have concentrated on 'insider perspectives', although in chapter 2 I also indicated the need for an 'outsider perspective' in developing a feminist perspective on childrearing. For the remainder of this concluding chapter, then, I intend to go beyond the research analysis presented in the main body of the book, both to explore some further issues and to raise additional questions. Furthermore, we need a specifically sociological contribution to this 'outsider perspective', and I will sketch in some ideas towards such a contribution to the study of childrearing, as this occurs in actual concrete experiences. I will first outline some thoughts and analysis about possible explanations/links between the women's childrearing accounts and other factors – specifically, factors related to class and occupational experiences, and factors related to intergenerational family dynamics. I will then turn to developing a preliminary sociological model of childrearing, by analysing the different ways in which mothers may position themselves in mediating between their children and others in a variety of social settings. These mediations return us to considerations about differences between public and private settings in social life, and the final part of the chapter will consider how we may approach the analysis of the inter-connections between public and private settings, or between family and wider 'social structures'. In this final chapter, then, I am making particular arguments about why the feminist study of the lives of women and children should be of central interest to sociologists, as well as considering how sociological analysis has a particular contribution to make to the study of childrearing.

Childrearing accounts in context

Class, occupations and childrearing reconsidered
In chapter 1 I noted the pervasive tendency within the existing literature to describe social class differences in childrearing, although both the descriptions and associated explanatory models are seriously flawed. In particular, traditional sociological approaches use women's husbands' occupations both to map, and then 'explain', differences in childrearing.

Traditional methods for the social class classification of women have been the subject of heated sociological debates (summarised by Abbott and Sapsford 1987), leading to a fundamental reassessment of the nature of these central concerns and concepts. Most obviously the debate leads to a reassessment of the purposes and scope of class analysis – what do we actually *mean* by this rather overworked concept, and what are we using it *for*? 'It is the very definition of class analysis itself – its rationale and objectives – that is implicitly being contested' (Marshall et al. 1988: 68). Such issues arise particularly strongly in relation to women-as-mothers and in relation to children's lives.

The issues lead on further, to raise questions of the nature of power, of social structure and its relations to social action, the links between the worlds of work and the family, between the spheres of public and private, between social reproduction and human reproduction. A core issue underlying the women-and-social-class debate concerns the centrality of production to the analysis of society, as distinct from culture and spheres of consumption and lifestyle, since traditional class theory starts from a model that presumes that the latter are dependent upon the former.

Some of the confusion in debates about women and social class arises, I believe, because the participants are *talking past each other*, being actually concerned with quite different issues. This is obscured by the pervasiveness of the use of occupation as the operational definition of class, while the underlying theoretical concepts of class may be quite divergent. Class is used in quite different ways by sociological theorists, and by a wide range of other social researchers, representing a divergence between (1) *class as a difference of culture and lifestyle*, and (2) *class as a position within the productive system*. In both cases occupation may be used as the operational definition, but the underlying concept and purpose of the class analysis may actually be quite different although unacknowledged.

Traditional sociological analysis of social class is concerned largely with class as a position in the productive system, and is oriented to explaining collective political and social action in the public sphere. It is thus rooted in masculinist activities and concerns. Even so, however, such debates are obliged to stray into a discussion of class as lifestyle and culture in order to develop satisfactory explanations of class formation (see e.g. Goldthorpe 1982, discussed by Ribbens 1990b).

Such discussions potentially open up the whole debate about whether and how class is defined and determined by reference to the system of production – in terms either of the occupation of the current head of household, or of the occupation of the individual's head of household during childhood (class of origin in traditional terms). However, if we recognise that class is in fact *conceptualised* more widely, it becomes possible to accept the use, for example, of women's educational qualifications as an aspect of class classification.

It may be objected that there is a danger in this of widening the concept of class beyond the point at which it can be seen as separate from the variables it is seeking to explain. To be used as an independent variable it must be clearly defined by reference to factors that are separate from the dependent variables at issue. While this may be a sound argument within the philosophy of scientific method, I am suggesting that this is not how the concept is used in practice, even within its traditional sociological definition. Goldthorpe (1982) himself has to invoke an intervening variable that refers to aspects of lifestyle and culture when seeking to explain the processes of class formation, and Osborne and Morris (1979) explicitly discuss how the concept of class as occupation lacks explanatory power.

Marsh (1986) suggests that a great problem for social class classification is how to incorporate a time perspective. In seeking to develop a way of considering women's class as individuals in their own right it is necessary to incorporate attributes that relate to key differences in experiences over the life time of the individual, whether class background, educational experience, or occupational experience. Much of this may seem irrelevant if women do marry men of similar experiences to their own, but this is an *empirical contingency* that will mean classification by reference to his occupation will correlate with her own characteristics anyway. Empirical contingency however is not the same as constituting a *theoretically adequate model.*

Class as lifestyle has not been theorized sociologically in the way that class as productive position has been. Consequently, most attention has concentrated on how class as productive position affects class as culture. However, I would suggest that we need *also* to consider that class as culture can have profound implications for class as productive position, both at the level of the individual and at the level of economic change more widely. This debate thus reveals how women's domestic lives become invisible within socio-logical theory through the assumption that the family is simply at the end of causal chains that originate elsewhere. The question is whether the analysis of this domestic arena is of central importance to the understanding of the social order or whether it has only peripheral significance. Thus, the women-and-class debate needs to be taken a great deal further to reconsider the role of the family in relation to the class system (Morgan, forthcoming).

In the present study, mothers' social class has been based on a view of women as individuals, using a multidimensional approach to social class that is not restricted to occupational issues. The study points to three main conclusions with relevance to the issue of class in women's lives as mothers:

1 the significance of women's social contacts (chapter 4, and Bell and Ribbens 1994); this issue particularly points to the relevance of locality in women's lives with young children, and we need to know a good deal more about how people come to live in the particular areas and houses that they do;
2 the presence of some autonomy of childrearing meanings within private families between women across the generations, such that we need to consider an analysis of family cultures as well as class cultures in women's lives with their children (chapter 4);
3 the significance of patterns over time, which suggest that women's lives may show important value orientations *prior* to their becoming members of particular social classes by virtue of their husbands' occupations, and these value orientations may themselves inter-relate with issues of internal family dynamics (see below).

Studies of women's class mobility through marriage show, firstly, a high degree of class endogamy (i.e. people marrying others of similar class to their own; in particular, people tend to marry others of similar educational levels), but secondly, that women are more mobile than are men via marriage (Hayes and Miller 1989). However, in order to understand such patterns we need to know more about how women come to marry the particular men they do, and also, what effects wives may have on their husbands' intra-generational occupational mobility (i.e. husbands' movement up or down occupational hierarchies within their professional lifetime). In the present study, the women's own educational and occupational experiences prior to marriage appeared significant. Only one woman in this sample had clearly been upwardly mobile through marriage as such.

Class by reference to husbands' occupations did not appear to have *direct* impact on these women's lives – the closest factor being level of income[1] – and there were no class patterns (in this traditional sense) discernible in relation to the variations in the women's childrearing perspectives (although we must of course bear in mind the small numbers involved in this study). However, if we consider how occupational experiences might be shown to relate to childrearing, via processes that are potentially *demonstrable and meaningful* at the level of individual women's lives, a number of possible issues might be considered.

Apart from income levels, the second most immediate way in which husbands' occupations might have a direct impact on the experiences of mothers is through the timetabling of their lives. This was on the whole a taken-for-granted backdrop that structured the lives of mothers in the present study, and set boundaries for shifting contexts of 'families with fathers' and 'complex maternal worlds' that did not include men. In the present study, there were men in both manual and non-manual occupations who worked unusually long or unpredictable hours, or spent days away from home at one time. Such minority patterns might either disrupt 'family life' by taking men out of the home too much, or they might disrupt the 'complex maternal worlds' if men were at home at unusual hours of the day. However, in neither case did such patterns represent class differences in any straightforward way.

Apart from these direct effects, there are three ways in which we could speculate that work experiences might relate to childrearing perspectives. First, women might indirectly draw upon their husbands' work experiences in developing their own childrearing ideas (but in this case, these indirect experiences would still of course be interpreted through the women's own frameworks of understandings). There was little evidence of this in the present study. Secondly, women might draw directly upon their own work experiences in seeking to understand their lives with their children. There was some limited evidence of this occurring in the present study (and see Stolz 1967). Further considerations here include whether or not women do see family lives as distinct from work lives or whether they see continuities between the two settings, such that lessons learned in one sphere are thought to be relevant to life in the other sphere, and how and why women themselves come to enter particular occupations in the first place. Thirdly, women might orient some of their childrearing ideas around considerations related to their children's anticipated future work lives. Again, while there were some marked contrasts in the degree to which parents took a future orientation *at all* in their childrearing, there was some limited evidence of this occurring in the present study. However, women were more likely to discuss their children's future educational lives rather than their future work lives. In regard to their children's educational futures, parents generally seemed reluctant to look too far ahead. It seems likely that important feedback mechanisms operate here, so that future aspirations are modified by reference to indications of current educational achievements.

Thus, while current, past and even future occupational experiences may indeed have relevance to childrearing ideas, we should be careful not to adopt (malestream) ideas of the central determinacy of work life for all areas of social life. Indeed, the ethnographic and case-study methodology used in the present study was intended to avoid giving automatic priority to the sphere of work as a site for explanations of childrearing, but to present some of the complex inter-relations between experiences in various settings in the lives of real people over time. One of the crucial questions raised by the present study concerns how people themselves construct boundaries between different settings, and perceive differences or continuities between them (see chapter 2, and David et al. 1993 for a fuller discussion of the concept of 'boundary'). Women varied as to how far they perceived the family/home as a particular sort of setting with its own particular considerations and understandings, different from other settings (discussed further below). Nevertheless, such questions are crucially important, about the possible *inter*-connections between experiences in 'public' and 'private' settings *over time*, if we are to develop a full feminist and sociological understanding of women's lives with their children. I will turn next to a further consideration of some of these processes over time.

Inter-generational family dynamics
While sociologists have focused on current class patterns as a way of describing and explaining childrearing, psychoanalysts and family therapists have directed our attention to inter-personal

family dynamics over time and the significance of parents' own childhood experiences. Sometimes these two themes coincide, via ideas of inter-generational cycles of deprivation.

Some variation in childrearing across the generations may be due to whether or not women feel happy about their own childhood memories. Byng-Hall (1985) offers us the concept of the 'family script' as a tool for analysis of family life, suggesting that family scripts are passed down across generations. In this regard, parents may develop replicative or corrective scripts. It was clear in many of the interviews, with men as well as women, that in some areas of childrearing they were engaged in the development of 'corrective scripts', deliberately seeking to put right what they felt had been in error in their own parents' approach. The depth of feeling involved in some of these corrective scripts seemed, however, to go beyond a simple desire to develop a 'better way of doing things'. In seeking to correct painful aspects of their own upbringings, parents may actually experience some sense of being able to put right their *own* memories of hurt, through a form of projection and then reparation through their own children as psychic extensions of themselves.

In the present study, such corrective programmes of childrearing might be discerned across a wide range of particular topics in the case-study families. A further question is whether some of these corrective and replicative programmes relate to patterned features of social life, and can thus be said to relate to social structure. Thus the example of the parent who wishes to 'spoil' children with gifts may clearly be systematically related to social structures of material deprivations. The 'spoiling' of children with sweets by grandparents seems to be systematically related in Britain to a generational experience of such deprivations as a result of wartime shortages.

A further issue for exploration, in relation to inter-generational family dynamics around childrearing, concerns patterns of gender identification. I am thinking here, not just of how the *child* makes a gender identification with the parent of the same sex (which is the more widely discussed issue), but also of how a *mother* may identify herself with her child of the same or different sex. Feminist writers have discussed some of the deep ambivalences that may arise between mothers and daughters from both sides of the relationship (see e.g. Flax 1978, Rich 1977). Such ambivalences may be an important reason why some daughters develop particular identifications with fathers, and why some mothers develop particular identifications with sons.

This raises issues well beyond the scope of the present study, but their relevance here is that identification by a girl with her father may lead to *discontinuities* across the generations of mother and daughter, with potential implications for the daughter's roles in both public and private settings. Such a daughter may find greater success than other girls in public settings of education and work (see e.g. Oakley 1984), but equally may find herself less inclined to use a straightforward replicative childrearing programme derived from her own mother, when and if she herself has a child.[2]

I am thus hypothesising that women who subjectively identify with their fathers more than with their mothers may experience a greater sense of questioning and self-doubt about their own approaches to childrearing than women who identify more fully with their own mothers. While not totally discarding their own mothers' approaches – which are the only ones they know from first hand – they are more likely than others to seek out alternative sources of advice. However, I would also suggest that such patterns relate not only to the daughter's level of identification with her mother, but also to the *mother*'s identification with her daughter. It is very striking in the present study that in three of the grandmother–mother pairs where the mothers (Emily, Christine and Clare) appeared most different from the grandmothers in their childrearing accounts, the grandmothers themselves described their daughters as more like their fathers than like themselves, and in two of these cases, where there was also a son, the grandmothers spoke of their own sense of identification with their sons.

The women interviewed may, of course, have felt a need to find a retrospective explanation for a current sense of difference between a mother and grandmother. However, such processes of gendered inter-personal dynamics within the home may have fascinating potential for understanding how and why men and women orient themselves in different ways to public and private settings, and thus to social life in its widest sense in terms of both continuity and change.

Mediating between public and private settings

The evidence presented here, whether from my own study or others, has stressed the position of mothers as mediators between their children and others. On the whole, I have paid particular attention to the ways in which mothers mediate family relationships within the household, and I developed a model of how different typifications of children implied different maternal responses relevant to these mediations. Here, I want to pay more systematic attention to the ways in which mothers may mediate between their children and others more generally, outside the home/family. I suggest that almost all women are put into this position of mediator, whether they like it or not, because of the way children are placed in contemporary Western societies as morally incompetent social actors (Cahill 1990).

New and David (1985) suggest that, in this role of maternal mediator *outside* the home, women are caught between love and understanding for their individual children's views, and pressures to make children conform. New and David thus conjure a strong image of the mother as looking two ways at once – towards her child, and towards others, with the woman herself placed between the child and these others, mediating the demands and requirements of each as she understands them. While women may vary as to how far they willingly take on and elaborate this mediatory role, they are almost all inevitably at times placed in the position of power-broker between their children and others. Furthermore, a woman may actively negotiate her own understandings of such situations. In particular, a mother may place herself more clearly (1) as advocate/agent acting on behalf of the child to seek other people's understanding and sympathy for the child's point of view, or (2) as representative/agent acting on behalf of wider society to bring the child 'into line' with other people's expectations.

In seeking to develop an analysis of mothers' position as mediators, there is scope for the development of a specifically sociological contribution to the understanding of maternal childrearing. However, it has been difficult to find an appropriate language for this analysis. I want to consider here how mothers with their children deal with the 'interface' between public and private lives. I am not seeking to describe differences between individual mothers, but between alternative courses of action which individual mothers may move between on different occasions and in different contexts. While I could have described these as alternative 'strategies', I have resisted doing so, because I did not want to use a language drawn primarily from public-world assumptions (Edwards and Ribbens 1991). Instead, I will develop an analysis of alternative 'approaches to mediation'. Thus the same woman may move between different approaches to mediation on different occasions.

The concepts of public and private are themselves of course also highly problematic (chapter 2, and Edwards 1993b), and I have somewhat glossed over these problems. In the substantive analysis of the women's childrearing accounts, I made a simple distinction between inside the home without outsiders present ('private'), and outside the home ('public'). While this worked as a starting point for analysis, it clearly oversimplifies very complex and subtle shifts of meaning of public and private. Not only may definitions of public and private settings be matters of degree and flexibility, it is also possible that the same setting might be *both public and private simultaneously*, from the point of view of different participants or issues. The work place may thus at times be experienced in ways that involve attitudes and forms of interaction more generally associated with private settings. Again, these are difficult if fascinating problems that cannot fully be unravelled here. For the present purposes what is relevant is that mothers themselves clearly drew boundaries between different settings, and regarded some settings as more public and others as more private.

Setting these conceptual difficulties to one side, I suggest that there are two dimensions relevant to the analysis of these approaches to maternal mediation: (1) weak or strong boundaries, and (2) high or low assertiveness.

The first question, then, concerns how far women perceive a strong boundary around the family, setting it apart from more public settings: are adult–child interactions in more public contexts expected to be the same as or different from those in the family/home? If a strong boundary operates, then public and private distinctions are maximised. While all social boundaries involve constructions from both sides (Wallman 1978), it is clear that those who feel on the weaker side of the boundary may defensively seek to develop a strong boundary. In the present discussion, I am concentrating on one side of the boundary, namely, mothers' own attitudes towards public/private distinctions. The social construction of such a boundary in children's lives is implied in the work of Newson and Newson (1978), where an important issue for the mothers of 7-year-olds was to teach their children to know the difference between behaviour that was acceptable in public and in private.[3] Hallden (1991) also found that her working class Swedish parents held different expectations about behaviour inside and outside the home, with greater conformity expected outside.

Secondly, how assertive are women in their attitudes towards settings outside the home: who is seen to have the power/authority to specify appropriate behaviour for children in public places? This dimension cross-cuts the first. *Whether or not* a woman perceives the family as strongly bounded, does the mother assert her *own* expectations about appropriate behaviour for her children, or does she give priority to *others'* expectations for her children and act as an agent on behalf of these others with her children? Clearly these two sets of expectations – the mother's and others' – may be related, but an assertive attitude means the woman is claiming greater power beyond the home, whereas a less assertive attitude gives greater priority to the wishes of others, and therefore gives them more power.

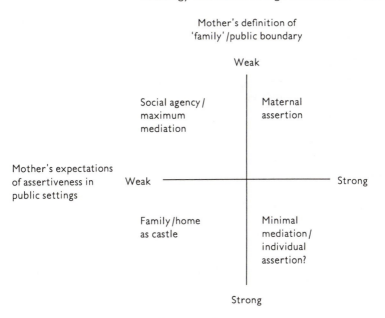

Figure 9.1 *Mothers' approaches to mediation*

When we superimpose these two dimensions, we create a four-fold typology.[4] In Figure 9.1, both the quadrants in the top half of the model concern a relatively open situation, such that boundary definitions are weak and continuity is expected between the home and elsewhere. This is divided by the assertiveness dimension, which describes the primary location of the mother's imagery and related expectations for children – is her imagery taken from ideas about the nature of public social life, and then imported into the family to understand childrearing (a less assertive attitude, found in the top left quadrant), or vice versa (a more assertive attitude, found in the top right quadrant)?

Both the quadrants in the bottom half of the figure concern a relatively closed situation with strong boundary definitions, such that different expectations are applied between the family/home and elsewhere. Again this is divided by the assertiveness dimension, the mother's attitude to settings outside the home – does she expect to be more or less assertive in settings outside the home? However, since she defines the family as different from these other settings, her level of assertiveness outside the family may be discontinuous with her ideas about childrearing inside the family/home.

It is possible to extend this model further, to combine it with the three typifications of children outlined in chapter 8. This logically generates twelve possible categories, and most of these potential categories could in fact be discerned within the accounts given by the women in this study. However, this does create a large number of rather speculative categories, and I will not elaborate all of them here, concentrating instead upon describing the four main approaches to mediation.[5]

Maternal assertion

In this approach, the boundary definition is weak, so that mothers expect continuity between the home and other settings. However, they are *assertive* towards non-family settings. Continuity between them thus depends upon the assumption that expectations that have been developed *within* the home may be extended to other non-familial social settings. In this case, expectations from the private setting are being applied to public settings, and childrearing typifications developed within the home are being taken as the basis for understanding how public life should operate. This is the approach to mediation which provides greatest scope for a woman to take ideas which she has developed in her childrearing within the home, and use them as a basis for asserting her ideas outside the home.

Social agency/maximum mediation

In this approach, there are also weak boundary definitions, so that again mothers expect continuity between the home and other settings. However, in this approach, the woman's attitude towards settings outside the home is *less assertive*. Thus her imagery of family life and childrearing at home is based upon her understanding and imagery of the relationship between the individual and the social group *outside* the home, and may indeed be rooted in imagery of the nature of 'society' as a whole. Thus expectations that depend upon perceptions of non-familial settings are taken into the home, and used as a basis for understanding interactions within the family. In this case, expectations from public settings are being drawn into private life, and the imagery used within the home is rooted in wider understandings of social life. Childrearing is thus typified by reference to what it means to be a member of society, and the mother's role within the home is understood as an agent acting on behalf of others. In this approach, then, the mother typifies the family as if it were a small model of society, and brings up her children accordingly.

The family/home as castle

Here there is a strong boundary definition, such that the family/ home is defined as a different sort of setting from more public interactions. However, in this approach the mother does not take an assertive attitude outside the home. This less assertive attitude means that individuals are expected to defer to others' social rules when moving outside the home, regardless of what is expected of them inside the home. In hierarchies outside the home, neither mother nor child can expect to be assertive against the wishes of those who are regarded as more powerful or authoritative. However, since this approach draws a strong boundary around the home/family, expectations of compliance to others' wishes which apply outside the home are not relevant within the home. In this approach, then, the weak level of assertion outside the home is limited by the family boundary, within which mothers may instead draw upon their own typifications of children. The family/home is thus a place where the mother feels able to develop her own ideas about childrearing and about appropriate personal relations, drawing on her own typifications of children, but outside she expects to defer to the wishes of others.

Individual assertion/minimal mediation?

Here there is again a strong boundary definition, but here there is also an *assertive* attitude outside the home in extra-familial settings. Different expectations apply within and outside the home, but these do not require the individual to take a less assertive attitude outside the home. On the other hand, since outside the home is different from inside, the mother's typifications of children are not seen as relevant beyond the home, opening the potential again for disjuncture between the two experiences.

In this approach, then, we find that the model itself does not contain necessary guidance within it as to what we may expect the mother's mediatory position to be. Outside the family/home is defined as different from inside, and yet the individual is not necessarily expected to defer to others, so how is the individual expected to behave? This approach thus leaves us with an open question as to *how* the mother will typify the relationship between individuals and social groups outside the home, since these are not implied either by her own typifications of childrearing, or by her deferential attitude to others. Furthermore, an examination of the mediatory practices apparent in the women's accounts suggests that this may be the approach which in fact minimises the mediatory role, since one possibility is that she will leave it to the child to assert her or his *own* wishes and views outside the home.

Overall, then, I have suggested three key dimensions for under-standing differences in women's childrearing perspectives across the various social settings within which women spend time with their children. There are thus three central questions to consider, the answers to which should provide considerable insights into the meanings underlying variations in mothers' dealings with their children across a range of substantive issues in their daily lives:

1 What is the typification of children being invoked in any particular circumstance?
2 What is the strength of the family boundary definition in any particular context?
3 What is the level of assertiveness in settings outside the family/home?

This model of approaches to maternal mediation is offered as a tentative basis for exploring a specifically sociological approach to issues of childrearing, by considering some of the ways in which childrearing within the home might relate to understandings of the relationship between the individual and social life in other settings. In this regard, the model allows for an analysis which moves across the different settings of more private and more public social life. It does not make assumptions about continuities between different social settings within the family and outside, but nor, where mothers do expect such continuities, does it make assumptions about the directions in which such continuities are thought to operate. It also suggests the possibility that different approaches to mediation may imply quite different maternal experiences of authority both inside and outside the home, such that women may at times use ideas they have developed in their mothering experi-ences within the home to assert these ideas in other settings.

This suggests that the assumptions underlying different images of children imply various understandings of the relationship between individuals and social life. The model draws attention to possible parallels between childrearing typifications and very longstanding issues of social and political philosophy, without presuming the direction of causality as to the origins of such philosophies. I shall explore such issues further in the next and final part.

Sociology and 'family life' – towards a feminist sociology

Sociological theorists tend to neglect family lives, and to treat society as if it occurs solely in public settings such as employment or the State (chapter 1). One likely reason for this concerns the fundamental division made in traditional sociology between macro and micro levels of analysis. This division tends to be paralleled by the distinction between structure and action, with social structure conceptualised by reference to the macro level of analysis. Since 'the family' is by definition a small scale unit, it tends inevitably to become marginalised within such analyses, and it is very difficult to see how a micro unit, such as 'the family', can have any 'causal' significance for structures occurring at the macro level. In this regard, Giddens' recent work (1991, 1992) is particularly welcome for paying attention to the implications of personal lives for the nature of modern social order. Nevertheless, I would suggest that this constitutes but the first step by a leading contemporary theorist towards the recognition of the centrality of family life, rather than its marginality, for any understanding of 'society'.

There is also a tendency for some parallel methodological divisions to occur, as for example between detailed empiricism based on localised settings, and abstract theorising about global settings. One area where such issues have been explicitly debated is that of educational ethnography:

> . . . if 'micro' researchers often seemed, like ostriches, to be so pre-occupied with the fine-grained detail of school and classroom life, that they rarely took their necks out of the sand to see what was happening in the world outside, theorists of 'the system' appeared all too often to have little contact with the 'real world' at all (Hargreaves 1985: 22).

Hargreaves suggests that one way of tackling this issue is for micro analysis to be linked with macro through a consideration of how interactions in macro settings relate to interactions in micro settings: 'even outside the school, policy still has to be negotiated and implemented through interaction, be this face to face, on the telephone, or via correspondence' (1985: 43).

I would like to go further, to suggest that we may need to abandon altogether the distinction between macro and micro levels of society, which intrinsically view society as hierarchically organised. While I am not disputing the hierarchical nature of much social interaction, I am suggesting that it is not helpful to use concepts that make a priori assumptions about the existence and social placing of such hierarchies. We need an approach that enables us to see 'structure' occurring even within small scale interactions, and 'action' occurring within large scale settings. Micro and macro would thus become a distinction, not between different levels of society, but between aggregative and interactive *forms of analysis*, which are relevant to all areas of social life. Historical sociology may have a particular contribution to make to such an approach.

Feminist theorists have of course paid much attention to the rather different concepts of public and private, which are also potentially dualistic and may even be viewed as inevitably hierarchical. However, I believe these concepts have been extremely fruitful in the present study, being open to a flexible analysis rooted within women's own understandings. Furthermore, they refer to a distinction that is central to women's lives with their children, and central to the marginalisation of women within the study of 'society' (Yeatman 1986). I suggest that the concepts of public and private, sensitively and sensibly applied, have considerable sociological potential, drawing our attention to a highly significant feature of contemporary Western societies and enabling an analysis that considers how boundaries are drawn both by large scale social policy institutions and by individuals in their own (small scale) everyday lives.

These concepts need careful use in research, just as we need to use the concepts of 'the family' and 'society' carefully. Furthermore, with all these concepts, we have to beware of their ideological overtones, and avoid reifying assumptions of their 'reality' as monolithic and fixed entities. Instead we must consider how they may be used by people themselves in their daily lives, not in terms of dualisms, but as constituting a flexible and diverse framework by which they make sense of their own subjective realities, in interactions and negotiations with others. However, I believe that the concepts of public and private carry far greater potential than the concepts of micro and macro for making women's lives visible, and, moreover, for seeing women as active social agents rather than as passive dependents within male social structures.

At the same time, there may be a danger within this discussion of falling into a sort of liberal pluralistic vision of the nature of social life, with people viewed as moving between different settings, constructing their own boundaries and negotiating their interconnections. What is missing so far in my discussion, of course, is any reference to *systematic differences of power* between or within different settings, or in the construction of particular settings in the first place.

Yet 'power' is another key sociological concept which, like 'social class', has been conceptualised from within male concerns with work and government in public settings, and cannot therefore be used in relation to women's lives without *careful reconsideration* from within the private sphere. Meyer (1991) points out how power has been discussed in ways that divide it rigidly from ideas about love, and Rich writes that, 'The language of patriarchy insists on a dichotomy: for one person to have power, others – or another –

must be powerless' (1977: 67). Rich suggests that women's power may be found, not in power *over* others, but in 'transforming power' (p. 99).

A reconsideration of the concept of power in line with meanings and issues relevant to parent–child relations – as viewed from *within* private settings – is a project beyond the scope of the present study. However, since the parent–child relationship is where we first experience social differences in power, it is a project of vital importance.

There have been some analyses of power within family lives, but these have tended not to call the concept itself fundamentally into question, defining power in terms of a capacity to create certain effects (Cromwell and Olsen 1975, Siltanen and Stanworth 1984). These writers do not question what purposes are being served by the exercise of this capacity, or how and why it is being evoked. A particularly important issue potentially raised by considering power within domestically based lives is the question of whether the exercise of power necessarily signifies a conflict of interests, or can rather be understood sometimes as an expression of caring. What Rich hints at is the possibility of power being a creative and energising force that need not necessarily be used *against* another.

Thus the *exercise of power* in the private sphere (even in what may appear as a fairly traditional form such as the discipline of children) may be regarded as itself *indicative of caring* – in an extreme form it may be seen in the remark 'We hit you because we love you' (see chapter 1). Within the childrearing accounts given in the present study, the exercise of power might be described as a duty that women are burdened with, which they are *obliged to exercise* to meet the needs of their children, despite any opposition from their children. Power in this case is being exercised to further the interests of the children, who are subjected to the power, rather than those of the mother, who exercises the power (see chapter 8). Indeed, it is on this basis that the exercise of power may be construed as caring.

Such an understanding of course presumes a close identification of interests between mother and child. While an important element of what could be regarded as ideological power may be involved here, through the presumption that adults are the people who know and define children's real needs and interests, even so, this ideological power may not always be obviously exercised so as to define children's interests in terms of the immediate interests of those adults. The exercise of power is here close to the exercise of dutiful responsibility.

Thus, for example, when a mother first lets her child play outside the confines of home and garden, she may feel obliged to exert a vigilant discipline to enforce the limits of the child's freedom of movement. She may regard this discipline as a burdensome obligation to exert power, which she nevertheless undertakes in order to further what she perceives as the *child's needs* for greater independence combined with safety. On the other hand, an approach which minimises the use of discipline may also involve mothers in exerting power in a different direction, in this case, in order to keep other adults at a distance, to create a particular social setting where children may be free to express their own needs without adult constraint (see chapter 8). In the longer-term view, childrearing may raise important issues about *how we conceptualise interests as attached to particular individuals* in the first place – how we define the boundaries of 'the individual' to whom interests are thought to be attached. Indeed, Bernardes and Keddie (1994) have discussed how the notion of citizenship might be extended beyond 'the individual' to 'the family' as a collective entity.

Power is a concept that is not often used in the discussion of family relationships, being more commonly associated with a discourse based in public settings. The language of power is ideologically excluded from the discourse of family life. Mothers themselves are unlikely spontaneously to discuss their interactions with their children in terms of a power struggle, even though they might describe family life as a battle ground. This discussion of power thus highlights the potentially political nature of family life, but it also raises further difficulties about how to find an appropriate language.

It is hardly a new notion to suggest that family life may involve issues akin to public politics: 'There is scarcely any less bother in the running of a family than in that of an entire state. Any domestic business is no less importunate for being less important' (Montaigne 1533–1592). This perspective suggests that we could analyse family politics as analogous to State politics, open to the same analysis of power as sociologists have applied to the analysis of public settings. However, there are limits to such an approach because we are uncritically borrowing analytical tools developed within public political life.

Siltanen and Stanworth (1984) suggest that one of the ways in which women's orientations are defined as apolitical is through malestream definitions of *moral issues* as lying outside the realm of politics. In this regard, one of the central conclusions of the present study is that women's childrearing perspectives can be analysed as the expression of *political and social philosophy*, since they involve fundamental considerations of the relationship between individuality and social life. Such considerations were apparent in the women's childrearing accounts, either through explicit discussion or through the use of images of children which implicitly assume such moral issues of political philosophy. There are clear parallels between the typifications of children and discussions of moral and wider political *philosophy* developed by men within the public setting.

Thus a key difference of childrearing was analysed as being rooted in one of two major images (chapter 7). The first image is a view of children as potentially destructive and anarchic (even evil) without the beneficial regulation of social life. This view clearly has parallels with a Hobbesian political philosophy which sees a Social Contract as the basis of moral and political principles which will regulate Man's amoral nature, in other words, individuals are destructive to themselves *and* others without the beneficial regulation of society. The second image of children concerns a Rousseau-esque conception of children as naturally innocent. In Rousseau's political philosophy any Social Contract should be minimised to allow maximum expression for the liberty of every individual: individuals are potentially creative and constructive if their nature is not distorted by the harmful influence of society.

The underlying issues at stake have very longstanding roots in Western culture at least. While these seventeenth and eighteenth century philosophers were concerned to develop a basis of social morality that was not rooted in religion, we can clearly also see parallels with *religious imagery* in mothers' typifications of children and appropriate maternal responses. Thus the directive typification is close to the religious view that the child's Will must be destroyed if his or her soul is to be saved, while the adaptive typification is closer to a view in which social life is in danger of distorting and destroying a childhood Garden of Eden through the introduction of adult Knowledge.

While these Western political philosophers were concerned with individuality within the burgeoning Nation State, this issue was also paralleled with a concern with equality, which is the basis for the third imagery of children described in the present study. Here children are typified as small people, such that there are no prior assumptions of hierarchies of control and authority. This implicit concern with equality in relation to children as small people is also expressed explicitly in political issues of children's Rights.

However, parents may view this typification as having limited relevance due to children's perceived irrationality, which is regarded as fundamental to children's Otherness from adults. Hobbes' views of the Social Contract were modified by Locke, who suggested that Man might have moral principles even outside the Social Contract, but only once rationality has been taught in childhood. Locke is thus particularly interesting here, since he specifically related his belief in children's need for regulation to a view of children as irrational. This view of the rational individual is also strongly related to notions of the Will as potentially destructive. Thus he suggests that Man should only have freedom to exercise his own Will if he has learned reason and may thus be *self*-governing, and he uses this as a basis for legitimising the power of parents over their children:

> The freedom then of Man and Liberty of acting according to his own Will, is grounded on his having Reason, which is able to instruct him in that Law he is to govern himself by, and make him know how far he is left to the freedom of his own Will. To turn him loose to an unrestrain'd Liberty, before he has Reason to guide him, is not the allowing him the priviledge of his Nature, to be free; but to thrust him out amongst Brutes, and abandon him to a state as wretched, and as much beneath that of a Man, as theirs. This is that which puts the Authority into the parents' hands to govern the minority of their Children. (Locke 1979: 242)

I am pointing here to some clear parallels between the analysis I have offered of the women's childrearing accounts in the present study, and longstanding issues of moral and political philosophy and religion that have been primarily developed by men in the public sphere. Furthermore, such images of children are widespread in a variety of contemporary discourses (see e.g. Warner 1989). There is, then, a further potential question of how these parallels have occurred and which social setting has been the primary source for the development of such ideas. I suggest we should avoid making assumptions about *how* such political philosophies are related to typifications of children as these are practised in child-rearing, and which determines the other, that is whether the typifications of children have been drawn from the political philosophies or *vice versa*.

Thus we should not *assume* that women's childrearing perspectives simply reflect these cultural themes as they are expressed in public discourses. As Warner hints, and as Chodorow and Contratto (1982) suggest more explicitly, adult images of the nature of children may be rooted within fantasies connected with our own childhoods. From this perspective, then, religious and political philosophies may also be rooted within the fantasies of our earliest years. Walkerdine and Lucey suggest that: 'fantasies and wishes also circulate at the social level through the production of meanings in scientific accounts (such as those about mothering in developmental psychology)' (1989: 148). Hints of such processes at work may also be found in sociology. Thus Sharrock and Watson, using an ethnomethodological orientation, characterise the notions of structure and agency as follows: 'The two seem inimical: "structure" apparently means givenness, constraint, stability, whilst "agency" seemingly implies creativity, autonomy, fluidity. How then do structure and agency relate in society: is it primarily one or the other? . . . Which should we favour?' (1988: 58).

This sounds very like some of the earlier characterisations given concerning the differences between directive and adaptive parenting. Thus Diane Bell writes: 'The division of things public from those private and things domestic from those political renders much of women's labour invisible and denies that constructions of self, forged in the little worlds of home, also give form to our cultural understandings of the socio-economic structures of the big world' (1990: 12).

We should therefore consider the possibility that a variety of features of social experience *in domestic settings* are actually the basis *upon which* more public settings have historically been constructed. We might refer here, for example, to the relevance of gendered family dynamics for gendered processes in public employment settings, as described by many feminist researchers. More fundamentally still, I have suggested that age divisions are basic to understandings of family lives, and constitute our primary experience of hierarchy. There is thus scope for an analysis of *age divisions in the domestic setting* as the primary basis for the development of *class divisions in public settings* (see e.g. historical evidence such as Clawson 1980).

In the discussion of maternal approaches to mediation, however, I have suggested a key issue concerning the boundedness of family lives, and whether or not continuities of meanings are expected to occur between public and private settings. Thus there are also *dis*continuities in the ways we ideologically construct private and public lives, such that in some respects domestic life is idealised as based upon fundamentally different assumptions from public life. Understandings of childhood in particular are intimately interconnected with understandings of dependency. Dependency creates vulnerability to others, and private settings are idealised as the place where such vulnerability may be protected and cared for. By contrast, in public settings any such vulnerabilities may be exploited against us for the benefit of others. It is for this reason that power may carry such different connotations within the two settings.

All of this of course represents idealisations rather than concrete experiences. Yet this idealisation helps to explain the importance attached to private lives in contemporary industrialised societies. We expect that our intimates within the domestic sphere will not take advantage of us, and we look for the family home to be truly a haven from a *heart*less world that is seen to be based on instrumental rationality (Lasch 1976, Zaretsky 1982). But in 'real' families and domestic units such expectations of safety and nurturance may often not be fulfilled. Hence the extreme *polarities of evaluations* that are used to describe modern family life – as progressively moving towards harmony and equality, a modern-day success story, or as a torture chamber of violent passions and mental illness. Indeed, Chodorow and Contratto (1982) suggest that such polarised images are *themselves* the result of a process which invests with reality the continuing fantasies of childhood, endowing care-givers with total power used either for complete gratification or for complete tyranny in relation to our infant helplessness.

However, just as these writers suggest that both of these polarised images of mothers are rooted within the same experiences of infant helplessness, I would also like to suggest that it is the continuation into adulthood of our childhood expectations of family life – as the place where our dependency needs will be met – that gives rise to both the attractiveness and the distress of family life more generally. It is not so much that some families are experienced as providing harmony and happiness for their members, while other families are experienced as violent and destructive, but that *both* experiences are the outcome of *similar* processes. Contradictions are indeed to be found at 'the heart of family life'. Favourable and unfavourable evaluations of 'the family' are thus rooted within the *same* central themes, of *power and vulnerability*, and the different ways in which these themes are experienced in public settings and private 'family life'. Furthermore, we cannot understand how they are experienced within one setting without also understanding how they are *experienced in the other*.

The primary group in which childcare occurs is the site in which we first experience social life, and develop understandings about its meanings. In contemporary Western society, this primary group is generally defined as 'the family' – even though the relevance of the father to childcare may be ambiguous. 'The family' may therefore in many ways give us our first knowledge of all that is experienced as good and bad about what it is to be a social being. It is within 'the family' that our needs as individuals are first given meaning and recognition, and it is here that we first experience the meeting (or otherwise) of those needs within a caring response. It is within 'the family' that we first experience dependency, and the obligations of the strong to meet such dependency needs. Nevertheless this dependency is itself structured in socially patterned ways which may be mediated in various ways by women-as-mothers.

However, it is also within 'the family' that we first experience differences, divisions and hierarchies, which in 'the family' are heavily structured around gender and age. Along with obligations to meet dependency needs, then, there may be reciprocal obligations of respect and deference to the strong. Thus the meeting of dependency needs also occurs alongside relations of power and control. If hierarchy is first experienced within 'the family', and hierarchy involves differences of power that are the basis of political life, then 'the family' is the site of the first political experience. It is in this sense that childrearing can be seen as a highly political activity. It is time we recognised that ideas about 'good' and 'bad' parenting are not based in objective scientific descriptions, but in fundamental differences of view about the nature of social life. We need a feminist sociology to develop such an analysis, since childrearing is truly the basis for the reproduction of 'society' as well as a central preoccupation in the lives of women.

Notes

1. In Britain particularly, however, sociologists have been at pains to distinguish class from income level, and these two variables do not simply map onto one another in British data on class patterns and income levels (see e.g. Hamilton and Hirszowicz 1987).

2. These ideas are elaborated further in Ribbens 1990a, chapter 9. While these thoughts are clearly highly speculative, they are in line with the evidence obtained from the eight grandmother–daughter pairs interviewed altogether for the present study.

3. See also some of the autobiographical accounts in Heron (1985). Harriet Gilbert, for example, discusses how she was taught that one set of rules about gender operated inside the home, but a different set operated when there were visitors or when she went outside the home.

4. I recognise that I am here introducing concepts beyond what could be regarded as topical terms, even though they are fundamentally rooted in social actors' own constructs. As with all typological models, there is a considerable danger of oversimplification at many different levels, but this may be worthwhile and insightful if we regard the simplification as an aid to thought, offering us signposts to the complexities of real lives, but not to be mistaken for any direct representation of social life. The model has been extended as a result of two interlinked processes: firstly, the application of theoretical writing about 'the family' and its relationship with non-familial settings, leading to the logical generation of further categories (what Barton and Lazarsfeld 1969 have described as a systematic typology), and secondly through a consideration of how these categories relate to the analyses of the women's actual childrearing accounts, leading to the introduction of further dimensions within these logically generated categories.

5. Readers who are interested in exploring the full model, describing all 12 categories, are referred to Ribbens (1990a), chapter 9.

Appendix: Further Details
of the Sample

Altogether, a total of 24 women were interviewed in three main stages of work. In the first phase I contacted eight women through intermediaries from my own friendship networks. For the main phase I approached women via playgroups (which meant of course that they had at least one other child of pre-school age as well as an eldest child aged 7), leading to 11 interviews. I then sought a further 'theoretical sample' (Glaser and Strauss 1968), chosen specifically to include women who were of interest in the light of the emerging analysis. The developing focus around issues of public/private boundaries led me to include women who had made different choices in relation to public settings, as regards either education or employment. Five women were contacted through intermediaries starting from my own personal networks, including two women who were in full-time employment, and three women who had made different decisions about their children's education: to use private education, to use a Steiner school, or to educate at home.

The decision to recruit the main part of my sample via playgroups was carefully made with regard to the crucial need to establish trust at the point of access. Playgroups provided for informal contact with women, previously unconnected with me, who had children of suitable ages. Playgroup registers also meant that I did not rely upon a volunteer sample, as in much qualitative research, and was able to include women who would certainly not have volunteered – in fact, there were no refusals from the playgroup sample, although some were unsure at first. Furthermore, in the main geographical area of study, I carried out a survey which established that 76 per cent of 3- and 4-year-olds were on a playgroup register or waiting list (Ribbens 1990a).

If we compare various characteristics of the resulting sample with national statistics, we find that as a group they were in line with national trends in lone parenthood but were more middle class than national figures – as one might expect from the general pattern in the South East of England. The households had incomes spread around the average income for home-owning households in the main county concerned. The employment position of the women was perplexing, with higher than average levels of part-time employment, but much of this very marginal and transient.

Overall characteristics

Children in each household

3 children................	7 households
2 children................	13 households
1 child	3 households

1 Down's syndrome child, 1 child with a fine motor disability, and 3 children with eczema and asthma.

Household income

£25,000 + ...	7	(in 2 cases this involved 2 full-time or almost full-time incomes)
£20,000–24,000	4	
£15,000–19,000	2	
£10,000–14,000	3	
Under £10,000.............	1	
Inconclusive answers given...	2	
Income level not asked......	4	

The average household income of borrowers with a major building society in the locality at this time was £18,000.

Mothers' employment status

Full-time.................	4	(including 2 working from home, and 2 theoretically sampled)
17+ hours weekly..........	5	
Under 17 hours............	6	
No paid employment	8	

Mothers' educational qualifications

None.....................	2	
O-levels/CSEs.............	6	
A-levels..................	1	
Teacher trained/graduate	3	
Graduate	3	
Other post-school training ...	8	(2 part-time)

Conventional class classification (derived from OPCS 1980 classifications)

Social class	Fathers	Mothers[1]
I Professional	3	0
II Intermediate	14	12
IIIA Skilled non-manual	2	10
IIIB Skilled manual	4	1
IV Semi-skilled manual	1	
Not known		1

[1] Based on the highest category of full-time employment the woman had had in her working life.

References

Abbott, Pamela and Sapsford, Roger (1987) *Women and Social Class*. London: Tavistock.

Abbott, Pamela and Sapsford, Roger (1990) 'Health visiting: policing the family?', in Pamela Abbot and Clare Wallace (eds), *Sociology of the Caring Professions*. Lewes: Falmer Press.

Abrams, Fran (1994) 'Part-time schooling from age three urged', *The Independent*, 18 March: 8.

Abrams, Philip (1982) *Historical Sociology*. Somerset: Open Books.

Adlam, Diana, Henriques, Julian, Rose, Nikolas, Salfield, Angie, Venn, Couze, and Walkerdine, Valerie (1977) 'Psychology, ideology and the human subject', *Ideology and Consciousness* 1(2): 1–56.

Agar, Michael H. (1980) *The Professional Stranger: an informal introduction to ethnography*. London: Academic Press.

Alanen, Leena (1990) 'Rethinking socialisation, the family and childhood', in Patricia Adler and Peter Adler (eds), *Sociological Studies of Child Development. Vol. 3*. Greenwich, Connecticut: JAI Press.

Alanen, Leena (1994) 'Gender and generation: feminism and the "child question"', in Jens Qvortrup, Marjatta Bardy, Giovanni Sgritta and Helmut Wintersberger (eds), *Childhood Matters: social theory, practice and politics*. Aldershot: Avebury.

Alibhai, Yasmin (1989) 'Burning in the cold', in Katherine Gieve (ed.), *Balancing Acts: on being a mother*. London: Virago Press.

Allan, Graham (1989a) 'Insiders and outsiders: boundaries around the home', in Graham Allan and Graham Crow (eds), *Home and Family: creating the domestic sphere*. Basingstoke: Macmillan.

Allan, Graham (1989b) *Friendship: developing a sociological perspective*. New York: Harvester Wheatsheaf.

Allan, Graham and Crow, Graham (1989) 'Introduction', in Graham Allan and Graham Crow (eds), *Home and Family: creating the domestic sphere*. Basingstoke: Macmillan.

Allan, Graham and Crow, Graham (1990) 'Constructing the domestic sphere: the emergence of the modern home in post-War Britain', in Helen Corr and Lynn Jamieson (eds), *The Politics of Everyday Life: continuity and change in work and the family*. London: Macmillan.

Alwin, Duane F. (1990) 'Historical changes in parental orientations to children', in Patricia Adler and Peter Adler (eds), *Sociological Studies of Child Development. Vol. 3*. Greenwich, Connecticut: JAI Press.

Anderson, Michael (ed.) 1971 *Sociology of the Family*. Harmondsworth: Penguin.

Atkinson, Paul (1979) 'Research design in ethnography', in *Research Methods in Education and the Social Sciences*, DE304. Milton Keynes: Open University.

Backett, Kathryn (1982) *Mothers and Fathers: a study of the development and negotiation of parental behaviour*. London: Macmillan.

Badinter, Elizabeth (1981) *The Myth of Motherhood: an historical view of the maternal instinct*. London: Souvenir Press. (First published by Flammeron, Paris, 1980.)

Barton, Allen and Lazarsfeld, Paul F. (1969) (first published 1955) 'Qualitative data as sources of hypotheses', in George J. McCall and J.L. Simmons (eds), *Issues in Participant Observation: a text and reader*. Reading: Addison-Wesley.

Baumrind, Diana (1967) 'Childcare practices anteceding three patterns of pre-school behaviour', *Genetic Psychology Monographs*, 75: 43–88.

Baumrind, Diana (1972) 'Socialisation and instrumental competence in young children', in Willard Hartup (ed.), *The Young Child: reviews of research, volume 2*. Washington: National Association for the Education of Young Children.

Baumrind, Diana (1975) 'Some thoughts about childrearing', in Urie Bronfenbrenner and Maureen A. Mahoney (eds), *Influences on Human Development* (2nd edn). Hinsdale, Illinois: Dryden Press.

Belenky, Mary Field, Clinchy, Blythe McVicker, Goldberger, Nancy Rule and Tarule, Jill Mattuck (1986) *Women's Ways of Knowing: the development of self, voice and mind*. New York: Basic Books.

Bell, Diane (1990) 'Doing anthropology at home: a feminist initiative in the bicentennial year', in Nurket Sirman and Kamala Ganesh (eds), *Anthropological Perspectives on Research and Teaching Concerning Women*. New Delhi: Sage.

Bell, Linda (1994) 'My Child, Your Child: Child-care structures and patterns of exchange between mothers in a Hertfordshire town', PhD thesis, London University (forthcoming).

Bell, Linda and Ribbens, Jane (1994) 'Isolated housewives and complex maternal worlds? The significance of social contacts between women with young children in industrial societies', *Sociological Review* 42(2): 227–62.

Bellah, Robert N., Madsen, Richard, Sullivan, William M., Swidler, Ann and Tipon, Steven M. (1985) *Habits of the Heart: individualism and commitment in American family life*. Berkeley: University of California Press.

Berger, Peter L. and Luckman, Thomas (1971) *The Social Construction of Reality: a treatise in the sociology of knowledge*. Harmondsworth: Penguin University Books. (First published in the USA 1966.)

Bernard Van der Leer Foundation (1992) 'Where have all the fathers gone?' *Newsletter*, No. 65, January.

Bernard, Jessie (1982) *The Future of Marriage*. New Haven: Yale University Press (2nd ed).

Bernardes, Jon (1985a) '"Family ideology": identification and exploration', *Sociological Review*, 33(2): 275–97.

Bernardes, Jon (1985b) 'Do we really know what "the family" is?', in P. Close and R. Collins, *Family and Economy*. London: Macmillan.

Bernardes, Jon (1986a) 'Research note: In search of "the family" – analysis of the (1981) United Kingdom census', *Sociological Review* 34(4): 828–36.

Bernardes, Jon (1986b) 'Multi-dimensional developmental pathways: a proposal to facilitate the conceptualisation of "family diversity"', *Sociological Review* 33(2): 275–97.

Bernardes, Jon (1987) '"Doing things with words": Sociology and "Family Policy" debates', *Sociological Review* 35(4): 679–702.

Bernardes, Jon (1988) 'Founding the *New* "Family Studies"', *Sociological Review* 36(1): 57–86.

Bernardes, Jon and Keddie, David (1994) 'Family Citizenship and Family Associationism', Paper presented to the conference, *Family Associations in Europe*, Milan, April.

Bernstein, B. (1971) *Class, Codes and Control Volume 1: theoretical studies towards a sociology of language*. London: Routledge and Kegan Paul.

Bernstein, B. (1975) *Class, Codes and Control Volume 3: towards a theory of educational transmissions*. London: Routledge and Kegan Paul.

Bertaux, Daniel and Delacroix, Catherine (1992) 'Where have all the daddies gone?' in Ulla Bjornberg (ed.), *European Parents in the 1990's: contradictions and comparisons*. New Brunswick: Transaction Publishers.

Berryman, Julia (1991) 'Perspectives on later motherhood', in Ann Phoenix, Anne Woollett and Eva Lloyd (eds), *Motherhood: meanings, practices and ideologies*. London: Sage.

Bhavnani, K. and Coulson, M. (1986) 'Transforming socialist-feminism: the challenge of racism', *Feminist Review* 23, Summer.

Birch, Maxine (1993) 'The Goddess/God Within: an initial exploration into alternative health-seeking practices and spirituality', Paper presented to the Sociology of Religion Study Group Conference, *Postmodernity and Religion*, University of Bristol, 31 March.

Bjornberg, Ulla (1992) 'Parenting in Transition: an introduction and summary', in Ulla Bjornberg (ed.), *European Parents in the 1990's: contradictions and comparisons*. New Brunswick: Transaction Publishers.

Blaxter, Mildred and Paterson, Elizabeth (1982) *Mothers and Daughters: a three-generational study of health attitudes and behaviour*. London: Heinemann.

Boh, Katya (1989) 'European family life patterns – a reppraisal', in Katya Boh, Maren Bak, Cristine Clason, Maja Pankratova, Jens Qvortrup, Giovanni B. Sgritta and Kari Waerness (eds), *Changing Patterns of European Family Life: a comparative analysis of fourteen European countries*. London: Routledge.

Boh, Katya, Bak, Maren, Clason, Cristine, Pankratova, Maja, Qvortrup, Jens, Sgritta, Giovanni B. and Waerness, Kari (eds) (1989) *Changing Patterns of European Family Life: a comparative analysis of fourteen European countries*. London: Routledge.

Bone, Margaret (1977) *Pre-school Children and the Need for Daycare*. London: HMSO.

Boulton, Mary Georgina (1983) *On Being a Mother: a study of women and pre-school children*. London: Tavistock.

Bourdieu, P. (1973) 'Cultural reproduction and social reproduction', in R. Brown (ed.), *Knowledge, Education and Cultural Change*. London: Tavistock.

Brannen, Julia and Moss, Peter (1988) *New Mothers at Work: employment and childcare*. London: Unwin Paperbacks.

Breen, Dana (1989) *Talking with Mothers*. London: Free Association Books.

Brodbar-Nemzer, Jay Y. (1986) 'Marital relationships and self-esteem: how Jewish families are different', *Journal of Marriage and the Family* 48(1): 89–98.

Bronfenbrenner, Urie (1958) 'Socialisation and social class through time and space', in E.E. Maccoby, T.M. Newcomb and E.L. Hartley (eds), *Readings in Social Psychology*. New York: Holt, Rinehart and Winston.

Bronfenbrenner, Urie (1979) *The Ecology of Human Development*. Cambridge, MA: Harvard University Press.

Bronfenbrenner, Urie and Mahoney, Maureen A. (eds) (1975) *Influences on Human Development* (2nd edn). Hinsdale Illinois: Dryden Press.

Brophy, Julia (1987) 'Motherhood and the Law', Talk given at the Thomas Coram Institute, London, 27 May.

Bruner, Jerome (1980) *Under Five in Britain*. London: Grant McIntyre.

Bryant, Bridget, Harris, Miriam and Newton, Dee (1980) *Children and Minders*. London: Grant McIntyre.

Burkitt, Ian (1991) *Social Selves: theories of the social formation of personality*. London: Sage.

Byng-Hall, John (1985) 'Family scripts: a useful bridge between theory and practice', *Journal of Family Therapy*, 7(3): 301–6.

Cahill, Spencer (1990) 'Childhood and public life: reaffirming biographical divisions', *Social Problems*, 37(3): 390–402.

Cheal, David (1991) *Family and the State of Theory*. New York: Harvester Wheatsheaf.

Chester, Robert (1986) 'The conventional family is alive and living in Britain', in Jeffrey Weeks (ed.), *Family Directory*. London: British Library Information Guide 1.

Chodorow, Nancy (1978) *The Reproduction of Mothering: psychoanalysis and the sociology of gender*. Berkeley: University of California Press.

Chodorow, Nancy and Contratto, Nancy (1982) 'The fantasy of the perfect mother', in Barrie Thorne and Marilyn Yalom (eds), *Rethinking the Family: some feminist questions*. New York: Longman.

Clawson, M.A. (1980) 'Early modern fraternalism and the patriarchal family', *Feminist Studies*, 6(2): 368–91.

Cohen, Stan (1973) *Folk Devils and Moral Panics*. London: Paladin.

Cole, Michael (1981) 'Society, mind and development', in Frank Kessel and Alexander Siegel (eds), *The Child and Other Cultural Inventions*. New York: Praeger.

Cooper, Jacqui (1989) 'Births outside marriage: recent trends and associated demographic and social changes', *Population Trends*, 63 (Spring): 8–18.

Cornwell, Jocelyn (1985) *Hard-Earned Lives*. London: Tavistock.

Cox, Kathleen (1990) '"The Cinderella Complex" in men with children', Paper presented to the Women in Psychology Conference, University of Birmingham.

Cromwell, Ronald and Olsen, David (eds) (1975) *Power in Families*. New York: Sage/John Wiley.

Crow, Graham (1989) 'The post-War development of the modern domestic ideal', in Graham Allan and Graham Crow (eds), *Home and Family: creating the domestic sphere*. Basingstoke: Macmillan.

Cunningham-Burley, Sarah (1985) 'Constructing grandparenthood: anticipating appropriate action', *Sociology*, 19(3): 421–36.

Cunningham-Burley, Sarah (1986) 'Becoming a grandparent', *New Society*, 7 February: 229–30.

Daniels, W.W. (1980) *Maternity Rights: the experience of women*. London: Policy Studies Institute.

Daniels, Denise and Moos, Rudolf H. (1989) 'Exosystem influences on family and child functioning', in Elizabeth Goldsmith (ed.), *Work and Family: theory, research and applications*. London: Sage.

David, Miriam (1988) 'Home school relations' in Anthony Green and Stephen Ball (eds), *Progress and Inequality in Comprehensive Education*. London: Routledge and Kegan Paul.

David, Miriam, Edwards, Rosalind, Hughes, Mary and Ribbens, Jane (1993) *Mothers and Education: Inside Out? Exploring family-education policy and experience*. Basingstoke: Macmillan.

David, Miriam, West, Anne and Ribbens, Jane (1994) *Mothers Intuition? Choosing secondary schools*. London: Taylor and Francis.

Davidoff, Leonore, L'Esperance, Jean and Newby, Howard (1976) 'Landscape with figures: home and community in English society', in Juliet Mitchell and Ann Oakley (eds), *The Rights and Wrongs of Women*. Harmondsworth: Penguin.

Davies, Bronwyn (1982) *Life in the Classroom and Playground: the accounts of primary school children*. London: Routledge and Kegan Paul.

Davies, Karen (1990) *Women, Time and the Weaving of the Strands of Everyday Life*. Aldershot: Avebury.

Davies, Lynn (1985) 'Ethnography and status: focussing on gender in educational research', in Robert Burgess (ed.), *Field Methods in the Study of Education*. Lewes: Falmer Press.

Davin, Anna (1978) 'Imperialism and motherhood', *History Workshop Journal*, No. 5: 9–67.

Dawe, Alan (1973) 'The role of experience in the construction of social theory: an essay in reflexive sociology', *Sociological Review*, 21(1): 25–55.

Denzin, Norman K. (1977) *Childhood Socialisation*. San Francisco: Jossey-Bass.

Denzin, Norman (1987) 'Postmodern children', *Society*, 24.

Devine, Fiona (1989) 'Privatised families and their homes', in Graham Allan and Graham Crow (eds), *Home and Family: creating the domestic sphere*. Basingstoke: Macmillan.

Dingwall, Robert and Eekelaar, J. (1986) 'Judgements of Solomon: pyschology and family law', in Martin Richards and Paul Light (eds), *Children of Social Worlds: development in a social context*. Cambridge: Polity Press.

Dizard, Jan E. and Gadlin, Howard (1990) *The Minimal Family*. Amherst: University of Massachusetts Press.

Doucet, Andrea (1991) *Striking a Balance: gender divisions of labour in housework, childcare and employment*, Working Paper No. 6, Sociological Research Group, Cambridge University.

Douglas, J.W.B. (1967) *The Home and the School: a study of ability and attainment in the primary school*. London: Panther. (First published 1964.)

Dreikurs, Rudolf with Soltz, Vicki (1972) *Happy Children: a challenge to parents*. Glasgow: Fontana/Collins. (First published in the USA 1964.)

Dreitzel, Hans Peter (ed.) (1973) *Childhood and Socialisation*. New York: Macmillan.

Dubois, Ellen, Buhle, Mari Jo, Kaplan, Temma, Lerner, Gerda and Smith-Rosenberg, Carroll (1980) 'Politics and culture in women's history: a symposium', *Feminist Studies*, 6(1): 26–65.

Dumont, Louis (1972) *Homo Hierarchicus*. London: Granada. (First published in France 1966.)

Duncombe, Jean and Marsden, Dennis (1993) 'Love and intimacy: the gender division of emotion and "emotion work"', *Sociology*, 27(2): 221–42.

Duvall, E.M. (1946) 'Conceptions of parenthood', *American Journal of Sociology*, 52: 193–203.

Edwards, Rosalind (1992) 'Pre-school home-visiting projects: a case study of mothers' expectations and experiences', *Gender and Education*, 1(2): 165–82.

Edwards, Rosalind (1993a) '"The University" and the "University of Life": boundaries between ways of knowing', in Miriam David, Rosalind Edwards,

Mary Hughes and Jane Ribbens (eds), *Mothers and Education: Inside Out? Exploring family-education policy and experience.* Basingstoke: Macmillan.

Edwards, Rosalind (1993b) *Mature Women Students: separating or connecting family and education.* London: Taylor and Francis.

Edwards, Rosalind and Ribbens, Jane (1991) 'Meandering around "strategy": a research note on strategic discourse in the lives of women', *Sociology,* 25(3): 477–89.

Eisenstein, Hester (1984) *Contemporary Feminist Thought.* London: Unwin.

Ellis, G.J., Lee, G.R. and Peterson, L.R. (1978) 'Supervision and conformity: a cross-cultural analysis of parental socialisation values', *American Journal of Sociology,* 84(3): 386–403.

Ferree, Myra (1985) 'Between two worlds: German feminist approaches to working class women and work', *Signs,* 10.

Ferree, Myra (1987) 'Family and job for working class women', in Naomi Gerstel and Harriet Engel Gross (eds), *Families and Work.* Philadelphia: Temple University Press.

Finch, Janet (1985) 'Social policy and education: problems and possibilities of using qualitative research', in Robert Burgess (ed.), *Issues in Educational Research: qualitative methods.* Lewes: Falmer Press.

Finch, Janet (1986) *Research Policy: the uses of qualitative methods in social and educational research.* Lewes: Falmer Press.

Finch, Janet (1987) 'The vignette technique in survey research', *Sociology,* 21(1): 105–114.

Finch, Janet (1989) 'Kinship and friendship', in R. Jowell, S.Witherspoon and L. Brook (eds), *British Social Attitudes: Special International Report.* Aldershot: Gower.

Firestone, Shulamith (1971) *The Dialetic of Sex.* London: Jonathan Cape.

Flax, Jane (1978) 'The conflict between nurturance and autonomy in mother–daughter relationships and within feminism', *Feminist Studies,* 4(2): 171–89.

Fletcher, Ronald (1966) *The Family and Marriage in Britain: an analysis and moral assessment.* Harmondsworth: Penguin.

Freely, Maureen (1994) 'Stop bashing the parents', *The Guardian,* 18 March: 24.

Friedan, Betty (1981) *The Second Stage.* New York: Summit Books.

Fromm, Eric (1942) *The Fear of Freedom.* London: Routledge and Kegan Paul.

Garfinkel, H. (1967) *Studies in Ethnomethodology.* Englewood Cliffs, NJ: Prentice-Hall.

General Household Survey (1982, 1985). London: OPCS, HMSO.

Gerson, Kathleen (1985) *Hard Choices: how women decide about work, career and motherhood.* Berkeley: University of California Press.

Gerstel, Naomi and Gross, Harriet Engel (1987) 'Introduction and Overview', in Naomi Gerstel and Harriet Engel Gross (eds), *Families and Work.* Philadelphia: Temple University Press.

Giddens, Antony (1991) *Modernity and Self-Identity: self and society in the later modern age.* Cambridge: Polity.

Giddens, Anthony (1992) *The Transformation of Intimacy: sexuality, love and eroticism in modern societies.* Cambridge: Polity Press.

Gieve, Katherine (ed.) (1990) *Balancing Acts: on being a mother.* London: Virago.

Gilbert, Harriett (1985) in Heron, Liz (ed.) *Truth Dare or Promise: girls growing up in the fifties.* London: Virago.

Gilligan, Carol (1982) *In a Different Voice: psychological theory and women's development.* Cambridge, MA: Harvard University Press.

Glaser, Barney (1969) 'The constant comparative method of qualitative analysis', in George McCall and J.L. Simmons (eds), *Issues in Participant Observation.* Reading: Addison-Wesley.

Glaser, Barney G. and Strauss, Anselm L. (1968) *The Discovery of Grounded Theory: strategies of qualitative research.* London: Weidenfeld and Nicolson. (First published 1967.)

Goffman, Erving (1956) 'Embarrassment and social organisation', *American Journal of Sociology*, 62: 264–74.

Goldthorpe, John H. (1982) 'On the service class, its formation and future', in A. Giddens and G. Mackenzie (eds), *Social Class and the Division of Labour.* Cambridge: Cambridge University Press.

Goldthorpe, John H. (1983) 'Women and class analysis: in defence of the conventional view', *Sociology*, 17(4): 465–88.

Gordon, Linda (1986) 'Feminism and social control: the case of child abuse and neglect', in Juliet Mitchell and Ann Oakley (eds), *What is feminism?* Oxford: Basil Blackwell.

Gordon, Tuula (1990) *Feminist Mothers.* London: Macmillan.

Graham, Hilary (1982) 'Coping: or how mothers are seen and not heard', in S. Friedman and E. Sarah (eds), *On the Problem of Men.* London: Women's Press.

Graham, Hilary (1985) 'Providers, negotiators and mediators: women as the hidden carers', in V. Olesen and E. Lewin (eds), *Women, Health and Healing.* London: Tavistock.

Gubrium, J. and Holstein, J. (1990) *What is Family?* Mountain View, CA: Mayfield Publishing Co.

Hallden, Gunilla (1991) 'The child as project and the child as being: parents' ideas as frames of reference', *Children and Society*, 5(4): 334–46.

Hamilton, Malcolm and Hirszowicz, Maria (1987) *Class and Inequality in Pre-industrial, Capitalist and Communist Societies.* Brighton: Wheatsheaf Books.

Hammersley, Martyn (1979) 'Analysing ethnographic data', in *Research Methods in Education and the Social Sciences*, DE304. Milton Keynes: Open University.

Hammersley, Martyn and Atkinson, Paul (1983) *Ethnography: principles in practice.* London: Tavistock.

Hargreaves, Andy (1985) 'The micro-macro problem in the sociology of education', in Robert Burgess (ed.), *Issues in Educational Research: qualitative methods.* Lewes: Falmer Press.

Harré, Rom (1986) 'The step to social constructionism', in Martin Richards and Paul Light (eds), *Children of Social Worlds: development in a social context.* Cambridge: Polity Press.

Harvey, Erika (1989) 'Teenagers: what parents worry about', *Good Housekeeping*, February.

Haskey, John (1990) 'Children in families broken by divorce', *Population Trends*, 61 (Autumn): 26–33.

Hayes, Bernadette and Miller, Robert (1989) 'The silenced voice: female social mobility patterns with particular reference to the British Isles', unpublished paper, Queen's University Belfast.

Heath, Christian (1988) 'Embarrassment and interactional organisation', in Paul Drew and Anthony Wootton (eds), *Erving Goffman: exploring the interaction order.* Cambridge: Polity Press.

Henderson, Ronald W. (1981) 'Home environment and intellectual performance', in Ronald W. Henderson (ed.), *Parent–child Interaction: theory, research and prospects*. London: Academic Press.

Hendrick, Harry (1990) 'Constructions and reconstructions of British childhood: an interpretive survey, 1800 to the present', in Alison James and Alan Prout (eds), *Constructing and Reconstructing Childhood: contemporary issues in the sociological study of childhood*. Lewes: Falmer Press.

Heron, Liz (ed.) (1985) *Truth, Dare or Promise: girls growing up in the fifties*. London: Virago.

Hess, Robert (1981) 'Approaches to the measurement and interpretation of parent–child interaction', in Ronald W. Henderson (ed.), *Parent–child Interaction: theory, research and prospects*. London: Academic Press.

Hewitt, Nancy (1985) 'Beyond the search for sisterhood: American women's history in the 1980's', *Social History*, 10(3): 299–319.

Hochschild, Arlie (1990) *The Second Shift: working parents and the revolution at home*. London: Piatkus.

Hockey, Jenny and James, Alison (1993) *Growing Up and Growing Old: ageing and dependency in the life course*. London: Sage.

Hodges, Jill (1981) 'Children and parents: who choses?', *Politics and Power Volume Three: feminism and socialism*. London: Routledge and Kegan Paul.

hooks, bell (1982) *Ain't I a Woman? Black women and feminism*. London: Pluto Press.

Hooper, Carol Ann (1993) *Mothers Surviving Child Sexual Abuse*. London: Routledge.

Huston, Aletha C. (1983) 'Sex-typing', in Mavis E. Hetherington (ed.), *Handbook of Child Psychology Volume 4: Socialisation, Personality and Social Development*. New York: John Wiley.

Ingleby, David (1986) 'Development in social context', in Martin Richards and Paul Light (eds), *Children of Social Worlds: development in a social context*. Cambridge: Polity Press.

Jackson, Brian (1983) *Fatherhood*. London: Allen and Unwin.

Jackson, Brian and Marsden, Dennis (1966) *Education and the Working Class*. Harmondsworth: Pelican. (First published 1962 by Routledge and Kegan Paul.)

Jackson, Stevi (1993) 'Even sociologists fall in love: an exploration in the sociology of the emotions', *Sociology*, 27(2): 201–20.

James, Alison and Prout, Alan (eds) (1990) *Constructing and Reconstructing Childhood: contemporary issues in the sociological study of childhood*. London: Falmer.

Jamieson, Lynn and Toynbee, Claire (1990) 'Shifting patterns of parental control 1900–1980', in Helen Corr and Lynn Jamieson (eds), *The Politics of Everyday Life: continuity and change in work and the family*. London: Macmillan.

Jenks, Chris (1982) 'Constituting the child', in Chris Jenks (ed.), *The Sociology of Childhood*. London: Batsford.

Johnson, Miriam M. (1988) *Strong Mothers, Weak Wives: the search for gender equality*. Berkeley: University of California Press.

Keddie, Nell (1971) 'Classroom knowledge', in M.F.D. Young (ed.), *Knowledge and Control*. London: Collier-Macmillan.

Kellerhals, Jean and Montandon, Cleopatre (1992) 'Social stratification and the parent-child relationship' in Ulla Bjornberg (ed.), *European Parents in the 1990's: contradictions and comparisons*. New Brunswick: Transaction Publishers.

Kelly, George (1955) *The Psychology of Personal Constructs*. New York: W.W. Norton.

Kelly-Gadol, Joan (1976) 'The social relation of the sexes: methodological implications of women's history', *Signs*, 1(4): 809–23.

Kerchoff, Alan (1972) *Socialisation and Social Class*. New Jersey: Prentice-Hall.

Kohn, M.L. (1959) 'Social class and parental values', *American Journal of Sociology*, 64: 337–51.

Kohn, M.L. (1963) 'Social class and parent–child relationships: an interpretation', *American Journal of Sociology*, 58(4): 471–80. Also reprinted in Michael Anderson (ed.) (1971) *Sociology of the Family*. Harmondsworth: Penguin, and in Urie Bronfenbrenner and Maureen A. Mahoney (eds) (1975) *Influences on Human Development* (2nd edn). Hinsdale, Illinois: Dryden Press.

Kohn, M.L. (1969) *Class and Conformity: a study in values*. Homewood, Illinois: Dorsey Press.

La Fontaine, J. (1986) 'An anthropological perspective on children in social worlds', in Martin Richards and Paul Light (eds), *Children of Social Worlds: development in a social context*. Cambridge: Polity Press.

Lambert, Susan J. (1990) 'Processes linking work and family: a critical review and research agenda', *Human Relations*, 43(3): 239–58.

Land, Hilary (1976) 'Women: supporters or supported?', in Diana Leonard Barker and Sheila Allen (eds), *Sexual Divisions in Society: process and change*. London: Tavistock.

Laosa, Luis (1981) 'Maternal behviour: sociocultural diversity in modes of family interaction', in Ronald Henderson (ed.), *Parent–child Interaction: theory, research and prospects*. London: Academic Press.

Lasch, Christopher (1976) 'The family as a haven in a heartless world', in Arlene Skolnick and Jerome Skolnick (eds), *Family in Transition*. Glenview, Illinois: Scott, Foresman and Co.

Lasch, Christopher (1980) *The Culture of Narcissism*. London: Abacus.

Lazarre, Jane (1987) *The Mother Knot*. London: Virago Press. (First published 1976.)

Lessnoff, M.H. (1973) *The Structure of Social Science: a philosophical introduction*. London: Allen and Unwin.

Lewis, Gail (1985) in Heron, Liz (ed.) *Truth Dare or Promise: girls growing up in the fifties*. London: Virago.

Lewis, Jane (1986) 'Anxieties about the family and the relationships between parents, children and the State in twentieth century England', in Martin Richards and Paul Light (eds), *Children of Social Worlds: development in a social context*. Cambridge: Polity Press.

Lieberman, Stuart (1987) 'The use of family trees in family therapy', talk given at the Institute of Family Therapy, 23 January.

Locke, John (1979) 'Paternal power: on the authority of mothers and fathers', in Onora O'Neill and William Ruddick (eds), *Having Children: Philosophical and Legal Reflections on Parenthood*. New York: Oxford University Press.

Locker, David (1981) *Symptoms and Illness: the cognitive organisation of disorder*. London: Tavistock.

Lukes, Steven (1985) 'Conclusion' in Michael Carrithers, Steven Collins and Steven Lukes (eds), *The Category of the Person: anthropology, philosophy, history*. Cambridge University Press.

Luster, Tom, Rhoades, Kelly and Haas, Bruce (1989) 'The relation between parental values and parenting behaviour: a test of the Kohn hypothesis', *Journal of Marriage and the Family*, 51: 139–47.

Maccoby, Eleanor E. and Martin, John A. (1983) 'Socialisation in the context of the family: parent–child interaction', in E. Mavis Hetherington (ed.), *Handbook of Child Psychology Volume 4: Socialisation, Personality and Social Development*. New York: John Wiley.

McGuire, Jacqueline (1991) 'Sons and daughters', in Ann Phoenix, Anne Woollett and Eva Lloyd (eds), *Motherhood: meanings, practices and ideologies*. London: Sage.

MacIntyre, Sally (1976) '"Who wants babies?" The social construction of "instincts"', in Diana Leonard Barker and Sheila Allen (eds), *Sexual Divisions and Society*. London: Tavistock.

Mann, Michael (1986) 'A crisis in stratification theory?' in Rosemary Crompton and Michael Mann (eds), *Gender and Stratification*. Cambridge: Polity Press.

Marsh, Catherine (1986) 'Social class and occupation', in Robert Burgess (ed.), *Key Variables in Social Investigation*. London: Routledge and Kegan Paul.

Marshall, Gordon, Newby, Harold, Rose, David and Vogel, C. (1988) *Social Class in Modern Britain*. London: Hutchinson.

Masserik, Fred (1981) 'The interviewing process re-examined', in Peter Reason and J. Rowan (eds), *Human Inquiry: a sourcebook of new paradigm research*. Chichester: John Wiley and Sons.

Mauthner, Natasha (1994) 'Post-natal depression: a relational perspective', unpublished PhD, University of Cambridge.

Mayall, Berry (1988) 'Health Visiting – theory and practice', Paper presented to a day conference, 17 March, organised by the Thomas Coram Research Unit, London.

Mead, Margaret (1962) *Male and Female: a study of the sexes in a changing world*. Harmondsworth: Penguin. (First published in the USA 1950.)

Meyer, Joan (1991) 'Power and love: conflicting conceptual schema', in Kathy Davis, Monique Leijenaar and Jantine Oldersma (eds), *The Gender of Power*. London: Sage.

Midgley, Mary and Hughes, Judith (1983) *Women's Choices: philosophical problems facing feminism*. London: Weidenfeld and Nicolson.

Mitchell, Juliet (1971) *Women's Estate*. London: Penguin.

Morgan, David H.J. (1975) *Social Theory and the Family*. London: Routledge and Kegan Paul.

Morgan, David H.J. (1985) *The Family, Politics and Social Theory*. London: Routledge and Kegan Paul.

Morgan, David H.J. (forthcoming) *Family Connections*. Cambridge: Polity.

Morrow, V. (1992) *Family Values: accounting for children's contribution to the domestic economy*, Working Paper Series, Sociological Research Group, Social and Political Sciences Faculty, University of Cambridge.

Moss, Peter (1990) *Childcare in the European Communities 1985–1990*. Women of Europe Supplements No. 31, August, Commission of the European Communities.

Nelson, M. (1989) 'Negotiating care: relationships between family daycare providers and mothers', *Feminist Studies*, 15.

New, Caroline and David, Miriam (1985) *For the Children's Sake: making childcare more than women's business*. Harmondsworth: Penguin.

Newson, John and Lilley, Jeanette (1989) 'Continuity and Change in Patterns of Infant Care during the First Year', Paper presented to the La Leche League (GB) National Conference, Oxford Polytechnic, 2–3 September.

Newson, John and Newson, Elizabeth (1965) *Patterns of Infant Care in an Urban Community.* Harmondsworth: Pelican. (First published by George Allen and Unwin 1963.)

Newson, John and Newson, Elizabeth (1968) *Four Years Old in an Urban Community.* London: George Allen and Unwin.

Newson, John and Newson, Elizabeth (1974) 'Cultural aspects of childrearing in the English-speaking world', in Martin Richards (ed.), *The Integration of a Child into a Social World.* London: Cambridge University Press.

Newson, John and Newson, Elizabeth (1976) 'Parental roles and social contexts', in Marten Shipman (ed.), *The Organisation and Impact of Social Research.* London: Routledge and Kegan Paul.

Newson, John and Newson, Elizabeth (1978) *Seven Years Old in the Home Environment.* Harmondsworth: Pelican. (First published by George Allen and Unwin 1976.)

Newson, John and Newson, Elizabeth (1989) *The Extent of Parental Physical Punishment in the UK.* London: Association for the Protection of All Children Ltd.

Newson, John and Elizabeth, Newson with Barnes, Peter (1977) *Perspectives on School at Seven Years Old.* London: Allen and Unwin.

Nice, Vivien (1988) 'In search of perfect mothers', *Social Work Today*, 20(14): 22–3.

Oakley, Ann (1976) *Housewife.* Harmondsworth: Penguin. (First published 1974.)

Oakley, Ann (1979) *Becoming a Mother.* Oxford: Martin Robertson.

Oakley, Ann (1980) *Women Confined: towards a sociology of childbirth.* Oxford: Martin Robertson.

Oakley, Ann (1981) *Subject Women.* London: Fontana.

Oakley, Ann (1984) *Taking it Like a Woman.* London: Jonathan Cape.

Oakley, Ann (1985) *The Sociology of Housework.* Oxford: Blackwell. (First published 1974.)

Oakley, Ann (1986a) *From Here to Maternity: becoming a mother.* Harmondsworth: Penguin. (First published 1979 under the title, *Becoming a Mother.*)

Oakley, Ann (1986b) 'Feminism and motherhood', in Martin Richards and Paul Light (eds), *Children of Social Worlds: development in a social context.* Cambridge: Polity Press.

O'Brien, Mary (1981) *The Politics of Reproduction.* Boston: Routledge and Kegan Paul.

O'Connor, Pat (1992) *Friendships Between Women: a critical review.* New York: Harvester Press.

O'Donnell, Lydia (1985) *The Unheralded Majority: contemporary women as mothers.* Lexington MA: Lexington Books.

O'Neill, Nora and Ruddick, William (eds) (1979) *Having Children: philosophical and legal reflections on parenthood.* New York: Oxford University Press.

Osborne, A.F. and Morris, T.C. (1979) 'The rationale for a composite index of social class and its evaluation', *British Journal of Sociology*, 30: 39–60.

Pearlin, Leonard (1972) *Class Context and Family Relations.* Boston: Little, Brown and Co.

Pearson, Geoffrey (1983) *Hooligans: a history of respectable fears.* Basingstoke: Macmillan.

Peterson, Larry R., Lee, Gary R. and Ellis, Godfrey J. (1982) 'Social structure, socialisation values and disciplinary techniques: a cross-cultural analysis', *Journal of Marriage and the Family*, 44(1): 131–42.

Phoenix, Ann (1987) 'Theories of gender and black families', in Gaby Weiner and Madeleine Arnot (eds), *Gender Under Scrutiny: new enquiries in education*. London: Hutchinson.

Phoenix, Ann (1991) 'Mothers under twenty: outsider and insider views', in Ann Phoenix, Anne Woollett and Eva Lloyd (eds), *Motherhood: meanings, practices and ideologies*. London: Sage.

Phoenix, Ann and Woollett, Anne (1991) 'Motherhood: social construction, politics and psychology', in Ann Phoenix, Anne Woollett and Eva Lloyd (eds), *Motherhood: meanings, practices and ideologies*. London: Sage.

Poster, Mark (1978) *Critical Theory of the Family*. London: Pluto Press.

Qvortrup, Jens (1990) 'A voice for children in statistical and social accounting: a plea for children's right to be heard', in Alison James and Alan Prout (eds) (1994) *Constructing and Reconstructing Childhood: contemporary issues in the sociological study of childhood*. Lewes: Falmer.

Qvortrup, Jens, Bardy, Marjatta, Sgritta, Giovanni and Wintersberger, Helmut (eds) (1994) *Childhood Matters: social theory, practice and politics*. Aldershot: Avebury.

Rapaport, Amos (1981) 'Identity and environment: a cross-cultural perspective', in James S. Duncan (ed.), *Housing and Identity: Cross-cultural perspectives*. London: Croom Helm.

Raphael-Leff, Joan (1983) 'Facilitators and regulators: two approaches to mothering', *British Journal of Modern Psychology*, 56: 374–90.

Rapp, Rayna (1979) 'Household and family', *Feminist Studies*, 5(1): 175–81.

Rapp, Rayna (1982) 'Family and class in contemporary America: notes towards an understanding of ideology', in Barrie Thorne and Marilyn Yalom (eds), *Rethinking the Family: some feminist questions*. New York: Longman.

Reason, Peter and Rowan, J. (eds) (1981) *Human Inquiry: a sourcebook of new paradigm research*. Chichester: John Wiley and Sons.

Ribbens, Geoffrey (1979) *Patterns of Behaviour: a comparative sociology text for the critical student*. London: Edward Arnold.

Ribbens, Jane (1989a) *Bringing up Our Children: whose practice and whose reality?* Paper presented to the British Sociological Conference, Plymouth Polytechnic, April.

Ribbens, Jane (1989b) 'Interviewing: an "unnatural situation"?' *Women's Studies International Forum*, 12(6): 579–92.

Ribbens, Jane (1990a) *Accounting for Our Children: differing perspectives on 'family life' in middle income households*. PhD, CNAA/South Bank Polytechnic.

Ribbens, Jane (1990b) *Class and the Private Household: the social and gendered worlds of childrearing across the generations*. Paper presented to the British Sociological Association Annual Conference, University of Surrey, April.

Ribbens, Jane (1993a) 'Standing by the school gate – the boundaries of maternal authority?' in Mariam David, Rosalind Edwards, Mary Hughes and Jane Ribbens (eds), *Mothers and Education: Inside Out? Exploring family-education policy and experience*. Basingstoke: Macmillan.

Ribbens, Jane (1993b) 'Having a word with the teacher: ongoing negotiations across home–school boundaries', in Miriam David, Rosalind Edwards, Mary Hughes and Jane Ribbens (eds), *Mothers and Education: Inside Out? Exploring family-education policy and experience*. Basingstoke: Macmillan.

Rich, Adrienne (1977) *Of Woman Born*. London: Virago.

Richards, Lynn (1990) *Nobody's Home: dreams and realities in a new suburb*. Melbourne: Oxford University Press.

Richards, Martin (1974) 'Introduction', in Martin Richards (ed.), *The Integration of a Child into a Social World*. London: Cambridge University Press.

Richards, Martin (1986) 'Introduction', in Martin Richards and Paul Light (eds), *Children of Social Worlds: development in a social context*. Cambridge: Polity Press.

Richardson, Diane (1993) *Women, Motherhood and Childrearing*. London: Macmillan.

Riley, Denise (1981) '"The free mothers": pronatalism and working women in industry at the end of the last war in Britain', *History Workshop Journal*, 11: 59–117.

Robinson, M. and Smith, D. (1993) *Step by Step*. New York: Harvester Wheatsheaf.

Rose, Nikolas (1989) *Governing the Soul: the shaping of the private self*. London: Routledge.

Rose, Sonya (1986) 'Gender at work: sex, class and industrial capitalism', *History Workshop Journal*, 21(1): 113–31.

Ross, Ellen (1979) 'Women and family'. *Feminist Studies*, 5(1): 181–9.

Ruddick, Sara (1982) 'Maternal thinking', in Barrie Thorne and Marilyn Yalom (eds), *Rethinking the Family: some feminist questions*. New York: Longman.

Sassoon, Anne Showstack (ed.) (1987) *Women and the State: the shifting boundaries of public and private*. London: Unwin Hyman.

Scheper-Hughes, Nancy (1987) *Child Survival: anthropological perspectives on the treatment and maltreatment of children*. Dordrecht: D. Reidel.

Schutz, Alfred (1954) 'Concept and theory formation in the social sciences', *Journal of Philosophy*, 51: 257–73. Also reproduced in John Bynner and Keith Stribley (1979) (eds) *Social Research: principles and procedures*. London: Longman/Open University Press.

Scott, J.W. and Tilly, L.A. (1980) 'Women's work and the family in nineteenth century Europe', in Michael Anderson (ed.), *Sociology of the Family* (2nd edn). Harmondsworth: Penguin. (First published 1975.)

Segal, Lynn (1985) *Is the Future Female? Troubled thoughts on contemporary feminism*. London: Virago.

Segalen, Martine (1986) *Historical Anthropology of the Family*. Cambridge: Cambridge University Press.

Sharistanian, Janet (1987) 'Introduction: women's lives in the public and domestic spheres', in Janet Sharistanian (ed.), *Beyond the Public/Domestic Dichotomy: contemporary perspectives on women's public lives*. New York: Greenwood Press.

Sharpe, Sue (1984) *Double Identity: the lives of working mothers*. Harmondsworth: Pelican.

Sharrock, Wes and Watson, Rod (1988) 'Autonomy among social theories: the incarnation of social structures', in Nigel Fielding (ed.), *Actions and Structures: research, methods and social theory*. London: Sage.

Siltanen, Janet and Stanworth, Michelle (1984) *Women and the Public Sphere*. London: Hutchinson.

Smart, Barry (1985) *Michel Foucault*. London: Tavistock.

Smart, Carol (1984) *The Ties that Bind: law, marriage and the reproduction of patriarchy*. London: Routledge and Kegan Paul.

Smith, Dorothy E. (1983) 'Women, class and the family', in Ralph Miliband (ed.), *The Socialist Register*. London: Merlin Press.

Smith, Dorothy E. (1988) *The Everyday World as Problematic: a feminist sociology*. Milton Keynes: Open University Press.

Smith-Rosenberg, Carroll (1975) 'The female world of love and ritual: relations between women in nineteenth century America', *Signs*, 1(1): 1–29.

Social Trends (1992) HMSO: London.

Stacey, Judith (1986) 'Are feminists afraid to leave home? The challenge of conservative pro-family feminism', in Juliet Mitchell and Ann Oakley (eds), *What is Feminism?* Oxford: Basil Blackwell.

Stacey, Judith (1990) *Brave New Families: stories of domestic upheaval in late twentieth century America*. New York: Harper Collins.

Stacey, Margaret (1981) 'The Division of Labour Revisited, or Overcoming the Two Adams', in Philip Abrams, Rosemary Deem, Janet Finch and Paul Rock (eds), *Practice and Progress: British Sociology 1950–1980*. London: George Allen and Unwin.

Stacey, Margaret and Davies, Celia (1983) *Division of Labour in Child Health Care: final report to the SSRC 1983*. Warwick: University of Warwick.

Stacey, M. and Price, M. (1981) *Women, Power and Politics*. London: Tavistock.

Statham, June (1986) *Daughters and Sons: experiences of non-sexist childraising*. Oxford: Basil Blackwell.

Steinkamp, Gunther (1983) 'Auf der Suche nach den sozialstrukturellen Bedingungen sozialen Handelns: Melvin L. Kohn' in *Zeitschrift für Sozialisationsforschung und Erziehungssoziologie*, 3(1): 105–16.

Stolz, Lois Meek (1967) *Influences on Parent Behaviour*. Stanford, CA: Stanford University Press.

Sutton, Geoff (1989) 'Parents in fear of attacks on young', *Daily Mail*, 6 January.

Swain, Scott (1989) 'Covert intimacy: closeness in men's friendships', in Barbara Risman and Pepper Schwartz (eds), *Gender in Intimate Relationships: a microstructural approach*. Belmont CA: Wadsworth.

Sylva, Kathy and Lunt, Ingrid (1982) *Child Development: a first course*. London: Grant McIntyre.

Taft, R. (1983) 'Presidential address: cross-cultural psychology as a psychological science', in C. Kagitcibasi (ed.), *Growth and Progress in Cross-Cultural Psychology*. London: Taylor and Francis.

Thompson, Paul (1981) 'Life histories and the analysis of social change', in Daniel Bertaux (ed.), *Biography and Society: the life-history approach in the social sciences*. Beverly Hills: Sage.

Thompson, Paul (1984) 'The family and child-rearing as forces of economic change: towards fresh research approaches', *Sociology*, 18(4): 515–30.

Thrower, S., Bruce, W. and Walton, R. (1982) 'The family circle method: integrating family systems concepts in family medicine', *Journal of Family Practice*, 15: 451–7.

Tivers, Jacqueline (1985) *Women Attached: the daily lives of women with young children*. London: Croom Helm.

Tizard, B. and Hughes, M. (1984) *Young Children Learning*. London: Fontana.

Tong, Rosemary (1989) *Feminist Thought: a comprehensive introduction*. London: Unwin Hyman.

Triandis, H.C. (1987) 'Individualism and social psccychological theory', in C. Kagitcibasi (ed.), *Growth and Progress in Cross-Cultural Psychology*. London: Taylor and Francis.

Tulkin, Steven (1975) 'An analysis of the concept of cultural deprivation', in Urie Bronfenbrenner and Maureen A. Mahoney (eds), *Influences on Human Development* (2nd edn). Hinsdale, IL: Dryden Press.

Ungerson, Clare (1983) 'Why do women care?' in Janet Finch and Dulcie Groves (eds), *A Labour of Love: women, work and caring*. London: Routledge and Kegan Paul.

Ungerson, Clare (1990) (ed.) *Gender and Caring: work and welfare in Britain and Scandinavia*. New York: Harvester Wheatsheaf.

Urwin, Cathy (1985) 'Constructing motherhood: the persuasion of normal development', in C. Steedman, C. Urwin and V. Walkerdine (eds), *Language, Gender and Childhood*. London: Routledge and Kegan Paul.

Van Every, Jo (1992) 'Who is "the family"? The assumptions of British social policy', *Critical Social Policy*, 33: 62–75.

Vetere, Arlene and Gale, Anthony (1987) *Ecological Studies of Family Life*. Chichester: John Wiley.

Waksler, Frances Chaput (1991) 'Beyond socialisaton', in Frances Chaput Waksler (ed.), *Studying the Social Worlds of Children: sociological readings*. Brighton: Falmer.

Walkerdine, Valerie and Lucey, Helen (1989) *Democracy in the Kitchen: Regulating mothers and socialising daughters*. London: Virago.

Wallman, Sandra (1978) 'The boundaries of "race": processes of ethnicity in England', *Man*, 13(2): 200–17.

Warner, Marina (1989) *Into the Dangerous World: some thoughts on childhood and its costs*. London: Chatto.

Warnes, A.M. (1986) 'The residential mobility histories of parents and children, and relationships to present proximity and social integration', *Environment and Planning*, 18: 1581–94.

Wartofsky, Marx (1981) 'The child's construction of the world and the world's construction of the child: from historical epistemology to historical psychology', in Frank Kessel and Alexander Siegel (eds), *The Child and Other Cultural Inventions*. New York: Praeger.

Weber, Max (1968) *Economy and Society – an outline of interpretive sociology* (Tr. by G. Roth and G. Wittich). New York: Bedminster Press.

White, Sheldon (1981) 'Psychology as a moral science', in Frank Kessel and Alexander Siegel (eds), *The Child and Other Cultural Inventions*. New York: Praeger.

Wilson, Patricia and Pahl, Ray (1988) 'The changing sociological construct of the family', *Sociological Review*, 36(2): 233–66.

Woodhead, Martin (1990) 'Psychology and the cultural construction of children's needs', in Alison James and Alan Prout (eds), *Constructing and Reconstructing Childhood: contemporary issues in the sociological study of childhood*. Brighton: Falmer.

Woodhead, Martin, Carr, Ronnie and Light, Paul (1991) (eds) *Becoming a Person*. London: Routledge.

Woollett, Ann and Phoenix, Ann (1991) 'Psychological views of mothering', in Ann Pheonix, Anne Woollett and Eva Lloyd (eds), *Motherhood: meanings, practices and ideologies*. London: Sage.

Yeatman, Anna (1986) 'Women, domestic life and sociology', in Carole Pateman and Elizabeth Gross (eds), *Feminist Challenges: social and political theory*. Sydney: Allen and Unwin.

Young, Michael and Willmott, Peter (1962) *Family and Kinship in East London*. Harmondsworth: Penguin. (First published 1957.)

Young, Michael and Willmott, Peter (1973) *The Symmetrical Family*. London: Routledge and Kegan Paul.

Yuen, Kay Chung (1985) 'At the Palace: work, ethnicity and gender in a Chinese restaurant', *Studies in Sexual Politics*, No. 3. Manchester: University of Manchester.

Zaretsky, Eli (1982) 'The place of the family in the origins of the welfare state', in Barrie Thorne and Marilyn Yalom (eds), *Rethinking the Family: some feminist questions*. New York: London.

Index

236 *Mothers a*